SCHOOLS OR MARKETS?
COMMERCIALISM, PRIVATIZATION, AND SCHOOL–BUSINESS PARTNERSHIPS

SCHOOLS OR MARKETS?
COMMERCIALISM, PRIVATIZATION, AND SCHOOL–BUSINESS PARTNERSHIPS

Edited by

Deron R. Boyles
Georgia State University

2005   LAWRENCE ERLBAUM ASSOCIATES, PUBLISHERS
Mahwah, New Jersey   London

Lawrence Erlbaum Associates, Inc., Publishers
10 Industrial Avenue
Mahwah, New Jersey 07430

Cover design by Sean Sciarrone

Library of Congress Cataloging-in-Publication Data

Schools or markets? : commercialism, privatization, and school–
    business partnerships / edited by Deron R. Boyles.
        p. cm.
    Includes bibliographical references and index.
ISBN 0-8058-5203-4 (cloth : alk. paper)
ISBN 0-8058-5204-2 (pbk. : alk. paper)
1. Industry and education—United States. 2. Commercialism
    in schools—United States. 3. Privatization in education—
    United States.   I. Boyles, Deron.
LC1085.2.S38   2004
371.19′5—dc22   2004043257
                                                        CIP

Books published by Lawrence Erlbaum Associates are printed
on acid-free paper, and their bindings are chosen for strength
and durability.

Printed in the United States of America
10 9 8 7 6 5 4 3 2 1

Contents

Foreword

Alex Molnar
Arizona State University

This volume provides a much needed analysis and critique of the breadth, depth, and character of corporate involvement in American public education. As the contributors point out, corporations are involved as business "partners" in K–12 education, as funders of think tanks, as media opinion shapers, as for-profit school managers, and as increasingly powerful shapers of post secondary institutions.

Over the past twenty-five years U.S. schools have faced chronic budget constraints. In this fiscal environment it is not surprising that turning to businesses as benefactors has become a commonplace response of parents, students, educators, and legislators. *Schools or Markets?* challenges the reader to consider critically what many corporations have come to call "strategic philanthropy" directed at schools and colleges.

The contributors to this volume argue that the greatest and most dangerous cost of the corporate make-over of public education is the threat that it poses to the historic purpose of public schools, the preparation of students for participation in democratic civic life. Trammell, for example, argues that the result of most business–school partnerships are "undiscriminating, gulping mental habits" that are valued over "discriminating intelligence." In Hewitt's view, curriculum designed to meet business needs will inevitably lead to "fill in the blank" curriculum that focuses on future "real world" needs instead of curriculum experiences that are built on the here-and-now realities of students' lives.

In a variety of ways the authors contend that schools cannot serve two masters because the demands of democracy are fundamentally different from the demands of corporations. The difference is revealed, for example, by the language used to talk about teachers and students. When "student" becomes "consumer," the authors would argue that the civic role of school is lost—so too, when schools adopt "business" methods that are touted as "tried and true." This volume asks what methods would be worth taking from Enron, Arthur Andersen, WorldCom, or any of the other businesses that have broken the law, cheated their shareholders, and violated the public trust.

As far as the contributors to *Schools or Markets?* are concerned, even as corporate ideology treats students as consumers to be manipulated, they are at the same time considered products in an industrial/marketing process. According to Boyles, for example, in the state of Georgia graduates of colleges of education are commodified and "guaranteed" by law. If the student is found to be "defective" in his or her teaching job, they can be "returned" to the college from which they graduated and be "fixed." Thus he argues, students, thanks in part to the successful advocacy of think tanks and legislators with pro-business, pro-market political agendas, are increasingly treated as cogs on a machine. Future teachers, then, are prepared in a way that treats them as a corporate-dominated system would have them treat their students. In the modern, market-oriented, high-stakes classroom, students are to be moved around the building and through the material as efficiently as possible.

The end point of corporate dominance of public education described by *Schools or Markets?* is schools that resemble the factory model envisioned by curriculum specialists such as Franklin Bobbitt and David Snedden. As these authors see it, in the factory now called school, students are hammered, chiseled, drilled, and bolted in the same routinized way until they are ready for the "real world," read *market.*

Despite its emphasis on the damage done—both direct and collateral—to public education's civic purpose *Schools or Markets?* also offers hope. Recognizing that business involvement in schools is going to continue for the foreseeable future the contributors provide examples of what, even in a corporate dominated context, genuine civic partnerships might look like and accomplish, of how corporate involvement in schooling can be used in lessons, and of ways teachers and students can examine not only the effects of specific business involvement but the reasons why businesses are involved in the first place.

The contributors are not naïve. They realize that challenging corporate influence in public education will not be easy. Americans are told in countless ways large and small that consumer values operating in a marketplace are essential to the American way of life. Indeed that it *is* the American way of life. For anyone interested in challenging the spread of those values to public education this book is a handy toolbox that deserves to be opened.

Preface

The goal of this book is to provide alternative views of business influences on and in schools. From the beginning, readers should know that the collection of writings assembled here represents a critical view of business involvement in schools. A presupposition of the book is that Americans are reared in a society that is so commercial that any questions raised about capitalism and commercialism are too easily dismissed without critical reflection. By investigating the variety of topics this book encompasses, the objective is to challenge the minds of readers to consider the *negative* consequences of commercial and business influences in and on schools.

Topics include the privatization of food services, commercialization and school administration, and business partnerships and parental concerns. The book also touches on themes that highlight the degree to which commercialism is evident in higher education, including marketing to high school students, intellectual-property rights of professors and students, and the bind in which professional proprietary schools find themselves. Also included is a critique of oil company ads that act as educational policy statements and a critique of teacher union complicity in the school–business partnership craze currently sweeping the nation. Additionally, the book considers education policy as "military-industrial complex policy in disguise" and includes a chapter that reveals the degree to which mass media coverage of educational issues is linked to corporate and conservative think-tanks. Finally, the point is made that exploitation is a two-way street. Specifically, the last chapter argues that commercialism and school–business partnerships promote consumer materialism, thwart critical agency, and negatively alter what it means to be a citizen. Instead, as is seen in the underlying and

unifying theme of the book, schools can benefit from school–business partnerships by exploiting them as object lessons for critical consumerism and
critical citizenship.

This book, like all texts, represents particular dispositions and values. In
this case, our disposition is to disrupt what many readers may take for
granted, namely, that schools benefit from and therefore need corporate involvement. Our values are represented in the topics chosen and this point
represents a double-edged sword. On the one hand, the breadth and variety
just mentioned is intended to spark further interest in the general topics of
commercialism, privatization, and school–business partnerships and provides a unique treatment of topics that otherwise rarely get addressed in the
literature. On the other hand, some specific areas of inquiry were not given
full treatment in this current edition. Educational management organizations (EMOs), for example, are not explicitly dealt with, even though the
questions surrounding privatization that are raised throughout the text
would apply to for-profit ventures. EMOs include companies like Edison
Schools, Education Alternatives, Inc., Alternative Public Schools, Eduventures, and even Sylvan Learning Centers. These organizations push the
agenda that privatizing public education will allow market forces to rid
schools of waste and will provide better instruction and a better "product" in
the form of students. Yet, as Alex Molnar points out, "Privatization schemes
are inevitably advanced in a deregulatory public policy environment, at least
in part promoted as cost-saving measures. But their proponents tend to omit
the essential element for realizing cost savings from such schemes—rigorous
oversight."[1]

Rigorous oversight was certainly not evidenced when Florida's state pension fund recently decided on investing $174 million in Edison Schools. As
Helen Huntley reported, the arrangement was made though one of the state
pension fund managers, Liberty Partners. Huntely notes, "The pension fund
has agreed to buy out the shareholders of Edison Schools Inc., taking the
New York company private. In effect, the fund that provides for the retire-
ment pensions of Florida teachers and other public employees will own a
company that has played a leading role in privatizing school management."[2]
Bizarre as it is to take public money that funds public school teachers to purchase a company that effectively tries to get rid of public school teachers and
public schools, the economics of the transaction belie the pro-business rhetoric. Edison Schools posted only one quarterly profit in its ten year history.
Shares of stock (publicly traded) crested at $36.75 in 2001 but fell to as low as

---

[1] Alex Molnar, *Giving Kids the Business: The Commercialization of America's Schools* (Boulder, CO:
Westview Press, 1996), 80.

[2] Helen Huntley, "State Fund Buys School Operator," *St. Petersburg Times* (23 September
2003). Online business section <http://www.sptimes.com/2003/09/25/Business/State_fund_
buys_schoo.shtml>. Accessed November 29, 2003.

$0.15 per share in 2002. Add to these facts the reality that Edison Schools is facing numerous lawsuits and one has to wonder about the logic, never mind wisdom, of the Florida decision. It might indicate, however, how perversely powerful pro-business ideologies are in the United States.

Indeed, the ideology that supports business interests carries a rhetoric that appeals widely in American culture. "Accountability," "cost-effectiveness," and "efficiency," are just some of the market logic terms that saturate conversations regarding Edison Schools, Educational Alternatives, Inc., Eduventures, and their distant higher education cousins, University of Phoenix, DeVry, and Argosy. Advertisements for these companies make it clear that "outputs" and "learning" are equivalent. They focus so squarely on profit that one wonders about the students. Where are they in these schemes? For Edison Schools, Educational Alternatives, Inc., and Eduventures, students are not even at the level of the consumer—their parents are. When students actually *do* become the consumer, as with the University of Phoenix, DeVry, and Argosy, they are enticed to believe that something substantial will come from little work. That the University of Phoenix and Argosy, specifically, elevate the notion of "convenience" to a primary criterion for learning seems to conflate drive-through lanes at fast-food companies for classrooms (online or not). By suggesting that students can "earn" their degree in a year or less, these institutions utilize technology for fiscal purposes, not educational ones. This point raises questions about the legitimacy of "distance learning" schemes that have aspects that are laudable, but realities that run contrary to the rhetoric. It *is* valuable for people in rural areas to have access to information they otherwise may not have. It *is also* so problem-plagued and expensive to start, run, and maintain the technology necessary to provide access that for those who actually stay enrolled in online courses, the cost is exorbitant. As a result, we have another irony: those in the habit of privileging corporate values like "cost-effectiveness" nonetheless push ahead with programs that are exceedingly costly and contrary to the very logic they maintain. The larger point is that such a topic does not get full treatment in the current text and there are likely other specifics that are not included. Readers are encouraged to develop these other areas and we think this text does a nice job of providing varied and unique treatments of some of the topics under the larger rubrics of commercialism, privatization, and school–business partnerships.

Indeed, this book fills a void. Although there are an increasing number of book-length treatments of issues surrounding commercialism and corporate influences on schools, the treatments tend to focus on one, two, or three major points. This book focuses on the central theme of commercialism but does so via such a distinctive multiplicity of examples that readers will arguably be struck by the sheer breadth and reach of corporate infiltration into schools and education policy.

OVERVIEW

Chapter one is by Carolyn VanderSchee, Georgia State University, and explores in great detail the privatization of food services. VanderSchee investigates the captive market of schools and the role cafeterias, caterers, and commercial fast-food chains have played in recent school policy initiatives. She looks at state and federal policy as well as, importantly, the health and nutrition issues concerning school lunch programs.

Leslie Trammell, Emory University, wrote chapter two. She explores two large advertising campaigns that ExxonMobil undertook and analyzes the newspaper ads ExxonMobil used to sway public opinion regarding education policy. Trammell's is a unique investigation of one company's ad and she demonstrates the kind of deconstruction that is necessary for students and general citizens alike in order to see through the imagery set up by corporate powers.

In chapter three, Randy Hewitt, University of Central Florida, provides a parent's view of his child's experiences in a school that encouraged school–business partnerships. Hewitt ultimately focuses on Deweyan philosophy to make sense of the role of the child, curriculum, and school in a purportedly democratic society.

A former school administrator, Donna Adair Breault, Georgia State University, raises questions about the role of school leaders who *will* be faced with deciding whether or which commercial enterprises will be embraced in various schools. Breault uniquely employs metaphor in chapter four as a way to illustrate what she calls a "consumption ethic" in the United States and she challenges educational administrators, with the rest of us, to rethink their responsibility to children and to society.

One might initially think that teachers' unions would be highly critical of outside, business influence, but Beth Weiss, Georgia State University, uses Web site information and other union material to reveal the degree to which teachers' unions actually promote school–business partnerships. In chapter five, Weiss charges that the unions, by making incautious connections to businesses, actually undermine their union imperatives to the advantage of commercial causes.

Judy Block, Georgia State University, takes a cue from Kenneth Saltman's book *Collateral Damage: Corporatizing Public Schools—A Threat to Democracy* and extends the war analogy by using "just war theory" as a means of evaluating education policy. In chapter six, she reveals the degree to which the military-industrial complex has not only not waned in its power, but has "advanced" on schools as the final homeland battlefield.

By comparing and contrasting "public" knowledge and the "private" domain in chapter seven, Benjamin Baez, Georgia State University, investigates the politics of intellectual property. Baez, a lawyer in addition to being a scholar, explores legal and theoretical issues concerning property rights, globalization, and the idea of private markets set against public goods. By exploring the degree to which higher education is an extension of the general concerns about school–business partnerships, he allows the reader to connect topics like materialism and citizenship, if in contentious ways.

Larry Stultz, former Dean of The Art Institute of Atlanta, wrestles with issues he faces in his daily work. In chapter eight, Stultz explores the role of professional, proprietary schools and the degree to which they must balance an admittedly commercial interest with issues of curriculum. In short, Stultz wonders whether a discipline-based arts education would provide the level of critique necessary to balance an otherwise overly vocationalistic and careerist orientation of schools like his.

In chapter nine, Gary Miller continues to explore issues in higher education, but ones that are directly linked to high school students. Miller investigates the "two-way street" of commodification. He challenges school rankings, like those done by *U.S. News and World Reports*, and, as an admissions professional, considers the aspects colleges focus on in order to lure prospective students. Part of his argument, connected to other chapters, is that students are seen not only as commodities, but as culturally developed uncritical consumers. For Miller, this means that colleges can send glossy "viewbooks" touting mini-kitchens and cable television links in dorms as "sure-fire" ways to attract students.

In chapter ten, Lynn Wilson, The Harbour Institute, investigates the degree to which conservative think tanks control the information citizens receive, especially concerning educational issues and policy. She reveals the degree to which the Heritage Foundation, Hudson Institute, Cato Institute, American Enterprise Institute, and the Brookings Institution effectively sponsor government officials and determine what information, especially information concerning education, gets the most "play" on what she calls "corporate media." Wilson also details and provides examples of the startling number of corporate executives that have held influential positions on boards, councils, and commissions that directly influence educational issues in the United States.

In the final chapter, I offer a definition of "exploit" that has two meanings. The argument is that school–business partnerships exploit schools in the first sense of the term, that is, to make unethical use of schools for their own advantage or profit. The ultimate intention of chapter eleven, however, is to champion the other definition of "exploit" in order to "make use of, turn to account, and utilize productively." Specifically, the chapter argues that school–business partnerships can be used as object lessons themselves to teach critical transitivity and critical citizenship.

The ultimate point, of course, is to consider and reconsider the roles and purposes of public schools in the United States. What this book shows is the degree to which commercial and corporate influences have saturated schools and the language we use to talk about schools. This book also high-lights the degree to which citizens accept and promote business logics even when it is detrimental for those same citizens to do so. The hegemony involved in commercialism, privatization, and school–business partnerships reduces the idea of community to markets and materialism. Greed under the guise of "free"-market entrepreneurialism appeals to rugged-individualist fears about cooperation and collective action. Consequently, capitalist expectations for competition and selfishness co-opt difference, pluralism, and critical study. These later characteristics are worth championing and we offer this book as one way of doing so.

—*Deron Boyles*
Atlanta, Georgia

ACKNOWLEDGMENTS

The authors wish to thank Alex Molnar for his time and consideration of their work. Thanks are also extended to the manuscript reviewer for LEA, Kenneth Saltman of DePaul University. This work would not have been possible without the interest and support of Naomi Silverman and the staff at LEA, including Erica Kica, Sara Scudder, and Sean Sciarrone. We thank them for their help and encouragement. Special thanks go to Philip Kovacs who helped bring this work to fruition.

REFERENCES

Huntley, H. (2003, September 23). State fund buys school operator. *St. Petersburg Times.* Retrieved November 29, 2003, from http://www.sptimes.com/2003/09/25/Business/State_fnd_buys_schoo./shtml

Molnar, A. (1996). *The Commercialization of America's Schools.* Boulder, CO: Westview Press.

Saltman, K. (2000). *Collateral Damage: Corporatizing Public Schools—A Threat to Democracy.* Lanham, MD: Rowman & Littlefield.

(Note: The Boyles chapter includes sections that have been published in *Educational Founda-tions* [Summer 2001, 63–75] and *Philosophical Studies in Education* [vol. 33, 2002, 115–126].) Reprinted with permission from Haithe Anderson and Alan Jones.

Chapter 1

The Privatization of Food Services in Schools: Undermining Children's Health, Social Equity, and Democratic Education

Carolyn VanderSchee

"Not satisfied with marketing to children through playgrounds, toys, cartoons, movies, videos, charities, and amusement parks, through contests, sweepstakes, games, and clubs, via television, radio, magazines, and the Internet, fast food chains are now gaining access to the last advertising-free post of the American Life": the public school.[1] The public school represents one of the last frontiers not already dominated by market segmentation, market penetration, and corporate profits. At the same time, the public school also represents one of the most, if not the most, strategically focused, captive, and lucrative markets in American society. It is no wonder that corporate America has invaded this new territory of impressionable consumers, a territory that provides access to the demographic segment with the greatest buying power. Corporations no longer prize children for their influence over adult spending; today children have become their own market holding significant spending power now and in the future.[2]

---

[1] Eric Schlosser, *Fast Food Nation: The Dark Side of the All American Meal* (New York: Perennial, 2002), 51.

[2] Jane Kenway and Elizabeth Bullen, *Consuming Children* (Philadelphia, PA: Open University Press, 2001).

Corporate presence in schools is growing from advertising in hallways, classrooms, buses, and rooftops, to writing curriculum. Labeled as "partnerships," corporate "sponsors" are actively pursued by many school boards, parents, and students. One area where partnerships are growing is in school food services.[3] Ten years ago, the school food service industry represented an estimated $4.8 billion market; in 1999, it was valued at $15 billion.[4] Cafeterias are portrayed as "untapped" markets and "some of the best buys in new advertising media."[5] A candid comment from Blaine Hurst, president of Papa John's Pizza, reinforces the notion that corporate sponsors have found their marketing utopia when he stated that offering Papa John's pizza in schools is, "more than a marketing tool ... clearly," he went on to say, "it's an opportunity for product trial."[6]

Today more than 20% of schools offer brand-name foods in their cafeterias.[7] Major corporate players include: McDonald's, Subway, Papa John's Pizza, Dunkin' Donuts, Pizza Hut, Dairy Queen, and Taco Bell. Four vendors in particular, Pizza Hut, Domino's Pizza, Taco Bell, and Subway, are the most aggressive and collectively provide approximately 73% of the brand-name fast foods available in schools.[8]

Widespread availability of soft drinks through vending machines complements greater prevalence of fast foods in the cafeteria. Currently, more than 20,000 schools have vending machines, offering an assortment of items including juice drinks, carbonated beverages, fruit juices, chocolate bars, cookies, and candies.[9] Although vending machines are not new to schools,

---

[3] Although the term "partnerships" is used throughout this chapter to describe school-based marketing schemes, its use does not legitimize the term's authenticity. Authentic partnerships are mutually beneficial; this chapter asserts that school-business partnerships only promote corporate interests.

[4] Ira E. Rodd, "McLunchrooms!" *The Nation* 255, no. 8 (1992): 276; Betsy Spethmann, "Cafeteria Lines," *Promo* 12, no. 12 (1999).

[5] Rodd, "McLunchrooms!" 276; Catherine M. Curran, "Misplaced Marketing," *Journal of Consumer Marketing* 16, no. 6. (1999): 534.

[6] Mark Hamstra, "Papa John's Hitting the Books for its School-Lunch Program," *Nation's Restaurant News* 3 March 1997: 20.

[7] Howell Wechsler, Nancy Brener, Sarah Kuester, and Clare Miller, "Food Service and Foods and Beverages Available at School: Results from the School Health Policies and Programs Study 2000," *Journal of School Health* 71, no. 7 (2001): 313–324. This figure has risen dramatically, when in 1990, only 2% of schools offered brand name foods. Government Accounting Office (GAO), *School Lunch Programs, Role and Impacts of Private Food Service Companies: United States GAO Report to Congressional Committees* (Washington, DC: Resources, Community, and Economic Development Division, 1996), GAO/RCED-96-217, ERIC, ED 400700.

[8] GAO, *School Lunch Programs, Role and Impacts of Private Food Service Companies*. Pizza Hut, Domino's, Pizza, Taco Bell, and Subway serviced 36%, 27%, 22%, and 6% of the schools respectively. For the purpose of this chapter, the terms "fast food" and "brand name fast food" are synonymous. Note that Pepsi Co. owns both Pizza Hut and Taco Bell.

[9] Kathleen Vail, "Insert Coins in Slot: School Vending Machines Generate Funds- and Controversy," *American School Board Journal* 186, no. 2 (1999): 28–31; Mary Story, Marcia Hayes, and Barbara Kalina, "Availability of Foods in High Schools: Is There Cause for Concern?" *Journal of American Dietetic Association* 96, no. 2 (1996): 123–126, 125. These six items were most frequently found in high school vending machines.

today, more than ever, they represent considerable profits for corporations and, to a lesser extent, schools.

In 1997, schools contributed an estimated $750 million to the vending machine service industry.[10] Today, almost 50% of all school districts in the country have contracts with a soft drink company like Coca-Cola, Pepsi-Cola, or Dr. Pepper.[11] In exchange for exclusive sales rights, soft drink companies offer schools lucrative signing bonuses and promotional packages that often include additional funding for sports equipment, extracurricular activities, scholarships, or technology. Nationwide, schools earn $750 million per year from fast-food and soda vendors.[12] School officials can also negotiate a contract entitling their school to a commission on sales. More savvy administrators engage in bidding wars that force vendors to compete for their school's business.[13] Partnership advocates claim that sponsorship arrangements represent "win-win" situations for both schools and businesses. As one school administrator said, "Why shouldn't schools get their share? In the end, everyone wins: the students, the schools, and the community. And for once, even the taxpayers get a break."[14]

This chapter is an examination of these alleged "win-win partnerships." The chapter begins with a description of the National School Lunch Program (NSLP), the rise of food service management companies (FSMCs), and the subsequent increase in availability of brand-name foods on school campuses. The historical account of school–business arrangements is followed by an analysis of profit-making pervasiveness in schools, the coinciding increase in privatization of school food services, and the resulting situation

[10]Vail, "Insert Coins in Slot." See also Sarah Jane Tribble, "Vending Machines Thrive in Today's Workplace," *The Charlotte Observer*, 30 June 2003. available from LexusNexus [http://web.lexis-nexis.com/universe]: Internet; accessed 8 December 2003. Tribble reports that the total vending machine industry's revenues were approximately $24.34 billion in 2001. Schools therefore represent a significant direct and indirect proportion of this total revenue. Directly, schools contribute to the total revenue through vending machine sales. Indirectly, schools contribute the vending machine industry by attracting loyal lifelong consumers who, after completing school, continue to patronize vending machines.

[11]Welcher, et al., "Food Service and Foods Available." Twelve thousand private nonprofit schools and residential childcare institutions participated in the School Health Policy and Programs Study sponsored by the Centers for Disease Control. The responses of 722 school districts were included in the food services component of the survey. Of the districts that had contracts with soda vendors: 79.2% received a specified percentage of the sales; 62.5% received incentives such as cash awards or donations for receipts that totaled a certain amount; 35.3% allow companies to place advertisements in the school building; 43% allow companies to place advertisements on the school grounds; 6.5% allow sales promotion by posters on school walls; 5.5% offer coupons; 3.0% allow school book covers to contain advertisements; and 1.1% allow companies to create lesson plans and curricula. The ramifications of these findings are addressed later in the chapter.

[12]Timothy Egan, "In Bid to Improve Nutrition, Schools Expel Soda and Chips," *The New York Times*, 20 May 2002, A(1).

[13]Robert Zorn, "The Great Cola Wars: How One District Profits from the Competition for Vending Machines," *American School Board Journal* 186, no. 2 (1999): 31–38.

[14]Robert Zorn, "The Great Cola Wars," 33.

where profits are prized more than children. Evidence to show that the "losers" of these partnerships are public schools and their children is also provided. More specifically, the data show how school–business partnerships
undermine children's health, social equity, and the promise of democratic
education.[15] Finally, the chapter closes with a description of the future of
these partnerships and recent attempts at curbing corporate interests and
"re-regulating" food services in schools.

HISTORICAL CONSIDERATIONS: INTRODUCTION
OF THE NATIONAL SCHOOL LUNCH PROGRAM

Since the inception of The National Lunch Act of 1946 and the creation of
the NSLP, U.S. schools have served more than 180 billion lunches.[16] In 2002,
the NSLP operated in 99,000 public and nonprofit schools and residential
child-care institutions. Despite reduced funding for this initiative over the
years, the program is still responsible for providing 28 million children with
daily lunches.[17]

During the late nineteenth and early twentieth centuries, private and philanthropic gifts to local schools supported school meals. In some instances,
local boards of education would incorporate a lunch program into its budget.[18] For the most part, food services in schools were ad hoc community efforts with no regulatory oversight. This practice continued until the 1930s
when a limited amount of federal support became available to needy children, in the form of federal work programs. It was not until the 1940s that the
NSLP received broader federal endorsement through the legislative action
of The National School Lunch Act of 1946.[19] This legislation was expanded

---

[15]See Kenneth Saltman, *Collateral Damage: Corporatizing Public Schools—A Threat to Democracy*
(New York: Rowman and Littlefield, 2000). Specifically see pages 13–15. Regarding the threat to
democratic education, I am referring to the erosion of the public sphere that accompanies privatization.

[16]Diane Allensworth, Elaine Lawson, Lois Nicholson, and James Wyche, ed., *Schools and
Health* (Washington, DC: Institute of Medicine, National Academy Press; 1997). At the federal
level, the United States Department of Agriculture (USDA) administers the NSLP and the
School Breakfast Program (SBP) through the Food and Nutrition Service. At the state level, the
respective Departments of Education are responsible for administering, dispersing funds, and
monitoring all lunch programs. States rely on the local school food authorities for the program's general oversight for one or more schools or an entire district.

[17]Government Accounting Office (GAO), *School Lunch Program, Efforts Needed to Improve Nutrition and Encourage Healthy Eating: Report to Congressional Requesters* (Washington, DC: United
States GAO, May 2003), GAO-03-506; available from <http://www.gao.gov/cgi-bin/
getrpt?GAO03-506htm>.

[18]Allensworth, et al., *Schools and Health.*

[19]National School Lunch Act of 1966, Pub. L. No 89-642, 80 Stat.885, 42 U.S.C. § 1751, et seq.
(1946).

in the 1960s, making free and reduced lunches available to all children who were members of low-income households.[20]

In the 1980s, federal and state governments drastically reduced the level of funding for the NSLP. A 1990 study conducted by the Citizen's Commission on School Nutrition found that funding for the NSLP was at only 58% of its initial 1946 level.[21] Researchers working with the Institute of Medicine believe that reductions in funding sent a clear message to local food authorities and school administrators to operate food services independent of public support.[22] Funding reductions gave an open invitation for corporations to enter the lucrative market of school food services.

INTRODUCTION TO
FOOD SERVICE MANAGEMENT COMPANIES

Over the last 30 years, regulatory and statutory changes have affected the administration and organization of the NSLP. In 1970, the USDA passed regulations allowing local food authorities to contract services with private corporations.[23] Known as FSMCs, these private corporations were responsible for a school's food services, facilities maintenance, staffing, accounting, as well as state and federal reporting. Recall that in the 1980s, the NSLP experienced massive funding reductions, which coincided with a rise in the number of schools that sought the services of FSMCs to operate their lunch programs. Since the 1980s, local food authorities most often turn to FSMCs for financial reasons, citing that outsourcing food services was the only way to maintain a fiscally viable lunch program because many nationwide FSMCs could generate higher sales volume with lower operational costs.[24] FSMCs came to schools promising to lower food service costs and increase student participation in the NSLP by offering a greater variety of food options. The

---

[20]United States Department of Agriculture (USDA), Food and Nutrition Service, *National School Lunch Program* (Washington DC: USDA, accessed 26 June 2002); available from <http://www.fns.usda.gov/cnd/Lunch/AboutLunch/faqs.htm>; GAO, *School Lunch Program, Efforts Needed to Improve Nutrition and Encourage Healthy Eating*, 6. The free and reduced lunch program is still in existence today. Children from families with incomes at or below 130% of the poverty level (below $22,945 for a family of 4) are eligible for free meals, children from families with incomes between 130–185% of the poverty level (between $22,945 and $32,653 for a family of 4) are eligible for reduced-priced meals. The program gives schools $2.14 reimbursement for free meals, $1.74 for reduced priced meals, and $0.20 for paid meals. Schools in areas that service a high proportion of needy children are also entitled to supplementary funding. In addition, schools receive commodity or "entitlement foods" valued at approximately $0.16 per meal served and "bonus" commodities available from agricultural surplus.

[21]Citizen's Commission on School Nutrition, *White Paper on School Lunch Nutrition* (Washington, DC: Center for Science and Public Interest, 1990) quoted in Allensworth, et al., eds., *Schools and Health*, 179.

[22]Allensworth, et al., *Schools and Health*.

[23]GAO, *School Lunch Programs, Role and Impacts of Private Food Service Companies*.

[24]Ibid.

local food authority is responsible for ensuring the FSMC's compliance with USDA and NSLP nutritional requirements.[25] Today, approximately 1,000 of the 15,000 school districts in the United States have contracted food services with FSMCs such as Marriott, Canteen, or ARAMARK.[26]

Increasingly, fast-food and soda vendors are marketing brand-name foods in school cafeterias. Although the USDA does not permit fast-food vendors to sell foods directly to students, vendors are permitted to sell items to schools or FSMCs.[27] Fast-food products can then be resold to students as à la carte items available in vending machines, canteens, and the cafeteria. Fast-food items, when coupled with other more nutritious items, can also become part of the NSLP's reimbursable lunch.[28] Fast-food products that are sold as à la carte, vending, or canteen items are not reimbursable and do not have to comply with the USDA's nutritional guidelines.

A comprehensive analysis of the FSMCs is beyond the scope of this chapter, however it is important to note that FSMCs also contribute to the problems endemic to all corporate–school partnerships.[29] For example, although FSMCs are under greater regulatory oversight when compared to fast-food vendors, the fundamental interest of both entities is to generate profits. Fast-food vendors are dependent on the FSMCs for their operational and managerial oversight. FSMCs contract with fast-food vendors because children purchase fast-food items at a higher rate than items that are more nutritious. FSMCs are very receptive to contracting with fast-food vendors because they generate greater profits with lunch sales that are independent of the

---

[25] Charlene Price and Betsy Kuhn, "Public and Private Efforts for the National School Lunch Program," *Food Review,* (May–August 1996): 51–57. In 1994, Congress passed the Healthy Meals for Healthy Americans Act (P.L. 103-448) stipulating that school lunches must meet federal nutrition requirements outlined in the Dietary Guidelines for Americans as established by the USDA and the US Department of Health and Human Services. These guidelines recommend that no more than 30% of calories can come from fat and less than 10% from saturated fat. Recommendations also state that school lunches must contain at least 1/3 of the Recommended Dietary Allowances for protein, Vitamin A, Vitamin C, iron, calcium, and calories.

[26] Ibid.

[27] GAO, *School Lunch Programs, Role and Impacts of Private Food Service Companies.* The USDA prohibits fast food vendors from selling food items directly to students unless they become the school's official FSMC. However, this rarely occurs as it would require the vendor to assume the entire management of the school's food services. It would also require the vendor to comply with the USDA and NSLP nutritional requirements.

[28] Ibid. However, a survey conducted by the GAO showed that 24% of schools that serve fast food items only offered them as a la carte items. Therefore, fast food items in those schools were unavailable to children who qualify for the free and reduced lunch programs unless the children paid the full fast food price for the item.

[29] Ibid. See this GAO study for additional concerns regarding FSMCs and their involvement in schools particularly surrounding issues of regulation and compliance of federal guidelines. Recall that FSMCs report directly to the local food authority. The local food authority is ultimately responsible for maintaining federal compliance. The GAO cited that in approximately 58% of the contracts between FSMCs and food authorities there were no stipulations regarding FSMC compliance with federal regulations. Since federal adherence was not contractually required, one wonders how the food authority enforces compliance.

NSLP.[30] Furthermore, there is also evidence showing that the role of FSMCs extends beyond the cafeteria and into the classroom.[31] However, this chapter does not address the supporting role that FSMCs play in distributing products; it focuses on corporations who are interested in buying children's brand loyalty.

INTRODUCTION TO COMPETITIVE FOODS

Brand-name foods offered to students in schools are widely referred to as *competitive foods*.[32] The USDA defines competitive foods as foods offered at school, other than meals served through the USDA's school meal program. The USDA further delineates two categories of competitive foods: foods of minimal nutritional value (FMNV) and all other foods offered for individual sale, typically brand-name foods.[33]

The USDA defines FMNV as foods that provide less than 5% of the U.S. Recommended Daily Allowance (RDA) for eight specified nutrients per serving. FMNV include water ices, soft drinks, most hard candies, and chewing gum.[34] Federal law governing the NSLP prohibits the sale of FMNV in the food service areas during the school meal periods.[35] However, it does not

---

[30]Ibid. This GAO survey reported that 75% of all cafeteria managers who offer brand name fast foods named "increased student participation" as the primary reason for offering them.

[31]Sharon Donovan, "Private Sector Adds to the Menu," *School Business Affairs* (September 1997): 18–20. Donovan describes school districts in the Pacific Northwest that are participating in an academic program with Marriott, their local FSMC. The program is entitled the *Marriott Career Classroom* and is offered as a one-credit elective course and is available to juniors and seniors at participating high schools. In addition to learning about Total Quality Management practices, students learn culinary skills, safety in food preparation, and general job skills. Advocates of the program also cite the numerous opportunities for student internships. The internships, of course, are conveniently "built into" Marriott's business. For a further discussion on how corporations promote their social and economic position by influencing the curriculum, see Alex Molnar, *Giving Kids the Business: The Commercialization of America's Schools* (Boulder, CO: Westview Press, 1996). See also Deron Boyles, *American Education and Corporations: The Free Market Goes to School* (New York: Falmer Press, 2000). Molnar and Boyles argue that corporations have a pro-business agenda for schools to adopt a training-oriented curriculum.

[32]Due to its widespread use, I will also use this term, but I do so reluctantly. It seems as though the term "competitive foods" is itself an endorsement of corporate ideology. I believe the term speaks to the pervasive use and universal acceptance of corporate language, but more importantly, it substantiates the appropriateness of using corporate metaphors in reference to children and schools. I will use the term competitive foods interchangeably when referring to fast foods and soft drinks throughout this chapter.

[33]USDA, Food and Nutrition Service, *Foods Sold in Competition with USDA Meal Programs: A Report to Congress* (Washington DC: submitted 12 January 2001, accessed 26 June 2002); available from: <http://www.fns.usda.gov/cnd/Lunch/CompetitiveFoods/competitive. foods.report.to.congress.html>.

[34]This chapter will primarily focus on the sale of soft drinks at schools due to their widespread availability and high rate of consumption.

[35]Federal law [7 C.F.R. 210.11(b)] regulates the sale of competitive foods in schools.

prohibit their sale outside food service areas or in the cafeteria at other times of the day.[36]

The second category of competitive foods includes all other foods offered for individual sale. These foods, although not officially designated as FMNV, are usually high in calories and fat, have low nutritional value, and include foods such as chocolate bars, pizza, hamburgers, and french fries.[37] Currently, no federal regulation governs the sale of these foods; consequently, schools can sell them at anytime or anywhere on campus. They are most often served as à la carte items in the cafeteria, vending machines, or in school canteens.

The almost 40-year regulatory history governing the sale of competitive foods in schools demonstrates that congressional decisions were repeatedly made to favor commercial interests over the health and welfare of children.[38] A look at the creation of soft-drink "pouring rights" provides a case in point.

SOFT-DRINK POURING RIGHTS AND BRAND-NAME FOODS

The soft-drink pouring rights saga begins in 1966 when the first soft-drink contracts were created.[39] These contracts allowed schools to place soda and snack vending machines on campuses. By the late 1960s, it was clear to school officials, parents, health authorities, and Congress that foods from vending machines were competing with the federally supported lunch program.[40] Therefore, in 1970, Congress passed legislation authorizing the USDA to regulate the sale of competitive foods in schools. The resulting USDA guidelines blocked all competitive-food sales in cafeterias and the sale of competitive foods campuswide until the end of the last lunch period. In addition, the USDA permitted schools to sell à la carte items only as components of reimbursable school meals. Consequently, many food companies and schools that became dependent on proceeds from the sale of competitive foods banned together to protest the USDA's decision.[41]

In 1972, Congress capitulated to pressure from protestors and amended the act to allow schools to sell competitive foods on the condition that sale proceeds support school organizations. Congress also permitted local and state agencies to govern the sale of competitive foods, effectively alleviating the

---

[36]GAO, *School Lunch Program, Efforts Needed to Improve Nutrition and Encourage Healthy Eating*, 8.
[37]Story, Hayes, and Kalina, "Availability of Foods," 123–126.
[38]Marion Nestle, "Pouring Rights: Marketing Empty Calories to Children," *Public Health Reports 2000* 115 (July/August 2000): 308–319.
[39]Ibid. This was done through congressional amendments to the Child Nutrition Act of 1966, which in turn revised the National School Lunch Act of 1946.
[40]National Soft Drink Association v. J.R. Block Secretary, Department of Agriculture, et al., 721 F.2d 1348 (US Court of Appeals, D.C. Circuit, 1983).
[41]Nestle, "Pouring Rights."

USDA's jurisdiction on the matter. Subsequently, vending machine use and food delivery services from outside the schools rose and school cafeterias began to offer more brand-name items to compete with vending machines.[42]

In 1977, under the Carter administration, Congress passed an amendment to restore the USDA's authority to establish regulations regarding the sale of foods in competition with the NSLP. However, Congress stipulated an important caveat: the USDA could not ban competitive foods from schools; they could restrict only the sale of foods inconsistent with a healthy diet. In 1980, after much debate, the USDA announced its final ruling: the sale of foods with minimal nutritional value from the beginning of the school day to the end of the last lunch period was prohibited.[43] Once again, the USDA's restriction meant significant revenue loss for companies and schools.

During the early 1980s, the National Soft Drink Association (NSDA) filed several lawsuits against the USDA forcing them to reconsider their ruling.[44] The USDA was unyielding, but on November 15, 1983, the U.S. Court of Appeals overturned the USDA's decision.[45] The court held that congressional intent was only to prohibit competitive foods being served in school lunch areas and not to prohibit the sale of all foods in competition with the NSLP. The court cited that the USDA had gone beyond congressional intent in establishing time and place provisions on food sales. Thus, current regulations regarding the sale of competitive foods at schools emanate from the federal court's intervention.[46]

The court's final ruling remains in effect today: the sale of FMNV is prohibited in the food service area during meal hours. Because it applies only to the sale of FMNV, this essentially only restricts the sale of hard candy and sodas in the cafeteria during mealtimes and does not forbid, for example, their sale outside the cafeteria doors at any time of the day.[47] Furthermore, because the regulations apply only to FMNV, there are no limits on the sale of other competitive foods, such as fast foods.[48] Although the court's ruling endorsed state and local authorities right to enforce additional restrictions, rel-

---

[42]Story, Hayes, and Kalina, "Availability of Foods."

[43]Nestle, "Pouring Rights." The USDA's 1980 regulations elicited an overwhelmingly negative response from the public. The initial proposal received more than 3,000 comments, however 562 of these were traced directly to PepsiCo. Nestle suggests that that the company likely endorsed in an employee-wide letter writing campaign.

[44]Story, Hayes, and Kalina, "Availability of Foods."

[45]National Soft Drink Association v. J.R. Block Secretary, Department of Agriculture, et al., 721 F.2d 1348 (U.S. Court of Appeals, D.C. Circuit. 1983).

[46]Nestle, "Pouring Rights." Nestle provides a more comprehensive description of the events described here in, "Select Events in the History of Regulations Governing Sales of Soft Drinks and Other Competitive 'Foods of Minimal Nutritional Value' in Elementary and Secondary Schools," 315.

[47]Story, Hayes, and Kalina, "Availability of Foods;" GAO, *School Lunch Program, Efforts Needed to Improve Nutrition and Encourage Healthy Eating.*

[48]Welcher, et al., "Food Service and Foods Available."

atively few states have taken any action.[49] For example, the court ruling did not specify when state and local authorities should impose further regulations, nor did it require state agencies to verify adherence or impose sanctions on schools that are out of compliance with the federal court ruling.[50] Most states do not have supplementary regulations and in the states that do, some schools do not even comply with the federal court ruling.

The NSDA does not act independently in its quest to manipulate legislation. Before the "Pizza Hut exemption," federal law mandated that all meat products were subject to strict laws governing their handling and inspection.[51] Rodd described how Pizza Hut successfully lobbied to have their pizza meat toppings served in schools excused from federal meat regulations. Essentially, Pizza Hut proposed that its meat toppings should not be considered meat, and therefore not subjected to costly health inspections. The bill was pushed through Congress by company ally, Representative Dan Glickman. In 1990, Pizza Hut was successful in exempting hospitals, offices, and university campuses; later that year public schools were added to the list.[52]

CONSEQUENCES OF PRIVATIZATION OF FOOD SERVICES IN SCHOOLS: UNDERMINING CHILDREN'S HEALTH

Nutrition professionals, school food personnel, and child health advocates argue that the current federal regulations are too lenient given the legislation's limited scope and laissez-faire enforcement requirements.[53] This chapter now focuses on three fundamental problems that corporate presence in school food services pose, namely, undermining: children's health, social equity, and public education.

The underlying premise of the NSLP is that schools are in a unique position to support and enhance children's health. Nutrition affects children's health, their ability to learn, and their potential for becoming healthy adults.[54] It is important for children to establish healthy eating patterns early on to ensure optimal growth and development, and to prevent illnesses later in life.[55] Because children receive approximately one third of their daily calories from lunch, school meals make an important contribution to a child's overall nutrition status.[56]

---

[49] Story, Hayes, and Kalina, "Availability of Foods."
[50] USDA, "Foods Sold in Competition."
[51] Rodd, "McLunchrooms!," 276.
[52] Ibid.
[53] Ibid.
[54] USDA, "Foods Sold in Competition."
[55] Welcher, et al., "Food Service and Foods Available."
[56] Ibid.

Researchers link diet as a risk factor for many health problems including obesity, asthma, diabetes, osteoporosis, tooth decay, and the nation's three leading causes of death: heart disease, cancer, and stroke.[57] Obesity is of particular concern to dietitians and health care professionals as it is linked to many of the aforementioned health problems. Since 1980, obesity rates among children and adolescents have doubled. Today, nearly 13% of children and adolescents are significantly overweight.[58] Furthermore, an estimated 25% of children have extremely high cholesterol levels.[59] David Satcher, the U.S. Surgeon General, says that failing to address obesity-related issues could negate some of the positive gains made in reducing the prevalence of other chronic health problems.[60]

According to Eric Schlosser, author of *Fast Food Nation*, "Fast food has infiltrated every nook and cranny of American society," and public schools are no exception.[61] Today, American children receive approximately one third of their total vegetable servings from potato chips or french fries. Schlosser goes on to report that, "In 1970, Americans spent about $6 billion on fast food; in 2001, they spent more than $110 billion. Americans now spend more money on fast food than on higher education, personal computers, computer software, or new cars."[62]

The increase in fast-food consumption parallels that of the soft-drink industry. Consumption today is nine times greater than it was in 1942 ac-

---

[57]Nestle, "Pouring Rights"; Welcher, et al., "Food Service and Foods Available." See also Michael F. Jacobson, *Liquid Candy: How Soft Drinks are Harming Americans' Health* (Washington DC: Center for Science in the Public Interest, 1998, accessed 1 July 2002); available from <http://www.cspinet.org/sodapop/liquid_candy.html>; Sally Squires, "Soft Drinks, Hard Facts," *Washington Post*, 27 February 2001, HE (10); R.F. Majewski, "Dental Caries in Adolescents Associated with Caffeinated Carbonated Beverages," *Pediatric Dentistry* 22, no. 3 (2001): 198–203; and Grace Wyshak and Rose E. Frisch, "Carbonated Beverages, Dietary Calcium, The Dietary Calcium/Phosphorus Bone Ratio, and Bone Fractures in Girls and Boys," *Journal of Adolescent Health* 15 (1994): 210–215.

[58]U.S. Department of Health and Human Services, *Over Weight and Obesity Threaten U.S. Health Gains* (Washington D.C.: Government Printing Office, 2001). According to the National Institutes of Health, "in children and adolescents overweight is defined as a sex-and-age specific BMI [Body Mass Index] at or above the 95th percentile, based on revised growth charts by the Centers for Disease Control and Prevention. There is no generally accepted definition for obesity for children and adolescents."

[59]Laura Shapiro and Patrick Rogers, "What's in a Lunch?" *Newsweek* (Summer, 1991): 66–69. A level of 170 or higher is considered extremely high. High cholesterol levels contribute to heart disease.

[60]David Satcher, *The Surgeon General's Call to Action to Prevent and Decrease Overweight and Obesity* (Washington D.C.: Department of Health and Human Services, 2001, accessed 15 July 2002); available from: <*http://www.surgeongeneral.gov/topics/obesity*> Internet. According to the report, obesity and excess weight are associated with 300,000 deaths annually. This was compared to 400,000 tobacco-related deaths annually. Furthermore, in 2000, the direct and indirect costs attributed to obesity were estimated at $117 billion.

[61]Schlosser, *Fast Food Nation*, 3.

[62]Ibid.

counting for one third of all refined sugar in the average American's diet.[63] Because of their poor nutritional profile, high in calories and low in nutrients, Nestle described soft drinks as the "quintessential 'junk-food.'"[64] Given this nutritional deficit, children's consumption rates are even more compelling as a serious public-health concern. Half of the country's children, aged 6 to 11, drink approximately 15 ounces of soda per day. Among adolescent boys who drink soda, the average daily intake is approximately 28.5 ounces, and among girls, the average soda drinker consumes around 21 ounces per day.[65]

For children, increases in soft-drink and fast-food consumption can have serious health implications. Although the privatization of food and drink services in schools is not solely responsible for all of these health consequences, their presence certainly makes a significant contribution. Multimillion-dollar marketing schemes increase the attractiveness of unhealthy foods and combining enhanced marketing efforts with increased availability at schools only exacerbates the problem.[66] In 1999 Coca-Cola spent approximately $867 million in advertising and PepsiCo spent even more—$1.31 billion.[67] According to the USDA:

> Students' appetites today are demanding, having been influenced by sociological changes ... the increase in convenience and processed foods, the proliferation of fast foods, and major marketing campaigns targeted to children and youth.... It is unrealistic to expect them to eat only healthful foods at lunch unless there is a concerted effort to make that happen.[68]

Current legislation does not require schools to make this concerted effort. Corporations take advantage of the permissive regulatory system governing fast-food and soft-drink sales on campuses. Consequently, the decision regarding which foods to offer in school cafeterias is often based on profitability rather than on nutritional profiles. Because fast foods and soft drinks have a higher sales rate and profit margin, they are the food of choice.[69]

---

[63] Jacobson, *Liquid Candy*. Jacobson reports that in 1997, Americans spent over $54 billion to buy 14 billion gallons of soft drinks equivalent to more than 1.6 12-ounce cans per day for every man, woman, and child.

[64] Marion Nestle, *Food Politics*, (Berkley, CA: University of California Press, 2002), 198.

[65] Jacobson, *Liquid Candy*.

[66] Ibid. In addition, soft drink companies have increased container sizes of soft drinks. In the 1950s the average container size was 6.5 ounces, today 12 ounce and 20 ounce servings are the norm.

[67] Nestle, *Food Politics*, 201.

[68] American Dietetic Association (ADA), "Position of The American Dietetic Association: Competitive Foods in Schools," *Journal of the American Dietetic Association* 91 (1991): 1123–1125. Author's note: this is no longer an official position of the USDA.

[69] Allensworth, et al., *Schools & Health*.

The fast-food and soft-drink industries have a difficult time reconciling the nutritional value of their products with the requirements for a healthy balanced diet. Fast-food and soft-drink companies defend their products citing that, when eaten in moderation, their foods can be a part of a healthy diet. Companies claim that studies on their products' association with health problems is inconclusive or conflicts with other research data. Corporations absolved themselves of any responsibility for these health problems by blaming the sedentary lifestyles of Americans. The NSDA even points to schools as a major contributor to children's health problems.[70]

Fast-food vendors and soft-drink vendors interpret select findings to support their interests, and choose to ignore important connections between the consumption of their products and compromised health. For example, NSDA literature repeatedly refers to a study conducted by Anne Mardis from the Center for Nutrition Policy and Promotion. The study examined the health effects of sugar intake. The NSDA reports that the study concluded that sugar consumption was not associated with chronic diseases such as diabetes, obesity, and hyperactivity in children. They quote Mardis' conclusion; "A focus on sugar as an independent risk factor for chronic disease and hyperactivity should be de-emphasized."[71] However, the Association fails to mention that Mardis' study confirmed well-established and intuitive data showing that obesity results when caloric intake exceeds expenditure. They also fail to mention that obesity and soft-drink consumption rates have risen in tandem. Today, some children receive up to 12% of their overall caloric intake from soft drinks; therefore, although it is possible that children exercise more to burn the additional calories, it is more likely that heavy consumption contributes to significant weight gain.[72]

Not only do competitive foods pose direct threats to children's health, they also deter children from eating foods that are more nutritious and reduce participation in the federal program. NSLP participation has steadily declined since the introduction of fast food and soft drinks in schools. Although school attendance has increased by 6.8% in the last 20 years, participation has decreased by 1.2%.[73]

---

[70]The National Soft Drink Association claims that schools are to blame for the health consequences typically associated with their products. The association asserts that if more school systems in the country provided daily physical activity for students, issues of childhood obesity would not have reached such "alarming levels."

[71]Anne Mardis, "Current Knowledge of the Health Effects of Sugar Intake," *Family Economics and Nutrition Review* 13, no. 1 (2001): 89.

[72]Jacobson, *Liquid Candy*. This figure is accurate for children in the 75th percentile of soft-drink consumption. Jacobson goes on to report that soft drinks are the fifth largest source of calories for adults, providing approximately 5.6% of their caloric intake. For 12 to 19 year old boys and girls, soft drinks provide approximately 8% and 9% of their caloric intake respectively. These figures are triple what they were in 1977–1978.

[73]Ibid. States that have restricted the sale of competitive foods have higher participation rates than the national average.

NSLP participation benefits for all children are well documented. A USDA study reported that NSLP participation is associated with higher than average intakes of protein-rich foods, vegetables, vitamin C, phosphorus, calcium, and lower intakes of sugars.[74] Advocates claim the program makes a significant contribution to social equity, particularly for those children that receive a healthy daily meal only through program participation.

Furthermore, schools arguably should be places where all children learn healthy consumption patterns. Offering unhealthy food options without critique or critical inquiry undermines nutrition messages that children receive in the classroom. Stated another way, "While health teachers are instructing kids on the food pyramid and the maligned effects of too much sugar, the message beyond the classroom door is to drink up—as long as you're drinking Coke, or Pepsi, or whatever brew is paying the bill."[75] This sends children the message their health is important, but not important enough to preserve when financial gains for the school are at stake.[76]

UNDERMINING SOCIAL EQUITY

The NSLP was established to ensure that every school-age child had access to a healthy meal; however, it embodied more than a tangible commitment to children. The entire program was not only a means of providing disadvantaged children with similar nutritional advantages as their more affluent counterparts; the program marked a new commitment to community, justice, and social equity.

Today, the NSLP is not assisting all the children who qualify for its services. More than 300 schools dropped out of the program from 1989 to 1993.[77] Many of these schools claim that they have too few students who qualify for federal reimbursement, and assert that they can provide for their students on their own by hiring private companies. Therefore, schools that serve a small number of poor students are at greatest risk for dropping out of the program.[78] This is consistent with findings showing that corporate vendors target a specific market segment; schools servicing a larger student pop-

---

[74]Mathematica Policy Research, Inc., *Children's Diets in the Mid-1990's: Dietary Intake and Its Relationship with School Meal Participation* (Washington DC: Final Report Submitted to the USDA, 2001) as quoted in USDA, *Foods Sold in Competition.*

[75]Majorie Williams, "The Soda Subsidy," *Washington Post* (3 January 2001): A 17.

[76]American Dietetic Association, "Position of the American Dietetic Association."

[77]Lisa Van Wagner, "Fed Up: Some School Districts are Booting Uncle Sam Out of Their Cafeterias," *American School Board Journal* 186, no. 2 (1999): 38–41.

[78]Van Wagner, "Fed Up." Van Wagner goes on to write that, "if your school system serves large numbers of low-income children, leaving the program probably isn't cost effective" (p. 39). Unfortunately, for today's students and the public school as an institution, cost-effectiveness trumps social justice and equity. Recall that schools only receive $0.20 reimbursement for students who do not qualify for the free and reduced lunch program. Therefore, schools with many students in this category do not feel as though the reimbursement adequately underwrites program costs.

ulation, suburban schools, and schools managed by FSMCs are most likely to partner with brand-name vendors.[79]

Although the expectation has always been that school lunch programs would be self-supporting, they were never earmarked as profit-making endeavors. The introduction of private, for-profit vendors has disrupted this unspoken understanding. Competitive foods, offered by private vendors, have decreased NSLP participation and diverted funds that would normally support the program.[80] Volume is the key to a fiscally strong program and when schools contract with private vendors to provide food services, they lay the tracks for the demise of their own NSLP.[81] This has put schools in the precarious position of competing with their own school meal programs for revenue. Thus, schools are partially responsible for decreased student participation in the school meal program, and the related loss of revenue for the federal program.

Other schools drop the program even though they may contain many students who qualify for the program but do not participate because of the negative social stigma. The USDA found that 4.1 million eligible students did not apply for the free or reduced lunch program; the study attributes the negative stigma associated with the program as a possible explanation.[82] Children with money can purchase more readily competitive foods for lunch, suggesting to all students that the NSLP is only for poor children rather than a nutritious option for all students.[83]

A privatized lunch program in Boulder, Colorado, sheds light on issues of equity and justice. In the early 1990s, two of the city's high schools decided to eliminate the federal program and contract the management and operation of lunch services with McDonald's. Because foods offered through McDonald's do not qualify for federal reimbursement, students who qualified for free or reduced lunches no longer received this benefit. However, as reporter Ira Rodd stated, "McDonald's came up with the kind of response Oliver Twist might have appreciated: Target those students ... to staff the McCafeteria ... (You want lunch? Work for it!)."[84]

---

[79]GAO, *School Lunch Programs, Role and Impacts of Private Food Service Companies*, 46. High schools were more likely to offer brand name foods when compared to elementary and middle schools; schools with brand name foods had an average of 730–885 students compared to smaller schools averaging 503–543 students; suburban schools were compared to urban schools and rural schools; and schools managed by a FSMC were compared to schools not run by a FSMC.

[80]In the GAO study, *School Lunch Programs, Role and Impacts of Private Food Service Companies* 82% of schools under contract with private vendors reported an increase in competitive food sales, invariably some of this money would have been otherwise spent on the NSLP.

[81]ADA, "Position of the American Dietetic Association."

[82]Allensworth, et al., *Schools & Health.*

[83]Recall that competitive foods do not qualify for federal reimbursement.

[84]Rodd, "McLunchrooms!" Since Rodd's article, the two high schools found that their decision to drop the NSLP was not as profitable as they had once envisioned. According to food service director Nancy Paluh, the costs of abandoning the program were too high because the district required the schools to provide lunch for eligible students.

Colorado's "work-fare" approach is not unique. In Henrico County, Virginia, the district abandoned the federal program to contract its services to fast-food vendors. As in Colorado, the high school has adopted a "good work ethics, no free lunch policy." According to Tim Mertz, the school district's assistant food service director, "'Any student who wants a free lunch, needy or not,' donates half of the lunch hour to a cafeteria task such as stuffing taco shells or stocking shelves."[85]

Other schools that have dropped the program *appear* to offer a more reasonable solution. These schools contend that through additional revenue generated from privatization, they are still able to offer free or reduced lunches to children who would have otherwise qualified for the federal subsidy. However, when profits fall or when too many children qualify for complementary lunches, private vendors have the freedom to reduce the aid they offer to needy students. Thus, the school is obligated to support student patronage of the private vendor to ensure the longevity of the free or reduced lunches program. As a result, the health of all children is compromised.[86]

Other problematic issues plague this arrangement. The benefit of regulatory oversight of nutritional standards that were once a social good provided for all students now becomes an entitlement available to only a few. Additionally, individual school boards have the authority to create their own guidelines to identify needy students. For example, in Chesterfield County, Virginia, the district specifies that only students who are foster children, belong to a family receiving food stamps, or receive Aid to Families with Dependent Children qualify for their "lunch program." Children outside these categories may "petition the principal for consideration and are reviewed for eligibility on a 30 to 60 day basis."[87] Therefore, many children that should qualify are relegated to the petition option. Children whose parents are not equipped, or choose not to petition suffer the loss of participation. Finally, meal tickets usually do not apply to more popular, less healthy foods. Consequently, healthy food options are stigmatized as being provided only for poor children.[88] This provides a social disincentive for affluent children to select healthy lunch options whereas, poor children are stigmatized as needing the alternative lunch.

Low participation rates and the subsequent elimination of the NSLP in many schools are directly attributed to the privatization of food services. Direct attribution occurs through offering foods that compete with the NSLP

---

[85] Diane Brockett, "School Cafeterias Selling Brand-Name Junk Food: Who Deserves a Break Today?" *School Board News* (October 1998): 58.

[86] Interestingly, this could create a cycle where affluent children are encouraged to consume more unhealthy food to subsidize the distribution of unhealthy food for the economically disadvantaged children.

[87] Wagner, "Fed Up," 40.

[88] Ibid.

and indirect attribution arises through subsidizing the costs of food services. The cost subsidization ensures that the program remains underfunded because it appears that the NSLP is fiscally viable when, in reality, the subsidies provided by privatization close the gap between federal funding and actual costs. The individual school's decision to discontinue the program poses a risk to the students who may have qualified for the benefits. However, discontinuing the program at the individual school level also jeopardizes the federal program's collective viability because lower school participation rates reflect decreased need for the program.

The loss of the NSLP is another assault on public education. In this case, aspects of public education shift, from being defined as a social good for all to an entitlement for a few. As Saltman writes:

> The significance of the shift should not be understated. Those public entities thought to be social goods, such as national defense, public roads, and policing, are considered universally necessary and unquestionable elements of a democracy. Entitlements, on the other hand, are less secure in that they are viewed as being in the special interests of a group rather than the entire of society.[89]

To be clear, the NSLP was originally established in 1946 to provide a social good to society. Shifting the program from one that provides an essential social good to one that provides an entitlement jeopardizes all students regardless of their social status. This is true because, offered as a social good, the program benefited the entire society by assuring a nutritious government-subsidized meal for all children; shifting the program to an entitlement provides a nutritious meal only to qualified children.[90] Even the future of this entitlement is questionable given the new decision-making process for reduced- or free-lunch eligibility.

UNDERMINING DEMOCRATIC EDUCATION

Privatization undermines democratic education because as corporations invade school services, schools relinquish their potential to be places that foster democratic action. Saltman refers to these phenomena as the "erosion of the public sphere." He wrote: "Educational privatization results in a deterioration of democratic space. The spread of privatization leaves fewer spaces for democratic decision-making, deliberation, and consideration of bolstering the common good. The result of this erosion of public forums is a transfer of power to private interests."[91]

---

[89]Saltman, *Collateral Damage*, 54.
[90]The entitlement refers to the free and reduced lunches only offered to children that qualify based on school or district designed criteria at schools.
[91]Saltman, *Collateral Damage*, 14.

The experiences of schools with Coca-Cola in Edison, New Jersey, illustrate three unsettling features of school–business partnerships, namely, the widespread community support, the dependency of school operating budgets on corporate partnerships, and the contrivances of corporate philanthropy. Furthermore, the case illustrates how the inherent features of privatization contribute to the devolution of democratic space.

In the fall of 1998, the school district of Edison, New Jersey, signed an exclusive 10-year contract with Coca-Cola, doubling the number of vending machines on school campuses. According to the contract, the district was entitled to scoreboards, scholarships, and other incentives in addition to payments of $3,000, $15,000, and $25,000 for each elementary, middle, and high school, respectively. Throughout the year, however, profits fell short of Coke's expectations, so in a number of now highly publicized letters written to school principals, Coke executives encouraged principals to employ various tactics to boost sales. Executives recommended that principals ensure easy accessibility to vending machines and suggested that principals permit students to bring drinks to class. Executives also reminded principals that if they did not meet their 70,000-case sales goal over the course of the first three years of the contract, the payments from Coke would be significantly reduced.[92]

In many cases, as in New Jersey, the most vocal supporters of school–business partnerships come from school boards, school officials, parents, and students.[93] Molnar writes: "It is rare to hear community leaders voice either ethical or educational objections to school-based marketing schemes."[94] Ironically, in some districts, the loudest protests come from competing cola companies who object to contracts that limit "freedom of choice" in the market place.[95]

School–business partnerships are comfortable exposing children to marketing messages, weakly defending their actions by pointing out the pervasiveness of advertising in society and claiming that there is no harm in advertising in schools.[96] Others claim that schools are simply one more venue for children to

---

[92]Marc Kaufman, "Fighting the Cola Wars in Schools," *Washington Post*, 23 March 1999, Z (12). This example of Coca-Cola executives pressuring principals to increase sales is not unique. Another highly publicized case involved Colorado Springs District 11. The district had signed an $8 million, 10-year contract with Coca-Cola. As in New Jersey, Colorado principals received letters from Coca-Cola executives urging them to implement necessary tactics to increase sales.

[93]Egan, "In Bid to Improve Nutrition," A(1). When legislators proposed to expel private vendors from schools in California some of the loudest protests were heard from students. Angelina Garcia, a high school student stated, "'first they take away our privacy; now they take away our food choice.'" Garcia's comment speaks to the widespread belief that privatization results in more choices for everyone and the assumption that more choices are inherently better. See Saltman, *Collateral Damage;* Boyles, *American Education and Corporations;* and Molnar, *Giving Kids the Business,* 25, for a discussion on the issue and lure of choice as it relates to privatization.

[94]Molnar, *Giving Kids the Business,* 25.

[95]Nestle, *Food Politics,* 197.

[96]Curran, "Misplaced Marketing."

express and refine their consumer potential. As a school board member in Wisconsin alleged, "'Our children are faced their entire lives with choices … and they need at the high school and middle school level to make these choices on their own.'"[97] Still others argue that students will leave the school premises if the school does not offer competitive foods. They reason that if a student is going down the road to purchase McDonald's anyway, the school may as well offer the product.[98] In their minds, this produces another "win-win" situation: The student remains on the school property and the school generates additional income. According to Alex Molnar, the fact that children have easy access to products outside of school is irrelevant and absurd. "That's the kind of logic that a parent wouldn't accept from a 7-year-old. Why should we accept it from a school district or school board members?"[99]

The recent trend toward brand exclusivity exemplified in Edison, New Jersey, is another lucrative scheme in corporate–school marketing that receives little community opposition in lieu of short-term monetary benefits.[100] The average cola contract pays schools between $3 and $30 per student a year in exchange for exclusive vending rights on campuses, including all school-sponsored events. For some districts, exclusivity can generate more than $1.5 million per year.[101] According to the Center for Commercial Free Public Education, more than 100 districts or schools have signed exclusive contracts with Coke or Pepsi.[102] In some instances, school board committees have negotiated for more than a year to create a multimillion-dollar contract.[103] Today, some districts even hire consultants to locate and negotiate the most profitable arrangement.[104]

---

[97] Hardy, "The Lure of Marketing," 24.

[98] The argument that students will leave school campuses in search of fast food if schools do not provide this option is erroneous given that 75% of high schools, 90% of middle schools, and 95% of elementary schools have closed campus policies in effect during the school day. Center for Science and the Public Interest (CSPI), *Pestering Parents: How Food Companies Market Obesity to Children*, (Washington D.C.: SPCI; November 2003); available from <http://cspinet.org/new/pdf/pestering_parents_final_part_1.pdf>.

[99] Molnar as quoted in Hardy, "The Lure of Marketing," 27.

[100] Kaufman, "Fighting the Cola Wars in Schools."

[101] GAO, *School Lunch Program, Efforts Needed to Improve Nutrition and Encourage Healthy Eating*, 14. However, the GAO report agues that all schools do not derive equal monetary benefits from these "partnerships." A district with a "less lucrative" student market may only be entitled to a one-time payment of $12,000 and yearly earnings of $4,800. Clearly, schools with students who have the greatest buying power enjoy more bargaining leverage.

[102] Nestle, "Pouring Rights."

[103] Lawrence Hardy, "The Lure of Marketing," *American School Board Journal* 186, no. 10 (1999): 26. Hardy describes a committee, working together on behalf of a consortium of seventeen school systems in Michigan, spent more than a year constructing a contract with Coca-Cola. After negotiations, the consortium secured a twenty-year contract giving them $10 a year per student, plus a proportion of the soft-drink sales. The consortium anticipates the contract will bring them an additional $4 to $5 million.

[104] Constance L. Hays, "Today's Lesson: Soda Rights: Consultant Helps Schools Sell Themselves to Vendors," *New York Times*, 21 May 1999, C (1,9).

Contract supporters claim that partnerships are fiscally sound and maintain that current funding formulas penalize districts for raising local taxes to pay for education. They assert that increases in local funding result in offsetting decreases in state funding. However, funding from corporate sources is counted as supplementary revenue that is not offset by the state.[105] Ostensibly, the fiscal advantages of school–business partnerships are inspiring, especially today as administrators and teachers face greater educational mandates with shrinking budgets. Therefore, lucrative offers made by soft-drink companies are not only financially compelling but also appear to be prudent solutions. It is this misconstruction, however, that makes partnerships most unsettling.

Those who perceive corporate partnerships as the panacea for school-funding problems fail to recognize the vulnerability of these partnerships and the subsequent unreliability of the funds. Corporations would not be involved in schools were it not for the promise of increased profits and market share. The privatization of school food and drinks is the result of a carefully constructed plan to allow corporations to increase profits through expanding their market. A 1996 U.S. GAO survey showed that schools offering competitive foods chose to do so because corporations promised increased revenue from student participation.[106] Profits are the bottom line and when actual revenue comes in lower than expected sales forecasts, schools do not receive all of the projected "perks." Increasingly, schools are using revenue generated from soft-drink sales to support instructional costs, and fast-food sales to support cafeteria costs.

The financial fallout when this money is taken away, due to broken contracts, changes in legislation, economic recessions, or any of a number of other reasons, worsens and sometimes even devastates the financial situation of the school compared to its precorporate condition. Many school administrators that once touted the success of establishing a school–business partnership now find themselves dependent on corporate profits to meet budgetary obligations. When this occurs, the authenticity of partnerships is exposed for their actual, contrived nature. This dependency contributes to the erosion of democratic public space, because public education is no longer inordinately supported by the public.[107]

For example, when Pinellas County School district in Florida unplugged vending machines until after the final lunch period, the district lost $500,000 in revenue that was budgeted for operational costs.[108] Suddenly the school district found itself unable to meet its financial obligations for the year. Similarly, when schools in Edison, New Jersey, experienced sales

---

[105] Vail, "Insert Coins in Slot."
[106] GAO, *School Lunch Programs, Role and Impacts of Private Food Service Companies.*
[107] Some aspects of public schooling, like busing, have already been privatized.
[108] Vail, "Insert Coins in Slot."

reductions, they risked losing anticipated revenue, placing them at the mercy of corporate interests.[109]

Furthermore, focusing solely on the financial arrangements of school–business partnerships diverts attention away from the corporate executives who are responsible for school underfunding in the first place.[110] Saltman, describing the funding desperation that schools are in, wrote:

> Such desperation leads to the portrayal of corporate profiteers as saviors rather than parasites. Of course, the corporate behavior that leads to the defunding in the first place is not commonly spoken of in mass media or in educational policy circles. A preponderance of mass media representations of corporations as responsible citizens works in conjunction with corporate volunteerism deceptively to portray corporations as concerned with the public good.[111]

Finally, corporate partnerships alleviate the "the burden off legislators who, instead of championing for adequate school funding, now push schools to find their own sources of funding through school–business partners."[112] "As one San Francisco school board official explained, 'Education cannot be funded by potato chip contracts … [C]ome back and talk to me about nothing being wrong with these contracts when there are Coca-Cola banners in the House of Representatives and members of the U.S. Senate can only have a TV set if they watch Channel One for 15 minutes a day.'"[113]

---

[109]Kenith Ervin, "District May Ban Daytime Sodas in Middle Schools," *The Seattle Times*, 17 June 2003, B(1). Another noteworthy case occurred in Seattle's School District. Ervin reports that in 1998 the district signed a five-year exclusive contract with Coca-Cola. In August 2003 the contract came up for renewal. At this time Coca-Cola told the district that if they renewed the contract without changes, the district would receive a signing bonus of $430,000 and annual payments of $195,000 to $245,000. On the other hand, if the district chose to alter the contract in any way, they would be financially penalized. The district found itself under pressure from parents, public-health advocates, and anti-commercial activists to stop or restrict the sale of sodas from schools. The district therefore chose to modify the contract by requiring "at least three slots of each vending machine or one-third of all slots in adjacent machines to non-carbonated soft drinks or water in both high and middle schools." Under the revised contract the district was only entitled to $190,000 per year. Therefore, even though soft drink companies like Coca-Cola claim to be interested in student health they penalize schools who choose to offer more healthy beverage options.

[110]Molnar, *Giving Kids the Business*, 7. Molnar argues that corporations have consistently shirked their responsibilities to provide an adequate tax base for public education. See also Saltman, *Collateral Damage*, 61. Saltman writes, "The corporate tax drain caused by successful corporate lobbying against taxes and social spending has contributed to public schools—particularly urban and nonwhite public schools—being incapable of raising sufficient funds."

[111]Saltman, *Collateral Damage*, 63. See also page 61, here Saltman discusses the reasons for the under-funding of educational He notes that, "the corporate tax drain caused by successful corporate lobbying against taxes and social spending has contributed to the public schools … being incapable of raising sufficient funds."

[112]John Sheehan, "Why I Said No to Coca-Cola," *American School Board Journal* 186, no. 10 (1999): 25.

[113]J. Wynns, "Yes: Selling Students to Advertisers Sends the Wrong Message in the Classroom," *Advertising Age* (June, 1999): 26, quoted in Nestle, *Food Politics*, 218.

Another problematic issue concerns the lack of candor surrounding the fine print written in partnership contracts. The school's contractual obligations requiring them to meet a specified sales quota often go unmentioned. At the same time, school administrators interested in additional revenue for their schools are also not forthright about the contract's details. Because the community remains unaware that "corporate donations" are contingent on revenue, corporations are viewed as authentic and altruistic partners. In reality, corporations use schools to conduct business in the same way they would for any other new market. This results in increasing profits for companies and has the unfortunate effect of also increasing the dependency of schools on corporations for their survival. This raises the issue of corporate philanthropy, or what Boyles refers to as contrived philanthropy: marketing schemes disguised as altruistic efforts.[114]

Boyles describes how it is the corporation, not the school or students, that garners benefits associated with school–business partnerships. Corporations benefit because they promote themselves as being interested in public education, students, and the community.[115] Furthermore, they are provided a forum to advertise and, in the case of soft-drink and fast-food venders, sell their products.

Particularly problematic is that contrived philanthropy remains predominantly underexamined. A comment made by Robert Zorn, the superintendent of the Poland, Ohio, school district, is indicative of the problem. Zorn writes, "When our new electronic two-line message, digital score-board, bigger than the ones used by many colleges, lit up at our first football game, fans loved it. They marveled at the fact that Pepsi had given it to us for free."[116] Although Zorn noted that the sign was not actually "free," his comment speaks to the pervasive and relatively unchallenged assumption that corporations have altruistic motives. He failed to recognize that Pepsi is the primary benefactor of this partnership. Not only do they get free access to the student population and the community, they have exclusive rights to sell their products at school-sponsored events, including football games.

Another quote from a Colorado high school principal who had just signed a three-year contract with Pepsi, further exemplifies this notion. The principal commented that, "The kids know all that Pepsi has done for the school ... and they really appreciate it." In this high school, Pepsi has sponsored academic and multicultural events, helped finance school landscaping, purchased jackets for the security staff, and supplied a scoreboard.[117] However, as Saltman points out, "If Coca-Cola [or any other of the cola companies] were genuinely

[114] Boyles, *American Education and Corporations.*
[115] Ibid., 72.
[116] Zorn, "The Great Cola Wars," 33.
[117] Kaufman, "Fighting the Cola Wars in Schools."

interesting in helping to fund American public education, it would not force schools to compete for the money or force them to sell Coke."[118]

The language used by the superintendent and the principal exemplify the insidious nature of corporate greed thinly, and conveniently, disguised as acts of altruism. To the critical citizen, however, the self-serving motives of corporate vendors are unambiguous and clear: The goal is to generate profits and coerce consumer loyalty at an early age. Competition between the cola rivals has caused them to search for new and younger consumers. They instill brand loyalty into young children by taking their aggressive, intensive marketing to a high-stakes environment: the public school. Schools offer corporations extensive audience reach and specific targeting capabilities to buy lifetime consumer loyalty. Moreover, at a rate price of $1.00 per drink from the vending machine, the profit generated from school sales far exceeds the lump sum bonuses, labor, overhead, and additional funds donated to the school district.[119]

PROSPECTS FOR THE FUTURE: GOVERNMENT INTERVENTION

Passing legislation to restrict the sale and advertising of competitive foods in schools is a daunting task. Advocates for greater restrictions claim that congressional leaders repeatedly favor corporate interests above the health and well-being of children. Election laws allowing legislators to accept large corporate donations implicitly oblige them to support a pro-corporate agenda.[120] Corporate lobbyists also impede efforts to limit school–business partnerships. In July 2001, lobbyists urged California legislators to reject a bill that would have shifted profits from the sale of competitive foods from sports programs, extracurricular activities, and so on, to school meal programs. The bill that

---

[118] Saltman, *Collateral Damage*, 61–62. Saltman goes on to write that, "However, even if Coke were to give public schools grants, this would reinforce a highly private way of thinking of education that is founded in volunteerism and philanthropy rather than in a recognition of the need for public support for public goods."

[119] Nestle, "Pouring Rights." Nestle writes that, when compared to profits generated from supermarket buyers of soft-drinks, the profit margin for vending machines is extraordinarily high. See also Curran, "Misplaced Marketing," 534–535. Curran provides a somewhat sarcastic commentary on school corporate "partnerships." While she disagrees with the fundamental premise of school–business partnerships she writes that school administrators have "grossly under priced" their services. Curran figures that based on average advertising costs outside schools and the profit margin within schools, school administrators should at least take a basic business course to "learn enough marketing so they set a price that asks a fair value for the product."

[120] Nestle, *Food Politics*, 217.

would have also imposed more stringent nutritional standards on the sale of competitive foods in schools was rejected in July 2001.[121]

In many cases, school boards, parents, and students cite the monetary benefits of partnerships in opposition to efforts to ban corporate presence on campuses. In Maryland, for example, the Captive Audience/Stop Commercialism in School Act of 2001 (S.B. 435) proposed by Senator Paul Pinsky (D-Prince George) was aimed at reducing advertising in public schools. It would have required each county to create policies to constrain corporate presence in schools. The proposed bill also banned exclusive vending machine contracts, and prohibited advertising on school buses.[122] Opposition from vending machine operators, soft-drink manufacturers, and other corporate lobbyists was expected.[123] Lobbyists claimed that the bill would "prevent them from participating in worthwhile programs that allowed them to donate money and services to students."[124] However, strong opposition from educators, school boards, and students was more disturbing. These groups cited that the bill financially burdened schools and their students. They claimed that lacking the additional revenue generated from partnerships would jeopardize school programs and pass extra costs on to students.[125] As a result, Pinsky was hard-pressed to find many advocates because school officials and students sided with corporate interests. As a result, the bill was defeated.

However, some communities and legislators are successfully challenging corporate powers. Legislators in New York, Florida, Connecticut, Kentucky, Louisiana, and Massachusetts have enacted stringent regulations to govern the sale of FMNV.[126] These states prohibit the sale of FMNV until after the final lunch period. Massachusetts is perhaps most progressive in dealing with the sale of competitive foods given that the sale of à la carte items is restricted unless the item is a part of the reimbursable school lunch program.[127] Not

---

[121] Robert Earl, "The Issue of Competitive Foods," *National Food Processing Journal* 3, no. 8 (2001): 24. However, California has been progressive in raising the nutritional standards of school food. State Senator Martha Escutia proposed the Pupil Nutrition, Health, and Achievement Act (SB 19). This bill limits fat and sugar in schools food by 2004. It was signed into law October 14, 2001.

[122] Daniel LeDuc, "Legislators Urge Ban on Ads in Md. Schools: Exclusive Pacts with Soda Companies Targeted," *Washington Post*, 21 February 2001, B (01).

[123] Ibid. Hearings on the bill elicited the services of some of the highest-paid and powerful lobbyists. Corporate lobbyists included Bruce Bereano for Safeway and the vending machine operators, and Alan Rifkin a Channel One representative.

[124] Ibid.

[125] Charles County, Maryland, recently signed a $10 million exclusive contract with Coca-Cola. Charles County officials claimed that the part of the revenue generated from the contract subsidized a $50 student fee that supported sport teams, culinary classes, and cosmetology classes.

[126] Recall that although the USDA cannot impose regulations, federal guidelines allow local and state authorities to establish additional restrictions on the sale of FMNV.

[127] Story, Hayes, and Kalina, "Availability of Foods."

only do these rules dissuade school–business partnerships, they also protect the nutritional integrity of school lunches and help preserve the NSLP.

State and local authorities have also created legislation to prevent advertising in schools. In 1999, state representatives from Wisconsin passed a bill prohibiting school boards from entering into contracts that grant exclusive advertising rights to a single vendor. The bill also prohibits schools from entering into contracts that disseminate advertising materials to students.[128]

In August 2002, a California school board, in one of the nation's largest school districts, voted to ban soft drinks from the campuses in the district's 677 schools during school hours. The ban was passed unanimously by the school board despite information showing that the ban would restrict profits generated from vending machine sales. Prior to the ban middle schools generated approximately $14,000, and high schools approximately $39,000 in additional funds. Although previous school board legislation had already banned soft drinks from its elementary schools, this legislation extended the ban to middle and high schools.[129]

On the federal level, a few Senators and other congressional leaders are also advocating the reinstatement of USDA's authority. Senator Patrick Leahy (D-Vermont) and Senator Richard Lugar (R-Indiana) have introduced the Better Nutrition for School Children Act of 2003 (S. 1007). The proposal seeks to give the Secretary of Agriculture more authority over the school lunch program, specifically allowing the Secretary to restrict FMNV in schools until after the final lunch period. The bill was introduced May 6, 2003, and to date it is still pending. The future of the bill is uncertain, given the changing climate, recent priorities, and influence of powerful corporate lobbyists on the U.S. Senate.[130] Currently, there is no overarching federal legislation to restrict school corporate partnerships or advertising in schools.[131]

UNITING COMMON ALLIES

For the most part, the actions of health professionals and citizens opposed to school–business partnerships remain mutually exclusive. The outcomes of a

---

[128] Also in 1999, a similar bill (AB 117) was passed in California.

[129] Louinn Lota, "L.A. School Board Bans Soda Sales," *Washington Post,* 28 August 2002.

[130] The bill has been read once and has been referred to the Committee on Agriculture, Nutrition, and Forestry. Senator Patrick Leahy introduced a similar bill in 2001 but it did not garner enough support for successful passage.

[131] Government Accounting Office (GAO), *Public Education, Commercial Activities in Schools* (Washington, DC: United States GAO, September 2000), GAO/HEHS-00-156. According to this GAO study 19 states have enacted regulations to restrict certain commercial activities in schools. Unfortunately, only five states have endorsed policies that are comprehensive in nature. The GAO writes that, "In 14 of these states, laws are not comprehensive and pertain only to some types of activities; in some states, laws prohibit or restrict activities while in other states, laws authorize activities" (p. 10).

collaborative effort between these two groups would arguably surpass the results of individual initiatives. At times, academic experts', namely health professionals, and nutritionists, cursory treatment of school–business partnerships is peripheral to their focus on children's health and the NSLP. Many fail to analyze the fundamental premise of school-business partnerships and connect issues of corporate greed and subversion to issues of health and nutrition.[132] An editorial comment from the *Journal of the American Dietetic Association* illustrates this point: "The key issue is not whether schools should have vending machines and school stores, but rather which foods are available to students. Emphasis should be placed on exposure and availability of healthful foods."[133]

The key issue, however, *is* whether schools should have vending machines on campuses. Many health professionals circumvent the issue that exposure and availability of healthful foods for the sake of children's health is antithetical to corporate philosophy. Corporations are fundamentally concerned with profits, not with children's health. This also overlooks the fundamental problem: Students have access to unhealthy foods *only because* of corporate involvement in legislation. Corporations have repeatedly engaged in ethical and moral malfeasance to manipulate legislation to suit their interests. Therefore, to solicit corporations to offer more healthy foods minimizes the fervor of their lobbying efforts against this over the past 40 years. Consequently, focusing on providing more healthy food options without also addressing the means of distribution of the unhealthy food is futile.

Nestle provides an explanation for nutritionists' reluctant stance on issues of corporate involvement in schools. In her book, *Food Politics*, she examined the ways in which nutritionists and health professionals have themselves been co-opted by the food industry.[134] She describes how corporations have strategically aligned themselves with academics, enticing them with lucrative financial incentives in an effort to garner their support. She writes, "They [corporations] routinely provide information and funds to academic departments, research institutes, and professional societies, and they support meetings

---

[132] Nestle, *Food Politics*. Marion Nestle's work is an exception to this. Nestle's research exposes strategies used by corporations to promote and protect their own interests. Nestle is among few researchers in the health profession to thoroughly document how corporate powers promotes sales to children by pursuing tactics such as lawsuits, Congressional lobbying, financial contributions, strategic alliances, and through public relations schemes.

[133] Story, Hayes, and Kalina, "Availability of Foods," 124. This author agrees that it is not the distribution channel of the vending machine that is problematic; it is the sponsorship of the products in the vending machine. However, Story, Hayes, and Kalina's assertion fails to recognize the antithetical relationship between vending machines and corporations, and exposure and availability of healthy food options.

[134] Nestle, *Food Politics*, 129. Nestle describes a study that found that 70–80% of nutritionists believed that school based marketing benefits schools. Moreover, these nutritionists believed that food companies should be allowed to provide schools with teaching materials.

conferences, journals, and other such activities."[135] For example, nutrition-related research journals have some of the following corporate sponsors: Coca-Cola, Mead Johnson, M&M Mars, Nestlé USA, and Kraft Foods (Philip Morris).

Corporate funding for academic research poses a number of ethical dilemmas, but in the area of nutrition, this problem presents a serious social concern and potential health risk. The most obvious dilemma relates to the limits placed on the researcher's academic freedom. Corporate involvement compromises a researcher's absolute freedom to determine their own research agenda. When funding is tied to corporate handouts, one has to question what kind of research gets supported and what types of questions are even raised. One must also consider whether the integrity of the research process is compromised, including its results and conclusions.[136]

CONCLUDING THOUGHTS

Schools have a tremendous influence on children acquiring healthy behaviors and lifestyles. Schools also hold great potential for alleviating social inequities and fostering a democratic society. School–business partnerships pertaining to school food services work against schools in reaching their potential and positive influence. Evidence shows that the privatization of food services ultimately undermines children's health, social equity, and democratic education.

Jane Kenway and Elizabeth Bullen believe that schools have become mired in a process of "double exchange." They wrote, "At the same time as the school is used by producers to sell products to consumers, school students have become commodities sold by schools and systems to producers."[137] The privatization of food services in schools embodies this double exchange; on one level, the school represents an expanded market for corporations to control and on another level, schools use the buying power of their students to barter for contracts with corporations. This results in a situation

---

[135]Ibid., 111.

[136]Ibid., 117. Nestle also provides disturbing evidence showing the extent of corporate influence in academic research (see specifically pages 116–121). She writes that individual academics are not alone in soliciting corporate partners. She describes how in 1998, the Department of Plant and Microbial Biology at the University of California, Berkley, a department researching issues of food science and food technologies, "auctioned" itself to a single company. The new partnership gave the corporation, Novartis, a Swiss agriculture and drug company, expansive control over traditional departmental jurisdictions. The partnership provided the corporation authority to: select faculty, have access to uncommitted research of faculty, negotiate licensing rights on research, veto faculty involvement on projects, negotiate with faculty on specific assignments, and integrate its own scientists as faculty.

[137]Kenway and Bullen, *Consuming*, 91. See also Sally Jhally, *The Codes of Advertising: Fetishism and the Political Economy of Meaning in Consumer Society* (New York: Routledge, 1990). Jhally expands on the media's role in consumer culture that creates the double exchange.

where schools are implicated in compromising, if not unethical, practices of marketing unhealthy products to students. School–business partnership advocates, especially teachers, students, and parents, should critically examine these alliances to determine whether the short-term profits are worth the long-term health, social, and democratic consequences.

REFERENCES

Allensworth, Diane, Elaine Lawson, Lois Nicholson, and James Wyche, ed. 1997. *Schools and Health.* Washington, DC: Institute of Medicine, National Academy Press.

American Dietetic Association. 1991. Position of the American Dietetic Association: Competitive Foods in Schools. *Journal of the American Dietetic Association* (91): 1123–1125.

Boyles, Deron. 2000. *American Education and Corporations: The Free Market Goes to School.* New York: Falmer Press.

Brockett, Diane. 1998. School Cafeterias Selling Brand-Name Junk Food: Who Deserves a Break Today? *School Board News* (October): 58.

Center for Science and the Public Interest. 2003. *Pestering Parents: How Food Companies Market Obesity to Children* [online]. Washington D.C.: Center for Science and the Public Interest [accessed 6 December 2003]. Available from the World Wide Web: <http://cspinet.org/new/pdf/pestering_ parents_final_part_1.pdf>.

Curran, Catherine M. 1999. Misplaced Marketing. *Journal of Consumer Marketing* 16 (6): 534.

Donovan, Sharon. 1997. Private Sector Adds to the Menu. *School Business Affairs* (September): 18–20.

Earl, Robert. 2001. The Issue of Competitive Foods. *National Food Processing Journal* 3 (8): 24.

Egan, Timothy. 2002. In Bid to Improve Nutrition, Schools Expel Soda and Chips. *The New York Times* (20 May): A1.

Ervin, Kenith. 2003. District May Ban Daytime Sodas in Middle Schools. *The Seattle Times* (17 June): B1.

Hamstra, M. (1997, March 3). Papa John's hitting the books for its school-lunch program. *Nation's Restaurant News*, 20.

Hardy, L. (1999). The lure of marketing. *American School Board Journal, 186*(10), 26.

Hays, C. L. (1999, May 21). Today's lesson: Soda rights: Consultant helps school sell themselves to vendors. *The New York Times*, pp. C1, C9.

Jacobson, Michael F. 1998. *Liquid Candy: How Soft Drinks are Harming Americans' Health* [online]. Washington DC: Center for Science in the Public Interest [accessed 1 July 2002]. Available from the World Wide Web: <http://www.cspinet.org/sodapop/liquid_ candy.html>.

Jhally, Sally. 1990. *The Codes of Advertising: Fetishism and the Political Economy of Meaning in Consumer Society.* New York: Routledge.

Kaufman, Marc. 1999. Fighting the Cola Wars in Schools. *Washington Post* (23 March): Z12.

Kenway, Jane and Elizabeth Bullen. 2001. *Consuming Children.* Philadelphia, PA: Open University Press.

LeDuc, Daniel, 2001. Legislators Urge Ban on Ads in Md. Schools: Exclusive Pacts with Soda Companies Targeted. *Washington Post* (21 February): B1.

Lota, Louinn. 2002. L. A. School Board Bans Soda Sales. *Washington* Post (28 August) available from LexusNexus [http://web.lexis-nexis.com/universe]: Internet; accessed 8 December 2003.

Majewski, R. F. 2001. Dental Cavities in Adolescents Associated with Caffeinated Carbonated Beverages. *Pediatric Dentistry* 22 (3): 198–203.

Mardis, Anne. 2001. Current Knowledge of the Health Effects of Sugar Intake. *Family Economics and Nutrition Review* 13 (1): 89.

Mathematica Policy Research, Inc. 2001. *Children's Diets in the Mid-1990's: Dietary Intake and Its Relationship with School Meal Participation.* Washington DC: Mathematica Policy Research. Quoted in United States Department of Agriculture, Food and Nutrition Service. *Foods Sold in Competition with USDA Meal Programs: A Report to Congress* [online]. Washington DC: submitted 12 January 2001 [accessed 26 June 2002]. Available from the World Wide Web: <http://www.fns.usda.gov/cnd/Lunch/CompetitiveFoods/competitive.foods.report.to.congress.html>.

Molnar, Alex. 1996. *Giving Kids the Business: The Commercialization of America's Schools.* Boulder, CO: Westview Press.

Nestle, Marion. 2000. Pouring Rights: Marketing Empty Calories to Children. *Public Health Reports 2000* 115 (July/August): 308–319.

Nestle, Marion. 2002. *Food Politics.* Berkley, CA: University of California Press.

Price, Charlene and Betsy Kuhn. 1996. Public and Private Efforts for the National School Lunch Program. *Food Review* (May–August): 51–57.

Rodd, Ira E. 1992. McLunchrooms! *The Nation* 255 (8): 276.

Saltman, Kenneth. 2000. *Collateral Damage: Corporatizing Public Schools—A Threat to Democracy.* New York: Rowman and Littlefield.

Satcher, David. *The Surgeon General's Call to Action to Prevent and Decrease Overweight and Obesity* [online]. 2001. Washington D.C.: Department of Health and Human Services [accessed 15 July 2002]. Available from the World Wide Web: <http://www.surgeongeneral.gov/ topics/obesity>.

Schlosser, Eric. 2002. *Fast Food Nation: The Dark Side of the All American Meal.* New York: Perennial.

Shapiro, Laura, and Patrick Rogers. 1991. What's in a Lunch? *Newsweek* (Summer): 66–69.

Sheehan, John. 1999. Why I Said No to Coca-Cola. *American School Board Journal* 186 (10): 25.

Spethmann, Betsy. Cafeteria Lines. 1999. *Promo* (11):12.

Story, Mary, Marcia Hayes, and Barbara Kalina. 1996. Availability of Foods in High Schools: Is There Cause for Concern? *Journal of American Dietetic Association* 96 (2): 123–126.

Squires, Sally. 2001. Soft Drinks, Hard Facts. *Washington Post* (27 February): HE10.

Tribble, Sarah J. 2003. Vending Machines Thrive in Today's Workplace. *The Charlotte Observer* (30 June). Available from LexusNexus [http://web.lexis-nexis.com/universe]: Internet; accessed 8 December 2003.

United States Department of Agriculture, Food and Nutrition Service. 2001. *Foods Sold in Competition with USDA Meal Programs: A Report to Congress* [online]. Washington DC: USDA [accessed 26 June 2002]. Available from the World Wide Web: <http://www.fns.usda.gov/cnd/Lunch/CompetitiveFoods/competitive.foods. report.to.congress.html>.

United States Department of Agriculture, Food and Nutrition Service. 2002. *National School Lunch Program* [online] Washington DC: USDA [accessed 26 June 2002]. Available from the World Wide Web: <http://www.fns.usda.gov/cnd/Lunch/AboutLunch/faqs.htm>.

United States Department of Health and Human Services. 2001. *Over Weight and Obesity Threaten U.S. Health Gains.* Washington D.C.: Government Printing Office.

United States Government Accounting Office. 1996. *School Lunch Programs, Role and Impacts of Private Food Service Companies: United States GAO Report to Congressional Committees.* Washington, DC: Resources, Community, and Economic Development Division. ERIC, ED 400700.

United States Government Accounting Office. 2000. *Public Education, Commercial Activities in Schools* [online]. Washington, DC: United States GAO [accessed 7 December 2003]. Available from the World Wide Web: <http://frwebgate.access.gpo.gov/cgibin/useftp.cgi?Ipaddress =162.140.64.88&filename=he00156.pdf&directory =/diskb/wais/data/gao.>

United States Government Accounting Office. 2003. *School Lunch Program, Efforts Needed to Improve Nutrition and Encourage Healthy Eating: Report to Congressional Requesters.* (Rep. No. GAO-03-506). Washington, DC: Author. Available from the World Wide Web: <http://www.gao.gov/cgi-bin/getrpt?GA003-506htm>.

Vail, Kathleen. 1999. Insert Coins in Slot: School Vending Machines Generate Funds-and Controversy. *American School Board Journal* 186 (2): 28–31.

Van Wagner, Lisa. 1999. Fed Up: Some School Sistricts are Booting Uncle Sam Out of Their Cafeterias. *American School Board Journal* 186, (2): 38–41.

Wechsler, Howell, Nancy Brener, Sarah Kuester, and Clare Miller. 2001. Food Service and Foods and Beverages Available at School: Results from the School Health Policies and Programs Study 2000. *Journal of School Health* 71 (7): 313–324.

Williams, Majorie. 2001. The Soda Subsidy. *Washington Post* (3 January): A17.

Wynns, J. 1999. Yes: Selling Students to Advertisers Sends the Wrong Message in the Classroom. *Advertising Age* (June): 26. Quoted in Nestle, Marion. 2002. *Food Politics.* Berkley, CA: University of California Press.

Wyshak, Grace and Rose E. Frisch. 1994. Carbonated Beverages, Dietary Calcium, the Dietary Calcium/Phosphorus Bone Ratio, and Bone Fractures in Girls and Boys. *Journal of Adolescent Health* 15 (3): 210–215.

Zorn, Robert. 1999. The Great Cola Wars: How One District Profits from the Competition for Vending Machines. *American School Board Journal* 186 (2): 31–38.

Chapter 2

Measuring and Fixing, Filling and Drilling: The ExxonMobil Agenda for Education

Leslee Trammell

The state of public education is a concern shared not only by students, parents, teachers, and school officials, but also by members of the business community.[1] For the past two decades, corporations such as ExxonMobil have been adopting education reform and applying market-influenced "solutions" such as "accountability" and "choice" initiatives to identify and "fix" what, in their view, is wrong with public schools. Such reform measures are controversial. Though public schools might improve by the use of choice (i.e., vouchers, charter schools, contract management, and so forth) and by being "held accountable" for student learning, some analysts hold that reforms based on free-market ideology,[2] whereby schools ultimately become profit-making, entrepreneurial entities, support an agenda to end all government participation in education.[3] These ideas coincide with the free mar-

---

[1]Mobil Corporation, "Are Schools Improving? Too Many Educated Guesses," *The New York Times* (25 February 1999). Mobil Oil became ExxonMobil in 1999.

[2]I use free-market ideology to mean the approach upheld by the marketplace, wherein, as with a private corporation, a school's "stakeholders" are punished for its failures, rewarded for its successes, and given guidelines for "improvement" of its "product" for its "customers." Outcomes of free-market ideology often reflect Darwin's concept of survival of the fittest.

[3]For example, see Kenneth J. Saltman, *Collateral Damage* (Oxford: Rowman and Littlefield, 2000), 1–33.

ket's self-promotional campaign to "establish itself as the true provider of equity and opportunity in the 'objective' realm of capital, and to provide so-called objective 'proof' of public sector failure."[4] The seemingly neutral terms *choice* and *accountability* are often used in the language of school reform. Behind these terms lies what Boyles refers to as a "language of economics"[5] that supports the agenda to transform public schools in the image of the marketplace. In other words, education should be reformed according to marketplace ideology using market-based techniques to meet the needs of the workplace.

In this chapter I take the position that some corporations involved in the education reform enterprise, specifically ExxonMobil, use a language of economics that supports an agenda to abolish public support of education. I examine two "op-eds"[6] produced by ExxonMobil that demonstrate how this particular corporation uses free-market ideology embedded in such terms and phrases as *measuring, fixing,* and *filling the education pipeline* to support the demise of publicly funded education.[7]

OPINION-EDITORIAL ONE: "FIRST MEASURE, THEN FIX"

The first ExxonMobil op-ed I examine is titled "First Measure, Then Fix."[8] The overt purpose of this ad is to publicize ExxonMobil's support of the Elementary and Secondary Education Act (ESEA) passed in 2001, which holds schools (grades three through eight) "accountable" for meeting "standards." The ESEA, according to the ExxonMobile ad, "is a way to ensure that educational systems across the country can improve[9] what they are supposed to do [sic], which is to educate every child," because, states the ad, "the only sensible goal is to ensure that children are educated."[10] The

---

[4] Erika Shaker, "Privatizing Schools: Democratic Choice or Market Demand," *Education, Limited* 1, no 3, i.

[5] Deron Boyles, *American Education and Corporations: The Free Market Goes to School* (New York: Falmer Press, 2000), 158.

[6] The opinion-editorials are advertisements produced by ExxonMobil in 2001. Op-eds published after the merging of Exxon and Mobil in 1999 are archived on the corporation's Web site. I use the terms "op-ed" and "ad" interchangeably to refer to these items for the purpose of this paper. I also refer a third ad published in *The New York Times* in 1999 by Mobil Corporation, as cited in footnote 1. This third ad is not part of the main structure of this paper, but it provides further evidence of ExxonMobil's agenda.

[7] Giroux holds that abolishing publicly funded education is the motive behind corporate involvement in schools. Henry Giroux, *Stealing Innocence* (New York: St. Martin's Press, 2000), 93.

[8] This ad was published in *The New York Times* (14 June 2001) and can be found at <http://www2.exxonmobil.com/files/corporate/140601.pdf> Accessed 9/4/02. I refer to this ad as the "measuring and fixing" ad.

[9] By using the term "improve," ExxonMobil seems to suggest that the schools are in fact not "doing what they are supposed to do," although the op-ed does not provide any evidence of this.

[10] ExxonMobil never explains what is meant by "educate." One can assume that, in the view of the corporation, test scores are the sole way to "ensure" that students are "educated."

op-ed outlines three components that are "especially relevant" for a "successful education system," which are as follows: (a) "Educational standards are needed to define what students can be expected to know," (b) "An educational system needs to measure the performance of students and schools," and (c) "An educational system needs to be accountable for results." A more *covert* message of ExxonMobil's ad is that the company supports the corporate agenda of privatizing education,[11] which I demonstrate by analyzing the main ideas behind the three components outlined by ExxonMobil: standards, measurement, and accountability.

The use of standards, measurement, and accountability in school reform conversation is due in large part to the neoconservative interest in education fostered in the Reagan era by the report *A Nation at Risk*.[12] This report claims that U.S. schools have deteriorated and that they compare badly with schools from other advanced countries, which threatens not only the economy but the nation at large. Though not backed by substantiated research,[13] the claims made in *A Nation at Risk* have been supported by corporations such as ExxonMobil[14] and embraced by the mainstream press. Consequently, the general public, including parents as well as school leaders, accept the re-

---

[11] According to the Wisconsin Education Association's Web site, privatization generally refers to the process whereby private efforts are used to supplant public programs. (<http://www.weac.org> Accessed 8/2/02). Applied to education, privatization engages a plethora of ways in which market ideology and corporate influences affect public schooling. The private sector provides both the diagnosis and the cure. Because of the lack of systematic corporate control, goes this logic, desired levels of optimum output are unattainable. If public money would dictate that education fit private specifications, if all followed the corporate model, the argument implies, then the schools would be able to achieve a state of "excellence."

[12] U.S. Commission on Excellence in Education, *A Nation at Risk* (Washington, D.C.: U.S. Government Printing Office, 1983). Sponsored by Secretary of Education Terrel Bell, prepared by a prestigious committee, and endorsed by President Ronald Reagan, the 1983 report *A Nation at Risk* links mediocre student performance on standardized national tests to the U.S.'s mediocre economic performance in the global marketplace.

[13] Although it has been taken for granted that schools are failing, Berliner and Biddle demonstrate that the American education system is in fact improving in modest ways. On average, students today are "at least as well informed as students were in previous generations ... [and] education in America compares favorably with education elsewhere." The problems that many schools do have are due to the fact that those schools lack resources and must contend with the worst social problems. Write Berliner and Biddle, "The major claims of the attack [by *A Nation at Risk*] turned out to have been myths," a "Big Lie." When these lies are believed and funds are used to alleviate a nonexisting crisis, "they are likely to confuse and derail efforts that are badly needed to help the neediest schools." David Berliner and Bruce Biddle, *The Manufactured Crisis* (Reading, MA: Addison-Wesley, 1995): 13, 127, 144.

[14] These claims are supported not only in ExxonMobil's corporate op-ed pieces that use terminology from *A Nation at Risk* to "prove" that education has become a "rising tide of mediocrity," but also through its membership in the "Partners in Education" program. This program involves collaborating with other corporations to "change the content and delivery of education services." Reads the ad published in The New York Times (30 December 1999), "We like to believe that business benefits when education truly works." Other corporate "partners in education" include AT&T, Chevron, BellSouth, and Bank of America. See <http://www.exxonmobil.com> Accessed 9/5/02.

port's theories as "common sense,"[15] so much so that proof of such a crisis has not been necessary because it has become a "given,"[16] a natural way of thinking. ExxonMobil has joined the business community in defining the purpose of schooling, which is to create an "educated and trained work force."[17] There is little questioning of these ideas by the news media or by national leaders.[18]

As the market ideology has crept into public policy in the past twenty years, parents, politicians, and business leaders have increasingly demanded "school accountability." Learning for the sake of learning has been replaced by attention to outcomes; education is measured in inputs and outputs and standardized via test scores so that each school and each student can be ranked.[19] Market-influenced reforms "use the tools for which the private sector can apparently take credit—strategic use of data through technology and standards."[20] The end goal is greater accountability to parents, to taxpayers, and ultimately, to the marketplace.

Fearing foreign competition would dominate the global market, Cuban writes that business-led coalitions forged political alliances among public officials, union leaders, educators, and community activists to draft public schools into preparing students for jobs.[21] According to Spring, "conservatives, socialists, Democrats, Republicans, progressivists, and unionists [alike] were convinced that a corporate model of schooling would provide industrial efficiency and equality of opportunity [as] the school functioned as a sorting machine to separate and train human resources to meet the demands of the labor market."[22] Through the mid-1980s to the present day, business leaders have embraced A Nation at Risk's claims that schools are failing and that they should be modeled after corporations to better produce an

---

[15] Saltman, Collateral Damage, x.

[16] Deron Boyles, "The Exploiting Business," Educational Foundations (Summer 2001): 69.

[17] Mobil Oil, "Are Schools Improving? Too Many Educated Guesses," The New York Times (25 February 1999). In this ad, Mobil Oil holds that "In the marketplace of the next century, our prosperity will depend on an educated and trained work force—people who can manage complex drilling projects, anticipate accidents before they happen or position our products in new niches." What is implied is that if schools did a better job of training workers, then oil accidents such as the 1992 Exxon Valdez spill would not happen.

[18] It is not only traditional conservatives who champion these ideas. President Bill Clinton emphasized extensive standardized testing, advocated charter schools, and supported corporate education policy lobbyists.

[19] A standardized curriculum that all students are required to take ensures which skills they are "getting." ExxonMobil's "measuring and fixing" op-ed states that it is "unfair to evaluate people in school or business when they do not understand what is expected of them," but it says nothing about the fairness of the "measuring" itself.

[20] Shaker, ii, op. cit.

[21] Larry Cuban, "Why Have American Public Schools Become an Arm of the Economy?" Sachs Lecture at Teachers College, Columbia University, New York, October 17, 2001. <http://www.tc.columbia.edu/newsbureau/INSIDETC/Oct01/1001sachs.htm> Accessed 9/5/2002.

[22] Joel Spring, Education and the Rise of the Global Economy (Mahwah, NJ: Lawrence Erlbaum Associates, Inc., 1998), ix.

efficient workforce and help America obtain a larger piece of the global market. Known as neoconservatism or neocapitalism, this line of thinking holds that private enterprise is a better catalyst for social change than are government programs, including public education,[23] and that market principles must be applied to virtually every aspect of public services, going so far as to argue for the privatization of *all* public services.

As economic imperatives overshadow democratic practices, public schools are in danger of becoming in large part vocational schools, the purpose of which is job training, and of neglecting the historic purpose of tax-funded public education: to transform children into civic-minded independent thinkers and socially responsible adults committed to democratic principles.[24] The "bottom line" for schools has become not teaching and learning but achieving higher and higher test scores.

In keeping with the neoconservative thinking referred to by Spring, the belief is that the quality of education will *necessarily* be enhanced by preserving the rules of the free market. If a school does not live up to the imposed standards, then parents have a "choice"; they are free to choose another school for their children to attend. ExxonMobil agrees with this ideology: The "key point," according to the company's op-ed, "is that only by setting standards, measuring results, and holding educational systems accountable can improvements be made and sustained." Furthermore, the "measuring and fixing" ad states, such improvement can be made through privatization initiatives, which include "options for parents to move children to other schools, charter schools[25] and much more."

Vouchers are one of the most controversial privatization issues in education today. Voucher programs and other "choice" initiatives (supported in the No Child Left Behind Act of 2001[26]) represent the view that market ideology produces optimal outcomes, in terms of both "efficiency" and social value, and they are embraced as a means of rescuing students from "failing" school systems. The argument for vouchers is that competition for students, coupled with the threat of losing funds as students leave failing schools, will

---

[23] See Wisconsin Education Association's Web site < http://www.weac.org/GreatSchools/Issuepapers/privatization.htm> Accessed 8/2/2002.

[24] Henry Giroux, "Education Incorporated?" *Educational Leadership* 56, no. 2, (October 1998). <http://www.ascd.org/readingroom/edlead/9810/giroux.html> Accessed 6/18/2002.

[25] A charter is defined as "an autonomous educational entity operating under a charter, or contract, that has been negotiated between the organizers, who create and operate the school, and a sponsor, who oversees the provisions of the charter." Michael Engel, *The Struggle for the Control of Public Education: Market Ideology vs. Democratic Values* (Philadelphia: Temple University Press 2000), 83. While charter schools remain publicly funded, they are often "deeply entrenched in an education market ideology, incorporating educational and financial Darwinism with grass-roots (decentralized) appeal." Shaker, x, op. cit.

[26] See the United States Department of Education's Web site <http://www.nochildleftbehind.gov> Accessed 9/15/02.

force schools to improve.[27] Critics such as Alex Molnar oppose vouchers in part because they hold that it is wrong to abandon the public school systems and the children left in them when those utilizing vouchers leave.[28] Molnar writes, "public schools are likely to lose their broadly based, bipartisan political support." Consequently, "what will be left is a public school system cast adrift politically that could quickly become an intensely segregated, chronically underfunded repository of the most disabled, the poorest, and the most difficult to educate children."[29] In a "choice" that seems to abandon everything public about public schools, Georgia parents who choose not to use vouchers may elect to have "supplementary education" provided by Sylvan Learning Center, yet another private venture.[30]

Another type of private involvement in public schools is contract management, or "contracting out." In this scenario, a private corporation is given a contract by a state or school board to manage an aspect of the district, such as food service or even the operation of the school itself—the company is given tax dollars that would otherwise go to the public school system to educate the students under private control. Owned by Chris Whittle, the father of in-school technology/marketing program Channel One, Edison Schools is one example of contract management that uses more technology and fewer, uncertified, and low-paid teachers in order to keep costs down. Education Alternatives, Inc. is another example of this type of venture. Recent research shows that neither has been very successful, financially or otherwise.[31]

The "measuring and fixing" op-ed states that "most parents seem to agree" with ExxonMobil's agenda for education reform: 83 percent of parents "support higher standards," and "more than three-quarters see value in evaluating the performance of teachers and schools."[32] However, Berliner and Biddle provide evidence that most citizens are happy with their own schools: "When parents were asked about the local school that served their children, a whopping 72 percent gave that school [a grade of] A or B."[33] Apparently "common sense" tells parents that whereas "their schools" are just fine, "those other" schools are indeed failing, which perpetuates the idea that public schools need "fixing."

---

[27] John Hood, "When Business 'Adopts' Schools: Spare the Rod, Spoil the Child," *Policy Analysis* no. 153 (5 June 1991). <http://www.cato.org/pubs/pas/pa-153.html> Accessed 7/22/2002.

[28] Many students cannot afford transportation or clothing to go to distant private schools that are out of their (often inner-city) neighborhoods.

[29] Alex Molnar, *Giving Kids the Business* (Boulder, CO: Westview Press, 1996), 118.

[30] See the Georgia Department of Education Web site, <http://www.doe.k12.ga.us> Accessed 8/8/02.

[31] At least ten class action lawsuits have been filed against Edison Schools for misleading investors, one of them by the firm handling a stockholder suit against Enron. Writes Woodward, "Private companies have had little success in running schools." Tali Woodward, "Edison's Failing Grade," Special to *Corpwatch* (20 June 2002). <http://www.corpwatch.org/issues/PID.jsp?articleid=2688> Accessed 9/9/2002. See also Deron Boyles, *American Education and Corporations: The Free Market Goes to School* (New York: Falmer Press, 2000):143–148.

[32] The ad does not state who was surveyed for this study or how many people participated.

[33] Berliner and Biddle, *The Manufactured Crisis*, 111–114.

ExxonMobil sums up its philosophy of education in its "measuring and fixing" ad: "As a company that depends on a highly educated and technically proficient workforce," reads the op-ed, "we have a stake in seeing more American students fully capable of entering a new technological society." As Spring puts it, the preparation of students for the ever-changing workplace has emerged as public education's single most important goal. He explains that, differing from the laissez-faire traditions of the nineteenth century, "neocapitalism calls for government intervention to promote and protect free markets" and for education to be evaluated as an "economic investment."[34] As a result, writes Cuban, early twenty-first century public schools have become an "arm of the national economy."[35]

In what seems to be an afterthought, ExxonMobil proclaims that "the reasons for improving education go far beyond business needs," but the op-ed fails to provide any of these. It glibly states that "a well-educated citizenry is a core strength of the United States, and an opportunity for a good education is something owed to every child," but as evidenced by Molnar, not every child receives this opportunity. This is, I assert, one of the greatest problems with market-based reform initiatives: They neglect the needs of the public in favor of the interests of the private. The second op-ed piece that I examine spells out how ExxonMobil infiltrates the curriculum with its corporate agenda to teach students to be workers by "filling" them with the technological skills necessary to become part of the workforce, thereby blurring the distinction between public education and private interests even more.

**OPINION-EDITORIAL TWO:
"FILLING THE EDUCATION PIPELINE"**

The second op-ed I examine, entitled "Filling the Education Pipeline,"[36] further links the goals of education with the goals of business. "The oil industry," the ad states, "now runs more on brainpower than horsepower." In other words, finding more oil "has become technically challenging." According to ExxonMobil, because today's drilling methods rely more on technologically educated workers than on manual labor, schools need to do a better job of training the workforce in these desired high-tech skills.[37] But, asks the ad, "are they up to the task?"

Apparently not, as ExxonMobil's "pipeline" op-ed states that by high school, U.S. students are falling behind other countries in math and science,

---

[34]Spring, x, op. cit.
[35]Cuban, op. cit.
[36]Published in *The New York Times* (12 April 2001). See ExxonMobil's Web site <http://www2.exxonmobil.com/files/corporate/120401.pdf> Accessed 9/5/2002. I refer to this ad as the "pipeline" ad.
[37]Alex Molnar writes, "American corporations invest less in worker training than their foreign rivals." (Molnar, *Giving Kids the Business*, 6.). Rather than spend funds for on-the-job training, corporations such as ExxonMobil support having this task performed by schools.

subjects that are important to the oil industry because of their high-tech focus. In a "technology-rich society, innovation and productivity fuel our way of life," ExxonMobil's "pipeline" ad asserts. The language of economics used here implies that the purpose of education is to prepare workers to ensure that the United States can sustain its culture, or its "way of life." As Boyles points out, "[such] language confuses sensibilities." In this instance, "A language of economics is utilized to advance the idea that schools should supply businesses with qualified workers ... [and to this end] the promotion of economics is masked by a vocabulary of [promoting American] culture."[38]

The "pipeline" op-ed, like the "measuring and fixing" op-ed, also supports privatization efforts: ExxonMobil proclaims, "We also believe that everyone—not just government—has a role in promoting education" (where "everyone" means corporations). In "market terms," says ExxonMobile, "it's a pipeline[39] issue. That means we can't just wait until students finish college and recruit them; we must encourage and nurture students through the pipeline, all along the way." ExxonMobil's agenda is to "fill" the "pipeline" with educated, skilled workers custom-made to fit industry needs, which includes getting involved with what is taught in schools and how it is taught, especially in math and science.

The task of "filling the pipeline" with potential employees calls for filling students with the skills desired by the marketplace. The corporate response is to bring "experts" in the form of mentors, technology, and curriculum consultation into the classroom. Let us instruct your teachers on what they need to know, they say. Let us help you figure out an "effective" administration policy in order to achieve the state of "excellence" held by the private sector. In short, the only way to fix the system is to turn over control of the schools to corporate interests. To this end, ExxonMobil's "pipeline" ad spells out the corporation's education doctrine. As with Freire's notion of "banking," where students are filled or "deposited" with facts (or skills) to be "withdrawn" at a later date for tests and jobs,[40] ExxonMobil holds that students should be trained with the skills necessary to join the workforce. States the corporation's 1999 ad, there is a "national consensus on what we want for our schools [which includes] curricula that prepare youngsters for

---

[38] Boyles, *American Education and Corporations*, 158.

[39] My dictionary states three definitions for pipeline: (1) a conduit of pipe, especially one used for the conveyance of water, gas, or petroleum products; (2) a direct channel by which information is privately transmitted; and (3) a system through which something is conducted, especially as a means of supply. It is interesting that ExxonMobil uses this term in the ad, as not only is a pipeline a tool used in their own industry to convey oil (definition 1), but it is also a "channel by which information" (e.g. the corporate curriculum) is "privately transmitted" by business to student (definition 2), as well as a "means of supplying" (definition 3) graduates to the workforce.

[40] Paulo Freire, *Pedagogy of the Oppressed* (New York: The Continuum Publishing Company, 1993), 52–67.

the demands of the workplace and an education administration that is more flexible and responsive"[41] to the marketplace. In ExxonMobil's view, employees are viewed as resources, whereas students are seen as apprentices for their inevitable roles as future workers, an ideology known as human capital.[42]

What is more, according to the "pipeline" op-ed, ExxonMobil funds "several math and science initiatives" such as the K–5 Mathematics Specialist program, which "helps elementary school teachers become better grounded in mathematics content, and more comfortable teaching it." As stated in the ad, ExxonMobil's education program addresses such topics as "good teaching practices and math education of teachers," and even instructs teachers on "how young children learn math." ExxonMobil's online material elaborates on the K–5 Mathematics Specialist program: "This program focuses on developing a math specialist per individual school. This specialist then becomes a pedagogical resource for the faculty, being able to advise colleagues on education and evaluation techniques."[43] The claim that an oil company is an expert on early childhood education and knows enough about pedagogical practices to train already certified teachers goes unsubstantiated in ExxonMobil's literature.

The corporate influence in public schools does not end with teacher training. In order to further exert their power over what is taught, businesses such as ExxonMobil often "team up" or form "partnerships" with the public sector in the form of in-school marketing and advertising, sponsored curriculum supplements,[44] exclusive product contracts, contests, and more. Linking their ideology and products to the goals of education, corporations infiltrate the schools by sponsoring such activities as reading programs and

---

[41]Mobil Corporation, "Are Schools Improving? Too Many Educated Guesses," *The New York Times* (25 February 1999).

[42]Human capital theorists hold that education should be thought of an investment in human resources that can benefit industry and fuel the national economy. See Berliner and Biddle, *The Manufactured Crisis,* 141.

[43]<http://www2.exxonmobil.com/Corporate/About/CommunityPartnerships/Corp_CP_Ed_PreCollege.asp> Accessed 9/4/02.

[44]Examples of ExxonMobil's curriculum supplements include "Products From the World of Chemicals," in which "a variety of chemical-based consumer items are used [in the classroom] to demonstrate how much our everyday life depends on chemicals," and thus, on ExxonMobil itself. According to the company's Web site, this program is designed to "increase [students'] interest in careers in the chemical field." See: <http://www.exxonmobil.com/chemical/education/around_globe/products.html> Accessed 9/9/2002. Another example is a video that Exxon offered to science teachers in 1992 after the *Exxon Valdez* spilled 11 million gallons of oil into Prince William Sound. Entitled "Scientists and the Alaska Oil Spill," the video was criticized for being "corporate propaganda" because it misrepresented the environmental effects of the spill and led viewers to believe that the damaged areas and organisms would recover quickly through natural processes. <http://www.textbookleague.org/36exx.htm> Accessed 9/2/2002.

rewarding students with gifts and coupons for products.[45] In addition, each year about half of all high school seniors take an economics course, and many of those students are "learning from textbooks, classroom activities, and Web sites paid for by corporate donors whose [market-based] ideological influence goes unrecognized."[46] ExxonMobil supports economics education by providing grant money and board members to the National Council on Economic Education[47] as well as partnering with Junior Achievement[48] to "improve the economic knowledge of students."[49] With national testing in economics to begin in 2005, and course materials influenced by corporations such as ExxonMobil being widely used, "economics courses are likely to swing even more toward a 'free-market' ideology"[50] with no questions asked. This involvement could inhibit inquiry and debate about economic theory in general, specific business practices, and what information is privileged in the classroom.

SCHOOL–BUSINESS PARTNERSHIPS: WIN-WIN SITUATIONS?

The ExxonMobil "pipeline" op-ed ends by encouraging "even more businesses to get involved [with schools], because the best news is, the benefits work both ways." In other words, ExxonMobil puts forth the idea that school–business partnerships are "win-win" for both the corporation and the school. Boyles holds that far from being win-win situations, "the benefits are [almost solely] for business."[51] "Inevitably," says Molnar, corporate involvement works "mostly to the advantage of the haves" [the private corporations] rather than the "have-nots" [the public schools].[52] School–business partnerships, Boyles writes, "represent a larger exploitative agenda" that is "pro-business, pro-capitalist, pro-careerist, and one that excludes questions" about the nature and purposes of the partnerships.[53] When corporations get

---

[45] Boyles provides detailed analysis of these examples. See Deron Boyles, *American Education and Corporations: The Free Market Goes to School* (New York: Falmer Press, 2000), 61–110.

[46] Mark Maier, "Corporate Curriculum," *Rethinking Schools* 16, no. 4. (Summer 2002). <http://www.rethinkingschools.org/Archives/16_04/Corp164.htm> Accessed 7/2/2002.

[47] See the National Council on Economic Education's Web site <http://www.ncee.net> Accessed 9/4/02.

[48] According to ExxonMobil's online education materials, Junior Achievement "educates and inspires young people to understand business and economics, and prepares them to enter the work force." See: <http://www.exxonmobil.com/chemical/education/around_globe/junior_achievement> Accessed 9/9/2002). For an analysis of the educational practices of Junior Achievement, see Deron Boyles, *American Education and Corporations*, 93–95.

[49] From ExxonMobil's "Pre-College Education" online material. <http://www2.exxonmobil.com/files/corporate/precollege.pdf> Accessed 9/9/2002.

[50] Maier, "Corporate Curriculum," 7.

[51] Boyles, "The Exploiting Business," 65.

[52] Molnar, *Giving Kids the Business*, 22.

[53] Boyles, "The Exploiting Business," op. cit.

involved in schools, it is often only the businesses who win; the "losers" are public education and, therefore, as several writers assert, democracy itself.

The purpose of education as put forth by such writers as Giroux stands in sharp contrast to the educational philosophies of ExxonMobil. Giroux writes, "One of the most important legacies of American public education has been providing students with the critical capacities, knowledge, and values that enable them to become active citizens striving to build a stronger democratic society."[54] Such a purpose, he says, "rightfully asserts the primacy of democratic values over corporate culture and commercial values."[55] Giroux further holds that "Schools are an important indicator of the well-being of a democratic society. They remind us of the civic values that must be passed on to young people in order for them to think critically, to participate in power relations and policy decisions that affect their lives, and to transform the racial, social, and economic inequities that limit democratic social relations."[56] When corporations such as ExxonMobil step in to "fix" schools, these civic values are often neglected in the agenda to privatize. According to Boyles, corporate involvement in public schools is inherently antithetical to the democratic ideals upon which our country was founded. Schools, he writes, "should be viewed as democratic public spheres" because they are "public places where students learn and know what it means to live in a democracy."[57] School–business partnerships reinforce the assumptions of ExxonMobil and other corporate entities that the purpose of schooling is first and foremost, as Boyles puts it, "to meet consumer-materialist desires."[58]

With the infiltration of corporations in schools on the rise, another type of school–business partnership, commercially motivated corporate "donations" to the classroom, have also increased in number.[59] Given the fact that children are required to be in school every day, and given the prominent role that school plays in society, the classroom is becoming one of the most lucrative locations in which to market to kids.[60] Research shows that the association with schools and education in and of itself virtually guarantees corporations a positive image in the community and therefore additional potential consumers.[61] Eager to attract young customers, many large corporations sponsor some type of in-school marketing program or promotional campaign. Multimillion-dollar contracts have turned schools into sales agents for Coke and Pepsi, and many cash-poor public schools find it difficult

---

[54]Henry Giroux, *Stealing Innocence* (New York: St. Martin's Press, 2000), 83.
[55]Ibid.
[56]Ibid., 84
[57]Boyles, *American Education and Corporations*, 184.
[58]Ibid., 105.
[59]Maier, 7.
[60]Ibid., 8.
[61]Erika Shaker, "Youth News Network and the Commercial Carpet-Bombing of the Classroom," *Education, Limited*, no. 5 (October 1999): 1–18.

to resist corporate-sponsored advertising and handouts, especially when they come with free computers or sports equipment. Molnar holds that in a school, everything that's going on is supposed to be good for you. When a private company takes that venue and exploits[62] it for a particular special interest, it damages children.[63] According to Molnar, corporate promotions turn teachers into salespeople, require that they take time away from teaching to keep program records, and force them to push products that may not be the best values or businesses that might not be the best choices for many families.[64] Because the school environment reinforces the legitimacy of the lessons taught within its doors, any move toward privatization or business "partnership" with a public school must, on my view, be scrutinized.

Corporations target schools not simply as investments for substantial profits but also as "training grounds" for teaching students to define themselves as consumers.[65] For instance, earlier this year CBS Evening News[66] ran a story about a privately owned company called The Field Trip Factory, the purpose of which is to coordinate "educational" field trips. One group of kindergartners took a field trip to learn about animals—at a Petco pet supply store. A group of fifth graders took a field trip to learn about sports—at a local Sports Authority sporting gear store. Petco and Sports Authority pay the owner of The Field Trip Factory to offer these trips to schools free of charge. What do the stores get in return? Again, a captive audience of consumers. Says The Field Trip Factory's owner: "These children have the potential to be the stores' future customers and not only their future customers but their future employees. It's one way stores can give back to the community." There's that pipleine again. What the corporations are "giving back" to the community are trained consumers ready to spend, spend, spend.[67] These trips appear not only to teach children to be consumers, but they also teach brand loyalty to children at what could be argued as an inappropriately young age. The story quotes one elementary school teacher as saying that these field trips teach students "to become better consumers," however, the lesson here seems to be not *critical* consumerism but shopping. I assert that these types of corporate-sponsored materials should have no "business" in schools, mean-

---

[62] Boyles demonstrates how these "partnerships" may be "exploited" to the good of the schools. See Boyles, "The Exploiting Business," op. cit.

[63] Molnar, *Giving Kids the Business*, 21–52.

[64] Ibid., 25. For instance, Molnar notes, fast food and soft drinks that are advertised in many schools gain a nutritional credibility that they may not deserve.

[65] See Boyles, *American Education and Corporations*, 4–39; and Kenneth J. Saltman, *Collateral Damage* (Oxford: Rowman & Littlefield, 2000), 57–75.

[66] CBS News. "Reading, Writing ... and Retail." (30 May 2002). <http://www.cbsnews.com/stories/2002/05/30/eveningnews/main510602.html> Accessed 7/22/2002.

[67] "It is small wonder that one business after another is rushing to exploit one of America's last marketing frontiers," Molnar writes, referring to public schools. "Teenagers spend $57 billion of their own money and about $36 billion of their families' cash." Molnar, *Giving Kids the Business*, 21.

ing that schools should not allow the materials into the classroom, and businesses should not be allowed to treat the classroom as a business venture.

Some school officials and parents argue that it shouldn't matter where the money and classroom materials are coming from as long as the students are learning (i.e., producing adequate test results). Writes Boyles, "The argument here is that it is better to get money for students in exchange for advertising and commercialism than to have students suffer in under-funded schools."[68] But corporate involvement in education is "the beginning of the end of public schooling,"[69] he writes, because free-market ideology turns schools into "reductionist institutions whose purpose it is to compartmentalize and transmit bits of information deemed 'marketable.'"[70] The "bits" deemed marketable by ExxonMobil are math and science; other corporations may privilege such bits as management or word processing.

Boyles writes that partnerships with the private sector "promote consumer materialism, thwart critical transitivity [e.g. the critiquing of such partnerships], and negatively alter what it means to be a citizen."[71] Privatization initiatives supported by the likes of ExxonMobil push "uncritical consumerism into what businesses no longer consider schools, but markets."[72] This practice reduces opportunities for democratic participation because it eclipses the goals historically attached to public education, which include creating informed citizens who function in a just society. Such goals of public education have been sidelined by economic uses of schools, whether they are filling the employment pipeline or incubating uncritical consumers. Free-market ideology has achieved a "common sense"[73] or hegemonic status that often goes unchallenged and thereby inhibits democratic debate, and it contradicts ideals put forth by Dewey and Freire that "schools cannot prepare students for democratic life by simply giving them masses of information to be used at some later time,"[74] whether on a test or on an oil tanker. Rather, education should prepare students for democratic life by involving them in "forms of democratic living appropriate to their age."[75] Noddings embraces the Deweyan notion that education should be viewed as a process of living and not a preparation for future living, and she holds that learning to participate in democratic life involves living democratically. In schools this would include having students collaborate on common problems and participate in the construction of their own educational goals; encouraging critical re-

---

[68] Boyles, "The Exploiting Business," conference version, <www.gsu.edu/~wwwsfd/2001/boyles.pdf> Accessed 9/2/2002.
[69] Boyles, *American Education and Corporations*, 105.
[70] Boyles, "The Exploiting Business," 66.
[71] Ibid., 67.
[72] Ibid., 72.
[73] Saltman, *Collateral Damage*, x.
[74] Nell Noddings, *Philosophy of Education* (Oxford: Westview Press, 1998), 34.
[75] Ibid.

flection and the concern for the welfare of others; and engaging in an open flow of ideas, rather than competing for grades. "From this perspective," Noddings writes, "student participation in democratic living serves as both an end in itself and as a means toward the achievement of adult democratic life."[76]

Dewey writes that the worth of a form of social life (e.g., education) can be measured by two points: "the extent to which the interests of a group are shared by all of its members, and the fullness and freedom with which it interacts with other groups." An "undesirable society," he holds, "is one which internally and externally sets up barriers to free intercourse and communication."[77] A democratic classroom free of corporate material would qualify as "desirable." An example of an undesirable society is an education system based on private ideology as mapped out by corporations such as ExxonMobil because they value competition and a "survival of the fittest" mentality over living democratically.

These thinkers ask the question: What is the role of education in a democratic society, and what is the public's role in promoting and providing education to its citizens? These are the questions, I assert, that must be asked again and again each time privatization initiatives are proposed. Most states and districts lack any comprehensive policies to determine where they draw the line between altruistic and manipulative business relationships, which is why it is important for teachers, parents, and all citizens to question such relations. Individuals in a democratic society have the ability—and the responsibility—to consider these issues. Giroux holds that the attack on public education through reform initiatives is a direct assault on the principles that make democracy work.[78] Ultimately, as I have attempted to demonstrate, these initiatives are an assault on democratic government itself to undercut public services. Writes Giroux, challenging corporate power is essential if democracy is to remain a defining principle of education and everyday life.[79]

Apple and Beane write that "rather than giving up on the idea of the 'public' schools and moving down the path toward privatization, we need to focus on schools that work."[80] Schools can become more democratic, they write, by giving students and teachers a "right to have their voices heard in creating the curriculum" by allowing teachers more control over their own professional work,[81] and, I hold, by not allowing the use of curriculum materials

---

[76] Ibid., 35.
[77] John Dewey, *Democracy and Education* (New York: The Free Press, 1916), 99.
[78] Giroux, *Stealing Innocence*, 83–88.
[79] Ibid., 101.
[80] James A. Beane and Michael W. Apple, eds. *Democratic Schools* (Alexandria, VA: Association for Supervision and Curriculum Development, 1995), 3.
[81] Ibid., 18–19. Apple and Beane provide examples of schools that operate on democratic principles.

sponsored by such corporations as ExxonMobil to go unquestioned. Giroux writes that teachers should recognize their roles as "public intellectuals," meaning that "the practice of teaching is ... by its very nature moral and political, rather than technical."[82] Saltman echoes this sentiment: "Teachers are not merely in the business of passing on knowledge but understand the significance of their practices as fostering particular social visions ... [and] critically engaging students and curricula with regard to issues of power and politics."[83] Molnar gives parents examples of ways to fight corporate sponsorships and lessen the hold that business culture has on public schools. "Parents can tell their child's school principal that they do not want their child being taught or evaluated for work done using corporate-sponsored materials or for participating in corporate promotions," he suggests.[84]

As I have attempted to demonstrate using the corporation's own advertisements, ExxonMobil's education agenda has arguably little to do with critical learning and a great deal to do with restructuring public life in the image of private, market culture.[85] Corporate involvement undermines the nature of public education while selling the integrity of the students and of the school itself. The only "winners" are the corporations. Molnar writes that the failure to change policies that govern commercialism in the public schools will result in solidifying the role of public education as delivery of corporate profits,[86] crystallizing the ExxonMobil agenda and others like it that wish to define the purpose of schooling as "measuring" education by holding schools accountable, "fixing" public schools in the image of private corporations, and "filling" students with the necessary skills (what Dewey calls a "narrow range of acts")[87] to custom-fit the needs of the marketplace.

REFERENCES

Berliner, David, and Bruce Biddle. 1995. *The Manufactured Crisis*. Reading, MA: Addison-Wesley.

Boyles, Deron. 2000. *American Education and Corporations: The Free Market Goes to School*. New York: Falmer.

Boyles, Deron. 2001. The Exploiting Business. *Educational Foundations* (Summer).

CBS News. 2002. *Reading, Writing... and Retail*. CBS News 2002 [Accessed 7 July 2002]. Available from http://www.cbsnews.com/stories/2002/05/30/eveningnews/main510602.html.

Cuban, Larry. 2002. *Why Have American Public Schools Become an Arm of the Economy?* [Lecture]. Sachs Lecture at Teachers College 2001 [Accessed 5 September 2002].

---

[82] Giroux, *Education Incorporated?*, op. cit.
[83] Saltman, *Collateral Damage*, 118.
[84] Molnar, *Giving Kids the Business*, 52.
[85] Giroux, *Stealing Innocence*, 98.
[86] Molnar, op. cit.
[87] Dewey, *Democracy and Education*, 121.

Available from http://www.tc.columbia.edu/newsbureau/INSIDETC/Oct01/ 1001sachs.htm.

Dewey, John. 1916. *Democracy and Education.* New York: Free Press.

Engel, Michael. 2000. *The Struggle for the Control of Public Education: Market Ideology vs. Democratic Values.* Philadelphia: Temple University Press.

ExxonMobil. 1999. Are Schools Improving? Too Many Educated Guesses. *The New York Times* (25 February).

ExxonMobil. 2001. Filling the Education Pipeline. *The New York Times* (2 April).

ExxonMobil. 2001. First Measure, Then Fix. *The New York Times* (14 June).

Freire, Paulo. 2000. *Pedagogy of the Oppressed.* Translated by M. B. Ramos. New York: Continuum Publishing Company. Original edition, 1970.

Georgia Department of Education Web site [Accessed 8 August 2002]. Available from http://www.doe.k12.ga.us.

Giroux, Henry. 1998. Education Incorporated? *Educational Leadership* 56 (2).

Giroux, Henry. 2000. *Stealing Innocence.* New York: St. Martin's Press.

Hood, John. 1991. When Business "Adopts" Schools: Spare the Rod, Spoil the Child. *Policy Analysis* (153).

Maier, Mark. 2002. Corporate Curriculum. *Rethinking Schools* 16 (4).

McLaren, Peter. 1989. *Life in Schools.* New York: Longman.

Molnar, Alex. 1996. *Giving Kids the Business.* Boulder: Westview Press.

National Council on Economic Education Web site [Accessed 4 September 2002]. Available from http://www.ncee.net.

Noddings, Nell. 1998. *Philosophy of Education.* Oxford: Westview Press.

Saltman, Kenneth. 2000. *Collateral Damage.* Oxford: Rowman and Littlefield.

Shaker, Erica. Privatizing Schools: Democratic Choice or Market Demand. *Education, Limited* 1 (3).

Shaker, Erica. 1999. Youth News Radio and the Commercial Carpet-Bombing of the Classroom. *Education, Limited* (5).

Spring, Joel. 1998. *Education and the Rise of the Global Economy.* Mahwah, NJ: Lawrence Erlbaum Associates, Inc.

U.S. Commission on Excellence in Education. 1983. A Nation at Risk. Washington, D.C.: U.S. Commission on Excellence in Education.

United States Department of Education Web site [Accessed 15 September 2002]. Available from http://www.nochildleftbehind.gov.

Wisconsin Education Association Web site [Accessed 2 August 2002]. Available from http://www.weac.org.

Woodward, Tali. 2002. *Edison's Failing Grade.* Corpwatch 2002 [Accessed 9 September 2002]. Available from http://www.corpwatch.org/issues/PID.jsp?article=2688.

Chapter 3

Priming the Pump: "Educating" for Market Democracy

Randy Hewitt

By a show of hands, how many of you like candy, you know, World's Finest® Milk Chocolate with almonds or the delicious Mint Meltaways® that everybody knows and loves? Many of you have raised your hands. This is absolutely great.

How many of you like cars, especially limousines with lunch in the back with your favorite person? Now, some of you aren't raising your hands. But I know something that absolutely everybody wants and that's money: cold, hard cash....

The preceding is an introduction similar to the one presented in the corporate-sponsored (OSP, Inc., a subsidiary of *Reader's Digest*) fund-raiser put on at my daughter's middle school. This presentation was designed to entice an assembly of sixth and seventh graders to help generate much needed cash for "economically strapped [insert name here] Middle School and to make [insert name here] Middle School the best darn school in Orange County, Florida."

If you want to be a part of something exciting and good, the perpetrators of this introduction went on, *if you want to help your school and community, then stand up and show that you are willing to take part in this wonderful opportunity. Come on, stand up! Some of you aren't standing. Look around at your friends. Come on, get them on their feet and make them a part of this fantastic opportunity.*

The presentation went on to suggest that the selling and consuming of candy, wrapping paper, stationery, Christmas candles, and various other overpriced trinket items are the essence of good community life. Therefore, the latter portion of the corporate "spiel" included a crash course aimed at schooling these children on how to be good public servants armed with the proper smile and techniques necessary to sell The Good Life®.

The commercialization of public schools concerns me as a parent who has kids in public schools that are becoming saturated with corporate advertising and commercialism. Furthermore, as a philosopher of education, I am concerned about what the unquestioned faith in corporate–school partnerships portend for the idea of a democratic education. Let me explain what I mean.

I teach a graduate course in the history and philosophy of American education framed around the ongoing problem of defining and securing "democratic justice"—the struggle over the meaning of "freedom" and "equality" in education. In this course, we go through the history of American education in order to get a more concrete sense of what the struggles over these concepts have been in the past and to understand what forms these struggles currently take.

A recurring task that I face while teaching this course is helping students understand the idea that there is no such thing as freedom in general but rather freedom or capacity (power) to do specific things within a given context or set of circumstances. Furthermore, they struggle to see that individuals do not always mean the same thing when they use terms appealing to a common social good. "Democracy," "freedom," and "equality" have been—and are—used to cover over all sorts of hegemonic relations and debilitating social arrangements. Perhaps the most difficult problem that I face teaching this course is leading students to recognize the possibility that public schools have been used and are used as a means to train obedient and uncritically minded workers who, unwittingly, are eager to serve as fodder for predatory capitalism. The difficulty does not stem from the students' inability to understand the causal relation expressed in the idea. They are quick to see that schools *can be* used as a means to quell critical analysis of social practices and, thus, to foster worldviews beneficial to the workings of the powerful. The difficulty stems from their immediate refusal to see that schools *are* used in this way. They are fast to point out that schools are used to indoctrinate and manipulate in communist countries such as Cuba and China but, the students hastily contend, schools are not used for such purposes in a democracy such as the United States. My attempt to confront their refusal with concrete examples, drawn from the ever-encroaching commercialization in schools and business–school partnerships, so as to suggest that corporations are using schools as a means to foster an unquestioning faith in the inherent benevolence of corporate America often is met with further resistance and scorn. To my students, any suggestion that business–school partnerships are in any sense forms of corporate exploitation, especially in a time when schools are so economically "strapped" as they are now, amounts to reckless cynicism and social irresponsibility.

Recurrent classroom discussions with my philosophy of education students about these matters give further evidence to the often heard complaint (expressed by philosopher John Dewey as early as 1922 in the brief article "Education as Politics") that public schools leave students ripe to be gulled by any and every form of socio-political bunk:

> Our schooling does not educate, if by education be meant a trained habit of discriminating inquiry and discriminating belief, the ability to look beneath a floating surface to detect the conditions that fix the contour of the surface, and the forces which create its waves and drifts.... This fact determines the fundamental criticism to be leveled against current schooling, against what passes as an educational system. It not only does little to make discriminating intelligence a safeguard against surrender to the invasion of bunk, especially in its most dangerous form—social and political bunk—but it does much to favor susceptibility to a welcoming reception of it. There appear to be two chief causes for this ineptitude. One is the persistence, in the body of what is taught, of traditional material which ... affords no resource for discriminating insight, no protection against being duped in facing the emergencies of today.... The other way in which schooling fosters an undiscriminating gulping mental habit, eager to be duped, is positive. It consists in a systematic, almost deliberate, avoidance of the spirit of criticism in dealing with history, politics, and economics. There is an implicit belief that this avoidance is the only way by which to produce good citizens. The more undiscriminating the history and institutions of one's own nation are idealized, the greater is the likelihood, so it is assumed, that the school product will be a loyal patriot, a well-equipped good citizen. If the average boy and girl could be walled off from all ideas and information about social affairs save those acquired in school, they would enter upon the responsibilities of social membership in complete ignorance that there are any social problems, any political evils, any industrial defects. They would go forth with the supreme confidence that the way lies open to all, and that the sole cause of failure in business, family life or citizenship lies in some personal deficiency in character.... The effect is to send students out into actual life in a condition of acquired and artificial innocence. Such perceptions as they may have of the realities of social struggles and problems they have derived incidentally, by the way, and without the safeguards of intelligent acquaintance with facts and impartially conducted discussion. It is no wonder that they are ripe to be gulled, or that their attitude is one which merely perpetuates existing confusion, ignorance, prejudice, and credulity. Reaction from this impossible naïve idealization of institutions as they are produces indifference and cynicism.[1]

---

[1] John Dewey, "Education as Politics," *John Dewey, The Middle Works, 1899–1924*, vol. 13, edited by Jo Ann Boydston (Carbondale: Southern Illinois University Press, 1983), 331–333.

The systematic avoidance of the spirit of criticism in the public schools not only keeps students ignorant that gross socioeconomic and political inequalities exist in their world but prevents them from developing the critical abilities to identify and evaluate the ideological justifications for such inequalities. In turn, schools deprive students of any real opportunity to define and struggle with their social responsibilities in these matters. As Dewey suggests, by fostering an undiscriminating gulping mental habit in students, schools produce citizens with a crippling artificial innocence about the social institutions that define them and an outright hostility toward individuals who call attention to the detrimental consequences associated with these institutions.

Insofar as Dewey's assessment of public education hits the mark and continues to be relevant, and if his assessment of schools is coupled with the fact of increasing corporate marketing in schools, then the suspicion is warranted that the conditions are ripe for schools to serve as means to produce a consuming, materialistic, product-oriented consciousness in students, whose bodies serve as hosts in which parasitic corporate greed infinitely may infest, feed, and multiply. Thus, in light of Dewey's criticism of twentieth century education, this paper will draw upon John Dewey's idea of social habit and his analysis of economic individualism as the philosophical underpinning of a capitalist democracy in order to suggest that public education primes students with the belief that the ability to consume is *the* mode and measure of participatory democracy.

SOCIAL HABIT

John Dewey's entire philosophy is predicated upon the fact that the human being, fundamentally a creature of habit, is thoroughly saturated by its environment, which is always social. Throughout his professional career, Dewey maintained that the acquisition of habit is the means by which the individual gains a more sensitive and controlled interaction with his or her environment. Put in the psycho-physiological terms Dewey would have used, habit amounts to the tendency to conduct nervous energy along a previously formed sensorimotor channel for the fullest coordination possible at the least cost. By virtue of acquiring habit, the individual comes to develop, widen, and enhance the significance of his or her interest in the world. In a word, habit means growth in one direction or another. This growth, however, can continue only by securing its proper conditions, which always includes attention to the specific needs, desires, expectations, and activities of other human beings. As Dewey pointed out, the inherent social nature of the individual constitutes a fundamental fact of existence:

> Since habits involve the support of environing conditions, a society, or some specific group of fellow-men, is always accessory before and after the fact.

Some activity proceeds from a man; then it sets up reactions in the surroundings. Others approve, disapprove, protest, encourage, share and resist. Even letting a man alone is a definite response. Envy, admiration, and imitation are complicities. Neutrality is non-existent. Conduct is always shared; this is the difference between it and a physiological process. It is not an ethical "ought" that conduct should be shared. It is social, whether bad or good.[2]

As Dewey maintained, the inherent social nature of the individual suggests that every one of the individual's habits is nourished and cultivated by means of association with others. The lives of others stimulate impulse and stoke emotion. Their occupations furnish purpose and sharpen skill. Their expressions conspire in memory, fuel imagination, and haunt plans. In other words, the joys and sufferings of others are metabolized into the very fiber of the individual's conduct:

> A being whose activities are associated with others has a social environment. What he does and what he can do depend upon the expectations, demands, and condemnations of others. A being connected with other human beings cannot perform his own activities without taking the activities of others into account. For they are indispensable conditions of the realization of his tendencies. When he moves, he stirs them and reciprocally.[3]

As indicated in the preceding quotation, Dewey well understood the mechanism of habit to be the basis for the psychological and social development of moral conduct.[4] He maintained that habit consists of a train of associated impulses, accumulated and modified over time according to the quality of consequences produced in the social environment and retained by the individual. The stimulation of one impulse calls up the train of others such that those called up check, inhibit, direct, and stimulate its further expression. That is, the associated impulses give social relation and significance to the inducing impulse: They serve as the standard for its measurement (the right) and constitute its good. Again, as Dewey puts it, "In this aspect, they are the law, the controlling power of that impulse. They determine in what form, under what conditions of time, place and quality, it may be satisfied. Thus they determine or measure its value."[5]

---

[2]John Dewey, *Human Nature and Conduct: An Introduction to Social Psychology* (New York: Henry Holt and Company, 1922), 16.

[3]John Dewey, *Democracy and Education: An Introduction to The Philosophy of Education* (New York: The Macmillan Company, 1916/1950), 14.

[4]See for example *Ethics, The Later Works*, vol. 7; *Human Nature and Conduct; The Study of Ethics: A Syllabus* (1894), *John Dewey: The Early Works, 1882–1898*, vol. 4, edited by Jo Ann Boydston (Carbondale, Illinois: Southern Illinois University Press, 1971).

[5]Dewey, *The Study of Ethics, The Early Works*, vol. 4, 248. Dewey most thoroughly explains the psychological basis of moral conduct in *The Study of Ethics*: "Psychologically, the mediation of impulse (a) idealizes the impulse, gives it its value, its significance or place in the whole system of action, and (b) controls, or directs it. The fundamental ethical categories result from this distinction. The worth of an impulse is, psychologically, the whole set of   (*continued*)

The upshot of this discussion so far has been to underscore the simple point that the social environment affects the growth of the individual and the individual affects the social environment, all for better or worse. Therefore, it is an ontological fact that individuals may affect patterns of thought and desire by way of affecting shared conditions and practices. As Dewey pointed out, "Social institutions, the trend of occupations, the pattern of social arrangements, are the finally controlling influences in shaping minds."[6] Now, in what sense does economic individualism serve as the philosophical underpinning of capitalist democracy and in what sense may it be said that schools provide the means by which this underpinning insidiously infects the consciousness of students?

ECONOMIC INDIVIDUALISM AS THE PHILOSOPHICAL UNDERPINNING OF CAPITALIST DEMOCRACY

Throughout his political works, Dewey suggested that the same forces that have made democratic forms of self-government possible also have served as the means by which laissez-faire capitalism flourishes. In *Liberalism and Social Action*, Dewey argues that whereas the concern about the essence of and proper relation between the individual, freedom, and the universal may be traced back to Greek thought, the modern formulation of this relation developed out of the empiricist-rationalist traditions, particularly out of the work of John Locke.[7] Since the early Enlightenment, philosophers had been strug-

---

[5] (*continued*)   experiences which, presumably (that is, upon the best judgment available) it will call into being. This, ethically, constitutes the goodness (or badness) of the impulse—the satisfaction (or dissatisfaction) which it carries. But the thought of the consequences which will follow, their conscious return back into the impulse, modify it—check it, increase it, alter it.... In this modification, through reaction of anticipated experiences, we have the basis of what, ethically, we term obligation—the necessity of modifying any particular expression of impulse by the whole system of which it is one part" (pp. 238–239).

[6] John Dewey, *Individualism, Old and New* (1929), *John Dewey, The Later Works, 1925–1953*, vol. 5, edited by Jo Ann Boydston (Carbondale: Southern Illinois University Press, 1984): p. 102. The evidence that Dewey was aware of and understood the need to combat powerful influences shaping social institutions is clear and prevalent. For example, Dewey writes, "It is indeed necessary to have freedom of thought and expression. But just because this is necessary for the health and progress of society, it is even more necessary that ideas should be genuine ideas, not sham ones, the fruit of inquiry, of observation and experimentation, the collection and weighing of evidence. The formation of the attitudes which move steadily in this direction is the work and responsibility of the school more than any other single institution. Routine and formal instruction, undemocratic administration of schools, is perhaps the surest way of creating a human product that submits readily to external authority, whether that be imposed by force or by custom and tradition, or by the various forms of social pressure which the existing economic system produces" ("Freedom," *John Dewey, The Later Works, 1925–1953*, vol. 11, edited by Jo Ann Boydston [Carbondale: Southern Illinois University Press, 1987], 253–254).

[7] John Dewey, *Liberalism and Social Action, The Later Works*, vol. 11, 6–9. For Dewey's understanding of the philosophical and historical development of democratic forms of self-government in relation to the development of laissez faire capitalism, see all of *Liberalism and Social Action; Freedom and Culture* (1939), *John Dewey: The Later Works, 1925–1953*, vol. 13, edited by Jo Ann Boydston (Carbondale: Southern Illinois University Press, 1988), 136–155; *The Public and Its Problems*, 75–109; and "The Future of Liberalism," *The Later Works*, vol. 11, 289–295.

gling to establish the idea that human beings are held together both physically and spiritually by constant laws permeating the universe. Philosophers from both the empiricist and rationalist traditions argued that all individuals have the capacity to sense and understand the laws of nature for themselves. Through test, intelligence, and effort, individuals could induce the constant truths of the universe and therefore enlighten themselves. This selfenlightenment, in turn, would lead to a freer and more just society, a society in which individuals forge a self-government in keeping with universal law. According to Dewey, by the late 1600s, Locke had worked out a set of moral and political implications from these metaphysical and epistemological tenets.

Locke maintained, according to Dewey, that all individuals have a right to seek and understand the universal laws for themselves, a right not bestowed upon them by any social organization but granted to them by nature itself. Furthermore, Locke suggested that it is a duty for individuals to conduct themselves according to their own understanding of the natural laws and, in turn, to forge a contract of collective regulation with others as they come to understand the natural laws for themselves. This duty rests upon the belief that the individual is the best judge not only of his or her own interests but of the best means necessary to bring these interests to fruition. According to the natural abilities and diligence of the individual in discovering his or her interests, the resulting industry and effort of the individual (the part) would contribute to the social good (the whole). Therefore, Locke argued, the individual must remain free of physical and intellectual coercion of all kinds, including binding tradition and corrupt authority, in order to help realize a better society and thus a more complete universe. Government, then, would not be an imposed or coerced arrangement but a contract of mutual consent entered into by the aggregate of individuals who are assumed to be free and clear about their personal interests beforehand. According to Dewey, democracy, both as a way of living together and as a form of self-government, grew out of the faith in the dignity and natural right of all individuals to realize freely the truths of the universe for themselves.

As Dewey points out, however, it followed from the tenet of the free individual that the human being has a natural right to the fruits of its labor, that is, a natural right to acquire property and profit. Without this right legally secured, the individual would be discouraged to exert energy toward an end that could be taken away, and, thus, social progress, which depends on the individual's industry, would suffer. Therefore, the natural right to own property required full protection from infringement and seizure. Because the tenet of the free individual entailed the dignity to determine one's own interest, any contractual relationship that the individual entered into was assumed to be done out of free choice and with the responsibility for understanding the conditions and consequences of such arrangements. Thus, contracts between individuals necessitated enforcement because they are a means to secure private property. The function of self-government, therefore, was to ensure that individuals remain free and nonobstructed in pursuit of their own interest:

> Economic "laws," that of labor springing from natural wants and leading to the creation of wealth, of present abstinence in behalf of future enjoyment leading to creation of capital effective in piling up still more wealth, the free play of competitive exchange, designated the law of supply and demand, were "natural" laws. They were set in opposition to political laws as artificial, man-made affairs. The inherited tradition which remained least questioned was a conception of Nature which made Nature something to conjure with. The older metaphysical conception of Natural Law was, however, changed into an economic conception; laws of nature, implanted in human nature, regulated the production and exchange of goods and services, and in such a way that when they were kept free from artificial, that is political, meddling, they resulted in the maximum possible social prosperity and progress.... The economic theory of laissez-faire, based upon belief in beneficent natural laws which brought about harmony of personal profit and social benefit, was readily fused with the doctrine of natural rights.... Each person naturally seeks the betterment of his own lot. This can be attained only by industry. Each person is naturally the best judge of his own interests, and if left free from the influence of artificially imposed restrictions, will express his judgment in his choice of work and exchange of services and goods. Thus, barring accident, he will contribute to his own happiness in the measure of his energy in work, his shrewdness in exchange and his self-denying thrift. Wealth and security are the natural rewards of economic virtues.... Under the invisible hand of a beneficent providence which has framed natural laws, work, capital and trade operate harmoniously to the advantage and advance of men collectively and individually. The foe to be dreaded is interference of government. Political regulation is needed only because individuals accidentally and purposely—since the possession of property by the industrious and able is a temptation to the idle and shiftless—encroach upon one another's activities and properties. This encroachment is the essence of injustice, and the function of government is to secure justice—which signifies chiefly the protection of property and of contracts which attend commercial exchange.[8]

According to Dewey, what the Enlightenment philosophers offered to early capitalist arrangements was a gritty account of man and matter and a reasoned excuse for the accumulation of private property as a natural inclination, right, and duty.[9] Dewey maintains that insofar as individual liberty and social progress were interpreted and identified strictly with the growth of economic liberty, as opposed to social and political liberty, then the Enlightenment

---

[8] Dewey, *The Public and Its Problems*, 90–92.
[9] Dewey, *Liberalism and Social Action, The Later Works*, vol. 11, 5–22; *Ethics, The Later Works*, vol. 7, 331–339. In "Authority and Social Change," Dewey writes, "The new economic forces also claimed the right to supreme authority on the ground that they were pure and literal expressions of natural law—in contradistinction to political laws and institutions which, in so far as they did not conform to the play of economic forces, were artificial and man-made. Economic forces, through their representatives, interpreters and agents—the official economists and industrialists—claimed the divine prerogative to reign supreme over all human terrestrial affairs. The economist and industrialist and financier were the new pretenders to the old divine right of kings" (*The Later Works*, vol. 11, 135).

principle of individual freedom sanctified the relations of capitalism such that its end became a shared moral compulsion. As Dewey suggests in *Ethics*, this compulsion rests upon "the notion that individuals left free to pursue their own advantage in industry and trade will not only best further their own private interests but will also best promote social progress and contribute most effectively to the satisfaction of the needs of others and hence to the general happiness."[10] According to Dewey, the social claim was and is made that the relations of capitalism rest upon the natural right to industry and profit and that this natural right is essential to the objective realization of the universal law and social good. This claim entails the idea that the objective realization of the universal law directly depends on the degree to which individuals bring their intelligence, industry, thrift, and tenacity to bear. Because the realization of the universal law is not complete as of yet, the only true measure of its present realization is in terms of the resources or wealth generated by industry and thrift. Therefore, the production and accumulation of wealth is claimed as a moral duty commanded by universal law.[11]

As Dewey suggests in *Liberalism and Social Action*, "When it became evident that disparity, not equality, was the actual consequence of laissez faire liberalism, defenders of the latter developed a double system of justifying apologetics" (p. 37). Dewey points out that appeal to the natural inequalities of individuals is used not only to account for the existence of exorbitant wealth along side heaping poverty but to justify this disparity as the fair workings of nature. That is, because it is a fact that individuals manifest various degrees of intellectual and physical abilities, the differences between wealth and poverty are claimed to be direct results of the differences in these natural abilities. As the argument runs, the laws of conflict and struggle inherent in nature expose those with the superior balance of intelligence and strength, who naturally emerge as the public stewards for those who are less able. Thus, the differences in social and political power are justified as natural.

Dewey suggests that to complete this justification, an appeal is made that the realization of a larger social good lies within each individual's capacity to be more self-reliant, judicious, industrious, and intelligent.[12] The appeal co-

---

[10]Dewey, Ethics, *The Later Works*, vol. 7, 331.

[11]See *Ethics, The Later Works*, vol. 7, 331–333; *The Public and Its Problems*, 90–92.

[12]Dewey, *Liberalism and Social Action, The Later Works*, vol. 11, 29–30. As Dewey was well aware, "Even when words remain the same, they mean something very different when they are uttered by a minority struggling against repressive measures, and when expressed by a group that has attained power and then uses ideas that were once weapons of emancipation as instruments for keeping the power and wealth they have obtained. Ideas that at one time are means of producing social change have not the same meaning when they are used as means of preventing social change. This fact is itself an illustration of historic relativity, and an evidence of the evil that lay in the assertion ... of the immutable and eternal character of their ideas. Because of this latter fact, the laissez faire doctrine was held ... to express the very order of nature itself. The outcome was the degradation of the idea of individuality until in the minds of many who are themselves struggling for a wider and fuller development of individuality, individualism has become a term of hissing and reproach, while many can see no remedy for the evils that have come from the use of socially unrestrained liberty in business enterprise, save changes produced by violence" ("The Future of Liberalism," *The Later Works of John Dewey*, vol. 11, 291).

mes with the promise that exhibiting and intensifying these virtues will create the opportunity for personal and social improvement. In keeping with the atomistic tenets of the Enlightenment philosophy, the appeal entails the assumption that all individuals, regardless of circumstance, are equally free to judge, choose, and execute what is in their best interests, insofar as their interests are consistent with the universal law. For example, as Dewey describes the matter, "In legal theory, the individual who has a starving family to support is equal in making a bargain about hours and conditions of labor and wages, with an employer who has large accumulated wealth to fall back on, and who finds that many other workers near the subsistence line are clamoring for an opportunity to earn something with which to support their families."[13] The outcome or degree of success, however, is claimed to be directly dependent on natural capacities and effort. As Dewey points out, the appeal entails extortion through fear. Those entrenched with great economic power make the claim that any disturbance of existing economic conditions will undermine both the just order of nature and the further realization of personal welfare and the public good:

> Their use of power to maintain their own interests is met, from the other side, by widespread fear of any disturbance, lest it be for the worse. This fear of any change is greatly enhanced by the complexity of the existing social scheme, where a change at one point may spread in unforeseen ways and perhaps put all established values in peril. Thus an active and powerful self-interest in maintaining the status quo conspires with dread ... to identify loyal citizenship with mental acquiescence in and blind laudation of things as they are.[14]

To state it simply, Dewey acknowledged the threat of overt force and implicit coercion as forms of power over others. In various places, he suggested that the interpretation and justification of the atomistic individual as the backbone of democratic liberty provides the sanction for governmental force against striking workers who supposedly violate their employment contracts, interfere with the capitalist claims to profit, and hence impede the so-called social good. He also understood that the ability to administer rewards and punishments in consequence of actions in support and protest of

---

[13] Dewey, *Ethics, The Later Works*, vol. 7, 335.
[14] Dewey, *Ethics, The Later Works*, vol. 7, 360. See also *Liberalism and Social Action, The Later Works*, vol. 11, 43–47. Although in somewhat different terms, Dewey, in *Individualism, Old and New*, suggests that the coercive power of capitalism lies in the threat that failure to support existing economic relations will jeopardize social progress. "Speeded-up mass production demands increased buying. It is promoted by advertising on a vast scale, by installment selling, by agents skilled in breaking down sales resistance. Hence buying becomes an economic 'duty' which is as consonant with the present epoch as thrift was with the period of individualism. For the industrial mechanism depends upon maintaining some kind of an equilibrium between production and consumption. If the equilibrium is disturbed, the whole social structure is affected and prosperity ceases to have a meaning" (*The Later Works*, vol. 5, 62).

capitalist relations enable those invested with great economic power to command attention to their demands as social claims of right. Dewey's recognition of physical threat and implicit coercion as means to command attention, coupled with his understanding of the influence of the social environment on the development of impulse and habit, suggests that power can be as productively oppressive as it can be suppressively oppressive. Now, how do schools serve as means by which to produce individuals motivated by values conducive to corporate profit?

Insofar as corporations weave their way into the schools ostensibly to serve as dutiful citizens doing their part to save an economically ailing public good, then corporations gain access to a captive and highly impressionable public. By means of deception, promise of reward, and implicit coercion (all embodied in corporate advertisements on school walls, in corporate-sponsored curriculum materials and programs, and through corporate-sponsored fund-raisers and contests), corporations come to influence the particular conditions that feed shared habits and therefore, in various degrees, command impulse, need, want, and desire. Insofar as the ends and means serving corporate interest—profit—become a—if not the—mediating law of shared habit, then this end becomes the standard of measurement regulating all associated impulses and emotions, working to inhibit, stimulate, or reinforce their expression. In this sense, corporations use schools (particularly if the leaders of which uncritically accept business–school partnerships as the touted "win-win" solution to their economic woes) as conduits by which to establish consumption as the ultimate expression of participatory democracy.

REFERENCES

Dewey, John. 1916. *Democracy and Education: An Introduction to The Philosophy of Education.* New York: The Macmillan Company.

Dewey, John. 1983 "Education as Politics." *John Dewey: The Middle Works, 1899–1924* vol. 13, edited by Jo Ann Boydston. Carbondale, Illinois: Southern Illinois University Press: 329–334.

Dewey, John. 1987. "Freedom." *John Dewey: The Later Works, 1925–1953*, vol. 11, edited by Jo Ann Boydston. Carbondale, Illinois: Southern Illinois University Press: 247–255.

Dewey, John. 1988. *Freedom and Culture* in *John Dewey: The Later Works, 1925–1953*, vol. 13, edited by Jo Ann Boydston. Carbondale, Illinois: Southern Illinois University Press: 63–188.

Dewey, John. 1987. "The Future of Liberalism." *John Dewey: The Later Works, 1925–1953*, vol. 11, edited by Jo Ann Boydston. Carbondale, Illinois: Southern Illinois University Press: 289–295.

Dewey, John. *Human Nature and Conduct: An Introduction to Social Psychology* (1922). New York: Random House, 1930.

Dewey, John. 1987. *Individualism, Old and New (1929)*. *John Dewey: The Later Works, 1925–1953*, vol. 5, edited by Jo Ann Boydston. Carbondale, Illinois: Southern Illinois University Press: 41–123.

Dewey, John. 1987. *Liberalism and Social Action (1935)*. *John Dewey: The Later Works, 1925–1953*, vol. 11, edited by Jo Ann Boydston. Carbondale, Illinois: Southern Illinois University Press: 1–65.

Dewey, John. 1927. *The Public and Its Problems*. Chicago: The Swallow Press, Inc.

Dewey, John. 1971. *The Study of Ethics: A Syllabus (1894)*. *John Dewey: The Early Works, 1882–1898*, vol. 4, edited by Jo Ann Boydston. Carbondale, Illinois: Southern Illinois University Press: 219–362.

Dewey, John and James Hayden Tufts. 1985. *Ethics (1908/1932)*. *John Dewey: The Later Works, 1925–1953*, vol. 7, edited by Jo Ann Boydston. Carbondale, Illinois: Southern Illinois University Press.

Chapter 4

Jesus in the Temple: What Should Administrators Do When the Marketplace Comes to School?

Donna Adair Breault

> Then Jesus went into the temple of God and drove out all those who bought and sold in the temple, and overturned the tables of the moneychangers and the seats of those who sold doves. And he said to them, "It is written, 'My house shall be called a house of prayer' but you have made it a den of thieves."[1]

It is a night like you will find in many schools. We are having a PTA meeting preceded by a joint performance of art, music, and drama—a night to celebrate the arts. That is what the flyer said that was sent to each home, and that is what the school's marquis announces in front of the building. Yet, as I enter the front door of the building, I am not inspired by displays from our art, music, and drama curriculum. Rather, I am overwhelmed by the brutal reality of what my school has become.

To my right, my school bookkeeper is sitting at a table selling "spirit wear"—shirts, hats, and other items that display our school's name and mascot. We ordered too many this year, and this spring PTA meeting will probably be the last opportunity we will have to unload them before they are put in a "half-off" pile next fall. Beyond the spirit wear table, teachers from the gifted program have a table where they are selling the school's literary maga-

---

[1] Matthew 21:12–13, *The New King James Version.*

zine. They work very hard each year to gather a representative sample of writing and art from each team, and the $7 charge merely covers the expense of publication. Across from the literary journal, a PTA volunteer sits at another table taking advanced orders for our school's yearbook. Thirty-five dollars seems a bit steep, but it is a nominal fee compared to the amount parents will pay for the high school yearbook.

As I walk down the hall and into the media center, I notice a large group of parents wandering around the Book Mobile kiosks. Each student had class time to come and review and purchase the books, posters, and games over the past week, but the media specialist wanted to keep the Book Mobile open during the PTA meeting so parents could buy more. After leaving the media center, I make my way into the cafeteria where the PTA is selling pizza for a dollar a slice along with 50¢ Cokes and brownies. They reasoned that many of the parents attending the meeting would come directly from work, so the pizza sale would provide a service for the parents as well as produce additional revenue for the Association. In the far corner, teachers have set up an additional table where they are selling baked goods. The proceeds from the sale will go toward our school's two Relay for Life teams.

This is middle-class America. Our parents, for the most part, come from very nice homes, and from all outward appearances, they are experiencing economic success. What harm is done? Parents look for opportunities to spend money on their children. Why not direct that tendency to spend in such a way as to benefit the school? In the past this rationale made some sense. Each small fund-raiser, each project that requires just a little money to keep it going seemed harmless enough. Yes, our school has a few families who cannot afford the extras we peddle at these meetings, and yes, I am sure some of our parents are overtaxed with debt even when they portray affluence at school functions. Yet, what harm is done when most parents can afford the monetary requests we make? Does "can" necessarily lead to "ought" regarding fund-raising? After wandering through my school this evening, I feel an overwhelming uneasiness. My mind keeps returning to a very clear call to consciousness and an equally clear and disturbing image: Jesus in the temple.

Like so many initiatives within schools today, fund-raising and other small-scale locally funded projects are easy to rationalize. For every project, for every promotion, we always seem to find many reasons to justify our participation. Those reasons are real. Who doesn't want students to have more books to read? Of course we want to encourage our students to write by publishing their work. My school's faculty has been hit very hard by the realities of cancer—both with those teachers and their family members who have survived and those who have not. How could anyone argue against supporting Relay for Life? All of these issues are very real, yet the message underneath the "money-changers tables" is real also. To what degree should our schools hold themselves responsible for institutionally promoting an ethic of consumption? At the expense of what other civic qualities do we consume?

THE CONSUMPTION ETHIC WITHIN U.S. SOCIETY

There is no doubt that Americans are obsessed with consumption. According to Twitchell, shopping has become the chief cultural activity in the United States.[2] He noted that we spend three to four times as much time in shopping malls than our European counterparts. As a society, we have four times as many things as Middle Europeans, consuming twice as many goods and services as we consumed in 1950. He added that this phenomenon is not relegated to the rich within our society. The poorest fifth of our current population spends more than the average fifth spent in 1955. Twitchell called this social phenomenon *mallcondo culture*.[3]

This mallcondo culture has not escaped our schools. It is evident within the many fund-raising activities and other initiatives that place money as the sole means for achieving a goal—be it philanthropic, instructional, social, or otherwise. Products are thrust on students through corporate sponsorship of school programs and activities, incentive programs, exclusive contracts, and sponsored educational materials.[4] In addition, direct messages to spend are reinforced daily through such mediums as Channel One's daily news program and ZapMe's Net-connected PCs.[5]

Furthermore, fund-raising has become big business within our nation's schools. There are approximately 2,000 companies that help schools generate fund-raising revenue. According to the Association of Fund Raisers and Direct Sellers (AFRDS), schools currently net $1.5 billion each year by selling wrapping paper and other goods via these fund-raising companies. The amount of money earned from consumption-promoting initiatives averages $30 million for every state, $13,000 for every school, and thus $30 for every student.[6] Based on a survey of principals, 90 percent of the schools surveyed responded that they use fund-raisers to supplement the money they get from district, state, and federal funding. More than half of the principals surveyed indicated that they have one to four fund-raisers every year, and more than

---

[2] J. B. Twitchell, *Lead Us Into Temptation: The Triumph of American Materialism* (New York: Columbia University Press, 1999).

[3] Ibid., 49.

[4] Alex Molnar, "Looking for Funds in All the Wrong Places," *Principal* 80, no. 2 (November 2000): 18–21.

[5] Sophie Bell, "Commercialism in Schools: An Interview with the Center for Commercial-free Public Education," *Radical Teacher*, 55 (1999), 4–8; Walter Minkel, "Zapped by Ads," *School Library Journal* 46, no. 8 (August 2000): 29.

[6] Vickie Mabry, "Product Fundraising: It's a Love-hate Thing," *Principal* 8, no. 2 (November 2000): 6–12.

one fourth of the principals surveyed noted that they raise over $10,000 a year with these initiatives.

When so much of a school or district's operating energy is influenced by or tied to an ethic of consumption, school leaders support this ethic through action or inaction. Said differently, the implications of Twitchell's mallcondo culture are not questioned.[7] Making money becomes a habit, one that is reinforced every time schools participate. Thus, a cycle is created. Successful fund-raising leads to more successful fund-raising until we no longer notice the excessive amount of energy we spend to spend more. We fail to recognize that the ethic of consumption leaves no room for the civic virtues we often espouse in our schools' mission statements.

A SCHOOL'S LIVING MISSION STATEMENT

So many schools, in true corporate fashion, have generated institutional mission statements. Often, these statements are proudly displayed in school lobbies, in teacher handbooks, in school improvement plans, and even in various school-to-home correspondences. In theory, a school's mission statement should serve two purposes. First, it should provide a clear purpose for the school. Second, it should identify worthy goals within the school. Ultimately, the mission statement should serve as a guiding document to set the direction and the climate of the school.[8] Yet, a statement on a wall or a slogan on stationery cannot compensate for a school's living mission statement. The focus of the school's time and energy, the nature of its climate and culture, the values it lives daily as well as those it ignores and thus denies all present a much clearer indication of the mission of the school and the vision (or perhaps lack of vision) of its leaders. Dufour concurred.[9] He noted that although most educators in North America have participated in developing and/or revising a mission statement, many school improvement initiatives within schools fail because schools lack a common purpose or central goals for student learning. He acknowledged that the problem for many schools is not the absence of a mission statement but, rather, an incongruity between the stated aims and the daily practices within the schools.[10]

When a school's official mission statement and its living mission are incompatible, ethical issues emerge. For example, whether explicitly stated or subtly implied, many schools relate their missions to notions of democracy and citizenship. Yet the consumption ethic that their living mission statements promote

---

[7]Twitchell, 49.

[8]Donald G. Coleman & Jessica Brockmeier, "A Mission Possible: Relevant Mission Statements," *The School Administrator* 54, no. 5 (May, 1997): 36–37.

[9]Richard DuFour, "That's Our Mission?" *Journal of Staff Development* 22, no. 1 (Winter, 2001): 68–69.

[10]Ibid.

undermines the very notion of democracy and what it means to be a critical citizen. Rather than focusing on a common good defined in terms of collaboration or sharing, many of the fund-raising activities encourage competition among students. The market mind-set focuses on self-interest rather than the egalitarian practices of citizenship. Giroux indicated that the market mind-set of schools is a result of educators looking to corporate rather than civic models when developing their institutions.[11] He reminds us that the corporate world is responsible for such things as savings and loan scandals, corporate buyouts, downsizing, and hostile takeovers—hardly the model we should esteem for our schools. Unfortunately, the consumption ethic in our schools is pervasive, and its implications are felt not only at the PTA meetings, but within the classrooms as well.

These implications extend beyond the immediate school mission to deeply affect the nature of a school's curriculum. As Boyles notes, the consumption ethic perpetuates a technorational way of being within schools and classrooms that supports intransitive consciousness or noncritical inaction rather than critical transitivity.[12] As a result, training replaces legitimate and democratic learning as the primary mode of knowing in classrooms. The civic project of educating is reduced to encompass only that which can be transmitted between the teacher and the student within the specific realm of schooling—the formal structures in which students learn. By reducing that which can be known to that which can be transmitted via the formal (and thus intended, official, presupposed/prescribed) system of schooling, schools limit the transformative potential of education itself. Boyles elaborated on this threat to critical transitivity:[13]

> While "training" is valuable (necessary?), the problem is that consumer materialism successfully (purposefully?) confuses "education" and "training" in order to reduce, and thereby limit, both content and criticality. Limited content and reduced criticality means stunted potential, increased gullibility and, as a result, an increase and perpetuation of consumer materialism.[14]

DEFICIT MENTALITY

According to Lichtenberg, society's ethic of consumption is not solely the result of wanting to appear better than the next person.[15] Rather, consumption is often a response to an individual or group's desire to be equal. For what-

---

[11]Henry A. Giroux, "Educational Leadership and the Crisis of Democratic Culture," Paper presented as keynote address at the UCEA Convention in University Park, PA, 1991.

[12]Deron Boyles, *American Education and Corporations: The Free Market Goes to School* (New York: Falmer, 2000).

[13]Ibid.

[14]Ibid., 14.

[15]J. Lichtenberg. "Consuming Because Others Consume," *Social Theory and Practice* 22, no. 3 (1996), 273–297.

ever reason, teachers and schools often equate having less with "being less." Thus, for teachers, parents, and schools to truly provide the advantages that they want for their students, they must consume more and more. Therefore, teachers often feel that their students will experience greater levels of success if they acquire more and more instructional materials. As a result, many teachers spend hundreds if not thousands of dollars from their own paychecks over the course of their teaching careers to supplement the materials in their own classrooms.

This accumulation phenomenon is not relegated solely to the individual teachers. Schools often support this line of reasoning as well by clamoring for more supplies, more instructional materials, and more equipment for various programs. This problem has become particularly noticeable with the influx of technology within the schools. Schools need more hardware and software as well as upgrades for the technology they already have. As technology advances, it becomes easier for schools to rationalize that neglecting such upgrades will put their students at a disadvantage.[16] How will students be able to compete in a global economy if they do not have all of the technological advantages available?

Interestingly enough, the pursuit of things for the sake of increasing levels of student achievement are most often seen within those schools that need it the least. For example, one district in the suburbs of Dallas and Forth Worth, Texas, maintains an annual operating budget of more than $90 million, yet they actively pursue corporate sponsorships and other initiatives to raise additional money.[17] One of the schools displays a large advertisement for Dr Pepper on its roof so travelers coming to and from the area's airport can see it. Meanwhile, the district as a whole has given Dr Pepper exclusive rights as a district soft-drink provider for the next ten years. In exchange, Dr Pepper paid the district $3.45 million and provided message boards and score boards for their arenas and athletic fields. Additional corporate sponsors pay the district between $1,000 and $10,000 annually to display advertising in athletic programs, arenas, and on buses. According to the district's superintendent, the district did not do a lot of soul searching when it made decisions about advertising within schools. As a result, what does the district gain from prostituting itself with the various corporations? The financial benefit, at best, accounts for a few hundred thousand dollars a year—approximately one third of 1% of their annual operating budget.[18]

---

[16]Deron R. Boyles, "Educational Technology Policy: Questioning Costs and Cultural Capital," *Educational Foundations* 11, no. 2 (Spring 1997): 83–94.

[17]Mike Kennedy, "Pubic Schools, Private Profits," *American School and University* 72, no. 6 (February 2000): 21–22.

[18]Ibid.

RESEARCH-SANCTIONED CONSUMPTION

At times, research-inspired initiatives also promote a sense of consumption among teachers and schools. The very nature of so much of our school reform focuses on the notion that schools will get results when they embrace simplistic adoption of reforms that have been abstracted to such a degree that they are hardly recognizable from their original positions. Hunch-of-the-month mentalities within schools motivate teachers and curriculum committees to run to teacher supply stores or educational-materials companies to find reproducible materials, software, and other easy-to-access instructional packages that will offer quick fixes to complex educational phenomena. To this degree, schools and teachers have become "Frank Schafferized."[19] Critical thinking, integrated curriculum, multicultural lessons, and the like are reduced to two-dimensional passive worksheet-like mediums conveniently packaged in moderately priced volumes. Teachers and schools mistake shallow, themed "units" for real integration; skill-based problem-solving worksheets as legitimate critical thinking; and tokenism in the form of famous African American word finds or crossword puzzles as authentic multicultural curriculum.

Furthermore, other research often directs teachers into new spending habits for their classrooms. As a supervisor, I often grimace when I see teachers proudly displaying the "mood lighting" they purchased for their classrooms and the expensive CD players they bring in to play Baroque music for their students—all in the name of "brain based" teaching. I have seen teachers who shifted their teaching of reading and writing from direct instruction with small groups to workshop formats, and I often notice that they invest more time, energy, and money in changing the physical setup of their classrooms than they spend focusing on the shifts they need to make in their methods of instruction and assessment. After all, it is easier to control the physical environment in the midst of change than to try to rethink practices. Changing one's perspective is often more difficult and takes more time and effort, particularly if the change involves rethinking deeply held beliefs.

Teachers' consumerist approaches to educational-reform initiatives may not only indicate desires to control their ever-changing educational landscapes, they may also demonstrate a "need" for individuals to communicate their identities as good teachers through the accumulation of things within

---

[19]Frank Schaffer is the brand name of teacher reproducible booklets marketed primarily to elementary school teachers. These materials offer worksheets and simple activities according to subject matter and/or themes. Elementary teachers often use these packets as "integrated curriculum units" even though they represent a false notion of integration. For example, a unit on fish might include a worksheet with math problems located within the shapes of fish. Upon completion of the math problems, students will color the fish according to the answers given.

their own classrooms. According to Lichtenberg, people often accumulate things in order to reveal something about themselves.[20] They want others to see those qualities within them that are not always easily seen, yet they are so essential when assessing their worth as teachers. Surrounding themselves with additional instructional materials and "things" for their rooms may help teachers project the image of a "good teacher" they want others to see.

ALTRUISM GONE AWRY

Philanthropic projects are yet another example of the consumption ethic entering our schools, and because the intentions of such projects are usually honorable, the consumerist notions on which the efforts are based often evade critique. For example, when my school introduced St. Jude's Math-a-Thon, the video students watched offered so much hype about competition and awards that I wondered whether the students would remember why they were participating.

My school also became a vehicle for the tried-but-true "dollar days." In order to collect more money for Relay for Life and other worthy causes, we often offered students the opportunity to bring their stuffed animals to school for a day or to wear hats or "silly socks." Each privilege was granted for any student presenting a dollar at the door as they came to school that day. The rationale behind these initiatives, "It's only a dollar," loses its credibility when these days follow one after another. In disillusionment, I have often wondered if it would not be more efficient to make the entrance to the school a toll entrance. Why not, if the proceeds go to a good cause? The only reason I haven't offered the suggestion in jest at various fund-raising committee meetings is for fear that someone might agree.

What message do schools send to students when they couch every act of good citizenship in economic terms? How powerful is the message that all of society's ills can be solved with money? How much ownership do students have regarding an initiative when all they have to do is grab a dollar from their parents as they walk out the door or ask their parents for a check? Do our schools help students esteem something greater than themselves when they project the good citizen and the good consumer as one in the same?

CURRICULUM AUDIT NEEDED

How can principals respond to the consumption ethic within schools? Each administrator needs to actively engage in a curriculum audit of his or her hidden curriculum. As Sergiovanni notes, school leaders must attend to the symbolic and cultural dimensions of school leadership as well as the educa-

---

[20]Lichtenberg, 1996.

tional and managerial issues.[21] To achieve this, administrators need to deal with a number of questions that address the symbolic and cultural dimensions of schooling:

1. How does my school spend its money?
2. What has my school identified as "needs," and how have we communicated those "needs" to our parents and community?
3. What is my school willing to do to acquire those things we have identified as "needs"?
4. How are my school's nonmonetary resources distributed?
5. What becomes the primary topics of discourse over my public-address system, during PTA addresses, and in faculty meetings?

If principals wrestle with these and similar questions, they will be able to gain a greater sense of their schools' culture—their hidden mission statements. With a better sense of the culture of their schools, principals can then work toward aligning their practices with their stated missions. To achieve this, principals should first choose their battles wisely. The consumption ethic runs deeply within our society; as such, it is impossible for principals to remove it completely from their schools. Second, principals should focus on the things they can change. Rather than trying to change the opinions of their parents and faculty, principals should try to change the conditions in which those opinions lead to pressure for fund-raising. Principals should be mindful of the manner and degree to which they and their schools blur the ideas of things they want and things they need. Finally, principals should clearly communicate the importance of their civic mission and the democratic principles they promote within their schools. Principals should lead their schools in efforts to continually seek ways to live out the democratic ideal in their daily practices. Thus, when civic rather than corporate principles become the focus of our work as educators, there will be very little space for the "moneychangers" to enter our school culture to distract us from the important work at hand.

REFERENCES

Bell, Sophie. (1999). Commercialism in Schools: An Interview with the Center for Commercial-free Public Education. *Radical Teacher*, 55: 4–8.
Boyles, Deron R. (1997). Educational Technology Policy: Questioning Costs and Cultural Capital. *Educational Foundations* 11, no. 2: 83–94.
_____. (2000). *American Education and Corporations: The Free Market Goes to School.* New York: Falmer.

---

[21]Thomas Sergiovanni, *The Principalship: A Reflective Practice* (Boston: Allyn and Bacon, 1995).

Coleman, Donald G. & Brockmeier, Jessica. (1997). A Mission Possible: Relevant Mission Statements. *The School Administrator* 54, no. 5: 36–37.

DuFour, Richard. (2001). That's Our Mission? *Journal of Staff Development* 22, no. 1: 68–69.

Giroux, Henry A. (1991). Educational Leadership and the Crisis of Democratic Culture. Paper presented as keynote address at the annual meeting of the University Council for Educational Administration, University Park, PA.

Kennedy, Mike. (2000). Pubic Schools, Private Profits. *American School and University* 72, no. 6: 21–22.

Lichtenberg, J. (1996). Consuming Because Others Consume. *Social Theory and Practice* 22, no. 3: 273–297.

Mabry, Vickie. (2000). Product Fundraising: It's a Love-hate Thing. *Principal* 8, no. 2: 6–12.

Minkel, Walter. (2000). Zapped by Ads. *School Library Journal* 46, no. 8: 29.

Molnar, Alex. (2000). Looking for Funds in All the Wrong Places. *Principal* 80, no. 2 (November 2000): 18–21.

Sergiovanni, Thomas. (1995). *The Principalship: A Reflective Practice.* Boston: Allyn and Bacon.

Twitchell, J. B. 1999. Lead Us Into Temptation: The Triumph of American Materialism. New York: Columbia University Press.

Chapter 5

Teachers, Unions, and Commercialization

Beth M. Weiss

> Don't scab for the bosses,
> Don't listen to their lies.
> Us poor folks haven't got a chance
> Unless we organize.
>
> (Which Side Are You On?,
> —Florence Reece, 1931)

Ask an education major why he or she wants to be a teacher and the answers vary.[1] Many will speak of their love of children; some mention a desire to foster learning; a commitment to helping future generations is often cited. The sweet song of summer vacations still calls to some. Whether the student is frivolous or scholarly, selling wrapping paper and writing grants for additional funding is never on this list. Yet, with funding shortfalls, teachers find themselves spending more and more time in extraneous fund development.

Teachers must explain fund-raisers to students and parents; teachers must encourage participation; they distribute materials; they tally results. Teachers, with their classes, might vie for the "most wrapping paper or-

---

[1] As an instructor for EPSF 2010, An Introduction to Educational Issues, I have the opportunity to interact with both "future" teachers and professionals already in the field. The question, "Why teach?" is standard and often discussed. My finding experience is consistent with the results reported by Newman. Joseph W. Newman, *America's Teachers: An Introduction to Education* (Boston: Allyn and Bacon, 2002), 3.

dered" recognition or the "most magazine subscriptions sold" distinction. Teachers, as directed by administration or a personal sense of purpose, are likely to encourage 100 percent participation from students and families. And teachers may deliver, with varying degrees of ceremony, awards to students who have met preset sales goals. Here is a disconnect between purpose and practice. Teachers, determined to serve their students and promote education in the classroom, find themselves reassigned sales managers, market promoters, and community organizers.

There is ample literature on the impact of commercial "partnerships" on school personnel and students. Time taken from teaching duties is an obvious concern. However streamlined the system, time spent tallying and sorting will never be time spent planning lessons and teaching. A teacher's credibility and professional posture may be compromised, sometimes decked out in logo-ed T-shirts, baseball caps, or other paraphernalia.[2] Should teachers be associated with products? Intentional or not, there is an implicit assumption of personnel endorsement of products used or marketed in schools.

The payoff to schools is predictably paltry compared to the benefits to the business partner and the payoff for the children may be the weakest of all.[3] The "bottom line" for kids is simple: "They are being subjected to marketing messages in school—some hidden, some obvious, but all quite powerful. The place where they might be learning how to deal with commercial pressures is thrusting more commercial pressure on them."[4] Children are attractive targets. They are a multibillion-dollar market opportunity that makes it good business to sell to kids.[5] The fact that children are harmed in the rush to commercialize schools makes them, according to Kenneth Saltman, "collateral damage" in the war for control of education reform.[6] That children are damaged seems inarguable, though there are proponents of school–business partnerships who deny the relationship is anything but supportive.

A student in my "Introduction to Educational Issues" class, currently working in special education, allowed how she recognized the issues regarding school–business partnerships, "But," she said, "you have to understand

---

[2] Deron Boyles, *School-Business Partnerships: Reading Between The Bottom Lines* [Internet] (Ohio Valley Philosophy of Education Society, 1999) [Internet] Accessed 10 July 2002; available from <http://www.geocities.com/Athens/Cyprus/6547/schoolbusiness.html>.

[3] Molnar, citing *The American School Board Journal*, indicates that "total corporate contributions to kindergarten through the twelfth-grade education in 1990 would run the nation's schools for less than two months." Alex Molnar, *Giving Kids the Business: The Commercialization of America's Schools* (Boulder: Westview Press, 1996), 7.

[4] Consumers Union, *Captive Kids: Commercial Pressures on Kids at School* [Internet] (Consumers Union Education Services, 1995) Accessed 20 June 2002; available from <http://www.consunion.org/>.

[5] Alex Molnar, *Giving Kids the Business*, 21.

[6] Kenneth J. Saltman, *Collateral Damage: Corporatizing Public Schools—A Threat to Democracy* (Lanham, Md.: Rowman & Littlefield, 2000).

that special education really *needs* this money." No doubt. When I asked her why she thought that the school budget could not or would not fund programs at the level needed to support required services, she was a bit stymied. The fact that corporations rarely pay their fair share in property taxes but make school contributions that support their own corporate bottom lines and still leave children without needed services (and teachers scurrying for grants and sponsors) takes a bit of the blush off the old rose of charitable giving. The fact that students become sales representatives or marketers for local businesses, bringing families together for school night at the local "Sweet Tomatoes" or "Chick Fil A" restaurant, spending a far greater percentage than the school will receive back in receipts, seems an abusive use of corporate power, as companies paint themselves as responsible neighbors while they contribute to the budget shortfalls in public services, including education. There are lessons learned in school–business partnerships that will affect children throughout their lives:

> This has consequences for the way in which children and childhood are understood both in and out of school. In the marketplace children are just another market segment to be studied so that they can be manipulated into thinking, feeling, and acting in ways that lead to the inevitable decision to consume something. The market takes all human desires such as love and transforms them into products that can be bought and sold. Lonely? Buy a candy bar. Feel ugly? Buy herbal shampoo. Feel powerless? Buy a convertible. All of this leads, I think, to a sort of cascading quietism that might be compared to the effect that television viewing seems evoke, i.e., an agitated passiveness. This is the death of the public sphere. It is also, from my standpoint profoundly immoral.[7]

With schools strapped for cash, it becomes difficult to turn down any income source. Surely, there are limits. Perhaps, but though it seems unlikely that we will see "Budweiser" scoreboards in high school gymnasiums, materials urging responsible drinking are already in circulation with the "Anheuser-Busch" logo. The company goes further, sponsoring a list of "Consumer Awareness and Education Speakers," whose presentations may be underwritten by local bottling companies and distributors pending a special and personal request from a teacher or other organizer to the company local.[8] Furthermore, speaker materials are copyrighted to Anheuser-Busch and marked with the corporate logo. This sets up a classic scenario for psychological cognitive dissonance. The alco-

---

[7] Alex Molnar, "The Commercial Transformation of American Public Education," lecture given at the annual meeting of the Ohio Valley Philosophy of Education Society, Dayton, Ohio. [Internet] Accessed 2 July 2003. Available from <http://www.asu.edu/educ/epsi/CERU/Documents/1999phil.html>.

[8] The Anheuser-Busch speaker's bureau can be found at <http://www.beeresponsible.com/programs.html>. I use Budweiser as an example only. It is representative of the kind of "curriculum" offered at many sites including other brewers as well as tobacco companies.

hol providers, once cognitively linked with problems and issues of drunk driving and underage drinking, now associate themselves with the charitable, though unlikely, role of prevention educators. I call this unlikely, not because I doubt the industry's sincerity and effort, but rather because of this unavoidable paradox: Anheuser-Busch, and other breweries, only makes a profit when people drink their products. Sales must always be part of the prevention equation. "We can't win for losing!" I hear them cry out in the boardrooms. And that is precisely the point. Without logo identification there is no payback for corporate generosity. Even for the teen who takes the message to heart and waits until he or she is 21, as I have every reason to think the beer industry hopes he or she will, there is the hope that the familiar logo and the corporation's warm image as a responsible community partner will encourage that new drinker to order with his or her memory. One way to resolve the cognitive dissonance caused by the competing characterizations of brewers is to simply conflate one belief with the other. Companies that sell alcohol, even when underage drinkers use the product, cannot be so bad when we see and consider the serious and valuable prevention efforts they put forth.

Kenneth Saltman speaks of the "cultural pedagogy" that is delivered through school–business partnerships. He aptly describes how corporatization "does a stealthy job of erasing the reality of certain social relations and producing new fictitious narratives in their stead."[9] Among the reframed narratives are: democracy equals capitalism; corporations are generous benefactors; commercialism solves problems; it is natural for schools to compete, market, and beg for funds.

There are, one must remember, ways for industry to support students without inherent conflicts. True charity works without logos and community recognition.[10] By paying its fair share in property taxes and other assessments that support public education, a business could ease the financial hardship in school budgets. Lose the logo and pay your taxes are simple, specific actions to describe. They are, in today's political climate, heretical to expect.

A PLACE FOR UNIONS

Teachers and school administrators need help resisting partnerships that are academically inappropriate, time-wasting, energy-draining, and professionally debasing. Fortunately, teachers and other public school employees have professional associations, unions that support educators' best interests. The National Education Association (NEA) and the American Federation of

---

[9]Saltman is referring specifically to Coca-Cola but the concept of a corporate pedagogy generalizes across business and provides a context, for example, to consider the changing image of brewers and cigarette companies. See Saltman, 65.

[10]Although it is worth wondering out loud whether public schools should be put in the position where, as institutions legislated to provide education to all students, they must depend on "charity."

Teachers (AFT), the nation's largest and most influential teacher organizations, have taken strong stands against privatization and the encroachment of private-sector commercialism into school life. Unfortunately, an examination of both organizations' Web sites reveals inconsistent messages about school–business partnerships and an apparent double standard for educators and unions.

Union opposition to privatization in public schools is resolute. Both the AFT and NEA oppose privatization trends by examining and explaining the pitfalls and the research that reveals the failure of private ventures in public schools. From the NEA site: "The National Education Association is strongly opposed to privatization because of the threat that it poses to the quality of education, the accountability of public schools to the communities that they serve, and to the well being of children in school."[11] (NEA, 2002). There is another understood truth; clearly privatization threatens the jobs of teachers and other union members. The AFT site is specific in its concerns regarding job security.

In school districts and colleges, privatization hits employees hard. They lose their jobs or are offered the same work at lower pay and benefits. Turnover rates increase, and employee morale suffers. Women and minority workers disproportionately bear the effects of contracting out.[12]

This reality need not taint these organizations' positions regarding privatization. Union opposition to privatization is much more meaningful and far-reaching than any apparent self-serving effort to maintain membership through jobs. There is philosophical and pedagogical support for their positions. What is necessary is a constant, consistent, comprehensive message. What is missing is a constant, consistent, and comprehensive message.

Although privatization and all of its ramifications are addressed directly and specifically and on both of these national organizations' Web sites, interestingly absent are critiques and criticism of commercialism as represented by school–business partnerships and fund development by public school administrators, teachers, children, and parents.[13] I cynically read into this omission a conflict of interest; unions—especially the AFT with its affiliation with the American Federation of Labor-Congress of Industrial Organizations (AFL-CIO)—must be "pro-business" in the largest sense. Commercial partners are often union partners. Material handlers, truckers, support workers—corporations are more than their executive office suites. It is possible that the NEA and the AFT are conflicted, seeing some advantage in activities that benefit many groups of employees.

---

[11]National Education Association, *NEA Mission Statement* [Internet] Accessed 17 August 2002; available from <http://www.nea.org/bt/6-association/6-2-q-a.html>.

[12]AFT, *AFT Mission Statement* [Internet] Accessed 19 July 2002; available from http://www.aft.org/about/index.html.

[13]There are clear, direct links on each union's homepage to privatization issues and information.

There are other ways to explain this philosophical discord. Professional associations may be unaware of the hazards that school–business partnerships present (an unlikely scenario) or, most likely, these teacher organizations simply assume that school personnel will be responsible and resolute in sifting through the elaborate maze of corporate cultures.

The NEA provides specific advice to "Beginning Teachers" through a series of web pages.[14] This is an interesting starting place to explore the organization's attitudes and practices related to commercialization. Missing from the pages is any introduction or overview, any statement of policy or position from the NEA. The page simply "is." It starts with a "Beginning Teachers" heading and then asks the following: "Looking for tips on launching your teaching career? The 'beginning teachers sections' of our Web site offers timesaving ideas honed by veteran educators, classroom management advice, and everything else you need to be successful." The page then goes on to present a series of questions with answers and advice. The homepage asks, "How can I tap resources like businesses, civic organizations, and volunteers?" What follows the interactive link encourages teachers to:

1. Define needs.
2. Target good partners.
3. Know the "shoulds" and "should nots."[15]

This may be a logical list—but the philosophical "why" is absent. Why are there needs? Why pursue partnerships? This is not just a question of economic reality. This is a question of political posture. Is entrepreneurialism a logical and principled position for teachers? These questions, rarely asked, seem incontestable when posed to educators. Given a choice between teaching and selling, teachers prefer to teach. However, in our market-driven system, to ask the question "why" is to ignore the growing cultural rhetoric that requires good teachers, and all of us, to be good Americans—good Americans who embrace business.[16]

Presented with the homepage question, "How can I tap resources like businesses, civic organizations, and volunteers," the new teacher logically

---

[14]The "Beginning Teachers" home is found at <http://www.nea.org/bt>. Links to subsequent pages follow in footnotes. The NEA Web site (www.nea.org) was "under construction" at the time of this writing. Some pages that had not yet been updated were available through cached sites via <www.google.com>.

[15]Ibid.

[16]I am reminded of President George W. Bush's advice to Americans who wondered how to response to the terrorist attacks of September 11, 2001. "Go about your business," he said. Patriotic shopping is born. George W. Bush, "Address to a Joint Session of Congress and the American People" [Internet] (September 20, 2001) Accessed 15 July 2001; available from <http://www.whitehouse.gov/news/releases/2001/09/20010920-8.html>. Noam Chomsky addresses the growing stature and power of business, stating that the "'corporatization of America' has been an attack on democracy …" leading to a redefinition of the "modern state/corporate era." Noam Chomsky, *Profit Over People: Neoliberalism and Global Order* (New York: Seven Stories Press, 1999), 132.

thinks, "I should be tapping resources. Tapping resources must be a good thing." Without any statements to the contrary, NEA positions itself in support of school–business partnerships (and other partnerships, as well). It is deeply frustrating that the NEA and AFT disregard this opportunity to define both the necessities and the very real drawbacks around this issue. NEA does, as the Beginning Teacher web pages continue, present specific "shoulds" and "should nots" for partnerships:

> Any business program or relationship with a business *should*:
> - Have real educational value and promote a love of learning.
> - Reinforce basic classroom curricula, not contrived activities.
> - Advance an education goal, not merely a public relations purpose.
> - Allow class participation to be decided at the school level.
> - Be open to students and parents who voluntarily choose to participate.
>
> It should *not*:
> - Offer trips, gifts, or prizes in exchange for teachers pushing commercial products in their classrooms.
> - Discriminate against any group of students.
> - Impede or interfere with student instructional time.
> - Require the purchase of a product by students or parents.
> - Require teachers, students, or parents, to promote a commercial product.[17]

This list addresses concerns and cautions educators ought to consider when establishing partnerships. The NEA also builds its own "school–business" partnerships and invites union "locals" to participate. How do these associations measure up to the advice to new teachers? Can unions abhor privatization with one hand and with the other hand press teachers toward commercial linkages? At what point is the integrity of the organization impugned, caught in the double-speak of a corporate mentality that pits immediate economic strain against strategic, pedagogic principles?

CONFLICT AND COMPROMISE

In the spirit of constant, consistent, comprehensive messages, it would be enough if the NEA read and followed its own guidelines. Are the union's Web site business links advisable according to NEA's own "shoulds" and "should nots"? Consider NEA's national, very visible project, Read Across America.[18]

This NEA program calls for every child to be reading in the company of a caring adult. The observance date is March 3, which coincides with "Dr. Suess'" birthday. The event can be small or a gala affair; NEA suggests that schools and communities make plans based on their needs and available

---

[17]NEA Web site: <http://nea.org/bt>. [Internet] Accessed 10 September 2002.
[18]NEA, *Read Across America: the Basics* [Internet]. Accessed 10 September 2002); available from <http://www.nea.org/readacross/basics1.html>.

budgets. Festive and fun, the "Cat in the Hat," Suess' beloved and well-known character, is the event's logo and mascot. This mascot, both full costume and trademark hat, are available for sale to help the kids and teachers create the mood for their "Read Across America" celebration. There is a "cat-alog" at the NEA site and a link to "Morris Costumes," for wholesale prices on merchandise.[19] These are darn cute items, sure to make the "Read Across" event memorable for the children (lest you think I am the "Grinch"). I wonder, and shouldn't others wonder, why Morris' is the outlet for costumes? I wonder why items are available wholesale and not "at cost"? There may be perfectly reasonable answers to these questions but they are not addressed on the site. There is, instead, a clear acceptance that this is a service. It is unquestioned that profits are part of life. But this recognition is the result of the "cultural pedagogy" that allows business to define the norms and expectations of a consumer society. NEA's participation, without explanation or rationale, is the first ripple in a subtle stream of hegemonic messages to its membership.

"Read Across America" comes with its own host of national sponsors and partnerships.[20] There is a specific, though unexplained, prohibition against local schools partnering with "fast-food restaurants" but schools are encouraged to seek assistance from the Saturn Corporation, a national sponsor. Indeed, the NEA Web site includes Saturn's corporate logo and the following text: "For the past three years, Saturn/UAW retailers across the country have taken part in *NEA's Read Across America*. Many have hosted birthday parties, cooked green eggs and ham, provided vehicles for Cat in the Hat appearances, supported reading contests, and most importantly, taken time to read to local schoolchildren. Contact your local Saturn/UAW retailer to see how they can partner in your *NEA's Read Across America* event."[21]

If the ban on fast-food partnerships is a statement about healthful eating, might the NEA have selected a car company whose product does not pollute with fossil fuels? Casting no aspersions on Saturn, I merely point out the inexplicable logic in NEA's position.

There are other "Read Across America" partners with links to Web sites from the NEA site. One partner, RIF, "Reading is Fundamental, Inc.," has many donation-with-purchase opportunities to support RIF programs. While looking for "Read Across America" at the RIF site, I was encouraged to buy Kraft, shop Albertson's, be a consumer at Toys-R-Us, and participate in Scholastic's special-edition *Clifford, The Big Red Dog* birthday promotion. A

---

[19] NEA, *Read Across America Cat-alog* [Internet]. Accessed 19 September 2002); available from <http://www.nea.org/readacross/catalog.html>.

[20] "The Basics: How to Celebrate from Start to Finish," NEA Web site. [Internet] Accessed 10 September 2002. Available from <http://216.239.37.100/cobrand_univ?q=cache:XNV1PXdILlcJ:www.nea.org/readacross/basics1.html+%22read+across+america%22++%22how+to%22&hl=en&ie=UTF-8>.

[21] NEA, *Read Across America* [Internet]. Accessed 19 September 2002; available from <http://www.nea.org/readacross/>.

portion of the proceeds from all of this shopping supports RIF. These donations support RIF; RIF supports NEA. In the arena of high-tech partnership, you are your partner's Web site. NEA's injunction against product promotion is demeaned by these "donation with purchase" campaigns.

NEA has a of history corporate connections in its own right. NEA's partnership page, cached as the Web site is being updated, lists projects and calls them "shining examples of school, community, and business partnerships that support our children's achievement and America's public schools."[22] On the list is Etienne Aigner, purveyor of upscale leather goods and accessories for women, and its NEA partnership to boost literacy. Aigner's literacy support effort entails placing reading corners in retail outlets with comfy chairs and books for kids. Presumably, children look at books, thus supporting literacy while their mothers shop. Call me cranky, but this just doesn't add up to a literacy effort. Simple questions about literacy and access to books lead to the obvious conclusion that this outreach offers gifts to the gifted. Remember NEA's advice to teachers? "Any partnership with a business should advance an education goal, not merely a public relations purpose." The Etienne Aigner reading program offers access to books whose families, based on socioeconomic demography, are the most likely to already be committed to literacy and value book ownership. Aigner's reading is linked to shopping, which brings us back to "cultural pedagogy," determined to make positive, albeit forced, associations between corporate culture and educational causes.

The AFT is not immune to issues of "cultural pedagogy." The AFT homepage offers an icon link to Powell's, a "union bookstore." A rationale for this commercial link is found when site visitors explore the "AFT Plus" member benefits page and then follow a link to the "List of Benefits and Merchants" page. The caveat, "No union dues are used to provide these benefits" follows a host of commercial-benefit descriptions. The question, "Does member participation in these opportunities benefit the union?" is not posed. Is there a business relationship between benefit providers and the AFT? It doesn't say.

Powell's is an exception. On the benefits site, AFT explains, "A percentage of each AFT purchase made online will be credited to the AFT Recovery Fund for the victims and families of the Sept. 11 attacks."[23] How and how much? I don't know. AFT encourages members "to take a peek at Powells. We [AFT] know you'll like what you see." This may not be an improper partnership but there is certainly a convoluted connection. The commerce-driven relationship is easy to find; direct links to Powell's exist on almost all

[22]NEA, *NEA Partnership Resource Page* [Internet] Accessed 25 July 2002; available from http://www.nea.org/partners/available cached: <http://216.239.51.100/search?q=cache:U9G4c3lrk-QC:www.nea.org/partners/+partnership&hl=en&ie=UTF-8>.
[23]AFT, "Powell's Bookstore Benefit." [Internet]. Available from <http://www.aft.org/aftplus/bookstore.html>. Accessed 15 July 2002.

AFT web pages. Information about the partnership is buried, taking a determined surfer three or four (more, for the less savvy) screens to find an explanation of the AFT–Powell's relationship. What's more, once at the Powell's
bookstore site, there is no mention or identification with AFT and no reference to the store's union connection.[24] This is a financial partnership.
Powell's gets AFT member purchases and the AFT gets a portion of the proceeds. Does this, then, become a model for local partnerships? The answer
must be, "Yes." AFT does nothing at its Web site to warn or dissuade schools
from donation for purchase business relationships.

HEGEMONY JOINS THE UNION

Teachers are committed to educating children. Educational unions and professional organizations exist to represent teachers in a supportive way. Mission statements from both the NEA and the AFT clearly state these unions's
positions.

NEA Mission Statement:

To fulfill the promise of a democratic society, the National Education Association shall promote the cause of quality public education and advance
the profession of education; expand the rights and further the interest of
educational employees; and advocate human, civil, and economic rights
for all.[25]

AFT Mission Statement:

The mission of the American Federation of Teachers, AFL-CIO, is to improve
the lives of our members and their families, to give voice to their legitimate
professional, economic and social aspirations, to strengthen the institutions
in which we work, to improve the quality of the services we provide, to bring together all members to assist and support one another and to promote democracy, human rights and freedom in our union, in our nation and throughout
the world.[26]

Commercialization and corporatization in public schools are antithetical
to ideals of democratic education. "The problem occurs," Deron Boyles argues, "at the point where private enterprise goals and free-market logics sub-

---

[24] Powell's Books, "Powell's Bookstore Homepage." [Internet] available from <http://
www.powells.com/>. Accessed 25 July 2002.
[25] NEA, *NEA Mission Statement* [Internet] Accessed 8 November 2002; available from
http://www.nea.org/aboutnea.html
[26] AFT, *AFT Mission Statement* [Internet] Accessed 8 November 2002; available from http://
www.aft.org/about/index.html.

sume pluralistic and democratic goals in the public, not private sphere."[27] Both the NEA and AFT commit themselves to quality education, human rights, and democratic values. Their incautious connections to corporations undermine these imperatives to the advantage of commercial causes. Logically, union support of school–business partnerships is a hegemonic association, working against the foundational principals of public education. Simply put, the foxes are in the hen house.

Antonio Gramsci, writing before the Second World War, defined hegemony as the predominance of one class over others. The underclass participates in its own demise by accepting and internalizing the values and politics of the dominant culture. Most interesting in Gramsci's theory is the concept of "common sense." "This represents not only political and economic control, but also the ability of the dominant class to project its own way of seeing the world so that those who are subordinated by it accept it as 'common sense' and 'natural.'"[28] This idea of "common sense," the obvious correctness of a philosophy, politic, or point of view, is completely relevant to question of commercialism in the public arena. George W. Bush's "No Child Left Behind" campaign is touted as "common sense education reform."[29] Common sense is a culture-driven commodity. Frequent testing of students to measure "success" and achievement, required by "No Child Left Behind" was not common sense to John Dewey.[30] Rewarding "successful" schools and penalizing "failing" schools would not be supported by Jonathan Kozol.[31] "Common sense, suggests Geoffrey Nowell-Smith, is 'the way a subordinate class lives its subordination.'"[32]

Common sense in education reform is corporate culture. Phrases like "fiscal responsibility," "accountability," and "quality management" come di-

---

[27]Deron Boyles, *American Education and Corporations : The Free Market Goes to School* (New York: Garland, 1998), 104.

[28]Kick Schouten, "Popular Music and Conservatism: Hegemony and the Power of Popular Music" [Internet] Accessed 25 July 2002; available from <http://home.planet.nl/~kick/hegemony/1.4johnfiske.htm>.

[29]J. Dennis Hastert, "Education Reform: No Child Left Behind Act" [Internet] (The Office of the Speaker, Accessed 22 September 2002); available from http://speaker.house.gov/default2.asp.

[30]Dewey introduces his concept that "educative growth ... and growing ... arouses curiosity, strengthens initiative." John Dewey, *Experience and Education* (New York: Collier Books, 1963), 38. Education is never an endgame based testing standards and information.

[31]Kozol's thesis throughout his work emphasizes the inequities in public education and the economic, governmental, and societal systems that maintain them. Withholding funds from "under-performing" schools and rewarding "schools of excellence" is business as usual framed, hegemonically, as education reform. Jonathan Kozol, *Savage Inequalities : Children in America's Schools* (New York: HarperPerennial, 1992).

[32]Kick Schouten, "Popular Music and Conservatism: Hegemony and the Power of Popular Music" [Internet] Accessed 25 July 2002; available from http://home.planet.nl/~kick/hegemony/1.4johnfiske.htm.[cited in Manuel Alvarado and Oliver Boyd-Barrett, *Media Education : An Introduction* (London: Open University, 1992), 51.]

rectly from business lingo.[33] The ideas that good schools are good business and that business is good for schools lash education to consumerism and the unions, by not being actively resistant, tie the knot.

Hegemony's enemy is resistance. School personnel, with the fiscal, governmental, and societal pressures they face, need assistance and encouragement to challenge the new norm of dependence on corporate influence and giving. The NEA and the AFT business connections are counterintuitive. They are not "common sense." The organizations must step forward, against trends, to meet their mandates in support of teachers, families, and public education. Or we are left to ask, "Which side are you on?"

POSTSCRIPT

There should be little surprise that Web sites have changed, grown, and developed since the original research for this chapter. As time passes, web addresses and "e-citations" become less reliable. Revisiting the sites noted, I find that questions of constancy and meaning continue. Conflicting messages regarding privatization and inconsistent advice regarding corporate involvement in schools are ongoing problems for teachers. The major teachers unions have not probed these issues. Unexamined, these messages become "normal," and the contradictions go unnoticed.

Again, in the time since the original research for this chapter, the national economy and state budgets for education have faltered. The pressure to find alternative sources of funding becomes more and more intense. Educators spend more time seeking for corporate charity and organizing local school fund-raisers. The cycle continues.

Educators and unions working together can examine these issues. Educational policy can be explored through various foundational lenses, restricting the privilege of the business sector. The evidence is all around us—the challenge remains.

REFERENCES

American Federation of Teachers. 2002. AFT Mission Statement. Available at http://www.aft.org/about/index.html. (Accessed 8 November)

Boyles, Deron. 1999. School-Business Partnerships: Reading Between The Bottom Lines. Presidential Address delivered to the Ohio Valley Philosophy of Education Society. Available at http://www.geocities.com/Athens/Cyprus/6547/schoolbusiness.html. (Accessed 10 July)

---

[33]The irony of this enculturation of business values is the very obvious lack of morals and ethics demonstrated in a variety of recent business debacles including Enron, Tyco, and WorldCom. This common sense in based in folklore not fact, created to ensnare and control public opinion, privileging the private sector and exploiting the public sector.

Boyles, Deron. 2000. *American Education and Corporations: The Free Market Goes to School.* New York: Garland.

Bush, George W. 2001. Address to a Joint Session of Congress and the American People. Available at <http://www.whitehouse.gov/news/releases/2001/09/20010920-8.html>. (Accessed 10 September)

Chomsky, Noam. 1999. *Profit Over People: Neoliberalism and Global Order.* New York: Seven Stories Press.

Consumers Union Education Services. 2002. Captive Kids: Commercial Pressures on Kids at School. Available at http://www.consunion.org/ (Accessed 20 June).

Dewey, John. 1938. *Experience and Education.* New York: Collier Books.

Hastert, J. Dennis. 2002. Education Reform: No Child Left Behind Act. The Office of the Speaker. Available at http://speaker.house.gov/default2.asp (Accessed 10 September).

Kozol, Jonathan. 1992. *Savage Inequalities: Children in America's Schools.* New York: HarperPerennial.

Molnar, Alex. 1996. *Giving Kids the Business: The Commercialization of America's Schools.* Boulder: Westview Press.

Molnar, Alex. 1999. The Commercial Transformation of American Public Education. Phil Smith memorial lecture given at the annual meeting of the Ohio Valley Philosophy of Education Society, Dayton, Ohio. Available at <http://www.asu.edu/educ/epsi/CERU/Documents/1999phil.html. (Accessed 2 July 2003).

National Education Association. 2002. NEA Mission Statement. Available at http://www.nea.org/bt/6-association/6-2-q-a.html. (Accessed 17 Aug).

Newman, Joseph W. 2002. *America's Teachers: An Introduction to Education.* Boston: Allyn and Bacon.

Saltman, Kenneth J. 2000. *Collateral Damage: Corporatizing Public Schools—A Threat to Democracy.* Lanham, Md.: Rowman & Littlefield.

Schouten, Kick. 2002. *Popular Music and Conservatism: Hegemony and the Power of Popular Music.* Available from http://home.planet.nl/~kick/hegemony/1.4johnfiske.htm. (Accessed 25 July)

Chapter 6

Children as Collateral Damage: The Innocents of Education's War for Reform

Judy Block

The trend toward corporatization of public schools reinforces and legitimizes the role of free market enterprise in American education. In education's war for reform, commercial marketeers and proponents of market-free schools vie for control of our nation's classrooms, setting education reform as their prize while rendering public school students its collateral damage.

Military war and education's reform war have something in common—both involve destroying innocents, creating *collateral damage*, to achieve a good end. In wartime we ask, "Is it really an accident when civilians die under an enemy's bombs?" In education's war for reform we ask, "Is it really an accident when a disproportionate number of students representing marginalized segments of the population drop out of school; are placed in vocational or remedial programs; either do not attempt to go to or fail postsecondary education as a result of the corporatization of education?" Even without the corporateer's intention to harm innocents, if innocents become victims again and again, can we truly call such acts accidents? In the case of education reform, do we truly want to justify some children as education's collateral damage?

IDEOLOGY AT WAR

The current struggle to reform public education is grounded in the basic assumptions of market ideology and democratic ideals. Peter Cookson addresses the commodification of schools and evaluates economics-driven choice by contrasting market ideology and democratic ideals as follows:

> At the heart of the democratic relationship is the implicit or explicit covenant: important human interactions are essentially communal. Democratic metaphors lead to a belief in the primacy and efficacy of citizenship as a way of life. The second metaphor is that of the market. At the heart of the market relationship is the implicit or explicit contract: human interactions are essentially exchanges. Market metaphors lead to a belief in the primacy and efficacy of consumership as a way of life.... For too long we have viewed education as a contractual relationship. The nature of this relationship is made most explicit by market advocates who speak of "educational products" as though education were something that could be manufactured and consumed. Learning is not something we can buy; it is something we must experience.[1]

Michael Engel locates four assumptions at the root of market ideology:

> Human nature is a more or less unchangeable assortment of basic character traits; society is best understood as an aggregation of individuals, and the social structure is best understood as the net result of their individual choices; self-interest is the primary motivator of these choices, and personal material reward is the primary goal; and protecting and maximizing the range of individual freedom of choice must be the primary purpose of any form of social organization.[2]

Subscribing to these assumptions or values requires individuals to turn over various tasks, such as education reform, to a market of:

> ... ongoing and unrestricted exchange of goods and services among producers and consumers in competition with each other. If individuals want a particular good or service, they should be prepared to pay its actual cost. It will be available to the extent that other individuals make a profit in producing it.... The market itself or regulate supply and demand. There will be no need for any external force to tell an individual what to produce, how to produce it, or what to buy.[3]

---

[1] Peter W. Cookson, *School Choice: The Struggle for the Soul of American Education* (New Haven CT: Yale University Press, 1994), 99.
[2] Michael Engel, *The Struggle for Control of Public Education: Market Ideology vs. Democratic Values* (Philadelphia PA: Temple University Press, 2000), 18, 19.
[3] Engel, *The Struggle for Control of Public Education*, 9.

In a free-market society, educating children becomes the good and service over which marketeers do battle, promoting their wares in the form of educational learning packets, technology, academic testing, school management, and school reform. Free-market proponents claim that their involvement in education promotes healthy competition for improved schools resulting in better education for children. In *Better Teachers, Better Schools*, Chester Finn, Jr., and Marci Kanstoroom applaud corporate involvement in education reform noting:

> America is beginning to adopt a powerful, commonsensical strategy for school reform. It is the same approach that almost every successful modern enterprise has adopted to boost performance and productivity: set high standards for results to be achieved, identify clear indicators to measure progress towards those results.... This strategy is sometimes called standards-and-accountability. It is a fundamental aspect of the charter school movement, and it undergirds many versions of systemic reform as well.[4]

Finn and Kanstoroom describe standards and accountability as measures key to charter schools; however, these measures reach beyond charter schools and into all public school classrooms in terms of what they teach, how they teach it, and how they test student "knowledge" in the form of standardized test-aligned curricula, teachers' manuals, and standardized tests. Teachers and schools are held accountable through student performance on these tests and, when necessary, corrected or replaced by individuals and/or remedies assumed to ensure children a quality education.

Many of Finn and Kanstoroom's strategies and measures for charter schools may sound familiar as they are repeated in George W. Bush's education plan, "No Child Left Behind." The Bush plan emphasizes core market concepts such as standards and accountability, competition, rewards, sanctions, and consumer choice. According to Pauline Lipman, there is "an explicit linkage of corporate interests with educational practices and goals. Business rhetoric of efficiency and performance standards and the redefinition of education to serve the labor market has become the common vocabulary of educational policies across the U.S."[5] In the context of free-market ideology, education is regarded as a consumer good; knowledge becomes a commodity and "schools and classrooms become marketplaces where commodities become available for students."[6]

---

[4]Chester Finn, Jr. and Marci Kanstoroom, *Better Teachers, Better Schools* (Washington DC: Thomas B. Fordham Foundation, 1999), 1.

[5]Pauline Lipman, "Bush's Education Plan, Globalization, and the Politics of Race." *Cultural Logic* 4, no. 1 (Fall, 2000), 1.

[6]Patrick Shannon, i*Shop, You Shop: Raising Questions About Reading Commodities* (Portsmouth NH: Heinemann, 2001), ix.

Henry Giroux describes the role of market-free public education as the following:

> [It is] one of the most important legacies of public education to provide students with the critical capacities, the knowledge, and the values to become active citizens striving to realize a vibrant democratic society. [Schools] remind us of specific values that must be passed on to young people in order for them to think critically; to participate in policy decisions that affect their lives; and to transform the racial, social, and economic inequities that close down democratic social relations.[7]

Claiming that corporatization of public schools "undermines the purposes for which schools exist," Michael Sandel differentiates commercial advertising and education.[8] Sandel notes, "Advertising encourages people to want things and to satisfy their desires: education encourages people to reflect on their desires, to restrain or to elevate them. The purpose of advertising is to recruit consumers; the purpose of public schools is to cultivate citizens."[9] Cultivating children for democratic citizenry is not easy and becomes even harder for teachers "to teach students to be citizens, capable of thinking critically about the world around them, when so much of childhood consists of basic training for a commercial society."[10] Democratic education promotes "[a] pedagogy that rewards openness, creativity, social awareness, and idealism [and can] flourish only when people are able to take control of their lives by controlling the direction of society, including the schools."[11]

"Growing up corporate has become a way of life for youth in the United States," claims Giroux, and "that as commercial culture replaces public culture, the language of the market becomes a substitute for the language of democracy."[12] Market ideology frustrates democratic ideals and fails students by constructing an educational system that "reduces them to commodities rather than developing human beings. Their value is measured in dollars, not in their humanity."[13] Engel condemns "the predominance of educational policies that literally devalue young people, or more precisely, see their value only in terms of return on investment."[14] The clash between commercial/corporate culture and democratic values spearheads the war for education reform.

---

[7] Henry Giroux, "Education Incorporated?" *Educational Leadership* 56, no.2 (October, 1998), 1.

[8] Michael J. Sandel, "Commercialism in Schools," *New Republic* 217, no. 9 (1 September 1997), 24.

[9] Ibid.

[10] Ibid.

[11] Engel, *The Struggle for Control of Public Education*, 2.

[12] Giroux, "Education Incorporated?" 2.

[13] Engel, *The Struggle for Control of Public Education*, 35.

[14] Ibid., 41.

COLLATERAL DAMAGE AND JUST-WAR THEORY

With market ideology and democratic ideals at war, education reform has become a battleground and public school students its collateral damage. William Saffire describes collateral damage as "a phrase used in restrained apology for casualties among civilians or to destruction of other than military targets…. The adjective came to mean 'ancillary, subordinated.' Where the adjective is used to modify damage, the meaning becomes 'unintended, inadvertent.' It is in the same league of regret as friendly fire."[15] Kenneth Saltman offers various usages of collateral damage, including the "military euphemism refer[ring] to the side effects of acts of war—bodies blown to bits, bloodied shreds of human flesh, the annihilation of people. [This] expression relies upon the meaning, additional, to erase the humanity of the victims of war by suggesting that the murder of noncombatants in the name of war is a side effect of a just primary act."[16] Saltman informs us that the term "also relies upon the economic meaning of collateral to transform people into incidental costs were incidental expenses incurred a transaction. The destruction of human life becomes a minor cost or justifiable risk incurred in pursuing the target."[17]

Collateral damage arises from the just-war tradition as formulated by Augustine and Aquinas and refined by various twentieth-century theorists including Elizabeth Anscombe, Paul Ramsey, James Turner Johnson, and Michael Walzer.[18] Just-war theory primarily focuses on the theoretical concepts of *jus ad bellum,* the justifiable recourse to war, and *jus in bello,* the conduct and means used during war. In short, just-war theory dictates the occasion, against whom, and in what manner we can do war justly. For Augustine, doing war justly is a matter of Christian charity that "condemns killing in self-defense [while] mandat[ing] killing in defense of others."[19] Augustine maintains his steadfastness toward charity by minimizing the force necessary against the aggressor in

[15]William Saffire, "Regime Never Good in Politics or Diet," *The Hamilton Spectator,* online edition (23 March 2002), 2.

[16]Kenneth J. Saltman, *Collateral Damage* (Lanham MD: Rowman and Littlefield Publishers, 2000), 77.

[17]Ibid.

[18]For early formations of Just-war theory see, Augustine, *De Libero Arbitrio Voluntatis,* (Charlottesville VA: University of Virginia, 1947) and *The City of God, XIX* (London: Dent, 1940); Thomas Aquinas, *Summa Theologiae,* II-II q. 40, q. 64. For twentieth century formulations see, G. E. M. Anscombe, "Mr. Truman's Decision," and "War and Murder" in *Ethics, Religion and Politics* (Minneapolis MN: University of Minnesota, 1981); James T. Johnson and George Weigel, *Just War and the Gulf War* (Lanham MD: Ethics and Public Policy Center, 1991); James T. Johnson, *Just War Tradition and the Restraint of War* (Princeton NJ: Princeton University Press, 1981); Paul Ramsey, *War and the Christian Conscience* (Durham NC: Duke University Press, 1961) and *The Just War* (Savage MD: Littlefield Adams Quality Paperbacks, 1968, 1983); Michael Walzer, *Just and Unjust Wars,* second ed. (New York: Basic Books, 1992).

[19]Timothy M. Renick, "Charity Lost: The Secularization of the Principle of Double Effect in the Just-War Tradition," *Thomist,* 58, issue 3 (July, 1994), 446.

defending an innocent's life. Paul Ramsey explains, "One may not maim the unjust opponent if it is possible to disarm him without doing so; one may not kill the opponent if it is possible to secure the desired end only by injuring him."[20] According to Timothy Renick:

> Christian charity may obligate us to seek a good effect (the saving of an innocent life) even though it causes an evil one (violence levied against an aggressor). But, the virtue of charity also places tight strictures upon the exercise of the obligation; it commands us to *minimize* the evil done.... Augustine's demands are far more exacting; we must use only as much force as is necessary to attain the good end, saving the life of the victim.[21]

Thomas Aquinas also presents a position on self-defense and taking the life of another, albeit different from that offered by Augustine. In his *Summa Theologiae*, II-II q. 64, Aquinas writes:

> A single moral act may have two effects, of which one is intended, while the other is incidental to that intention. But, the way a moral act is to be classified depends on what is intended, not on what goes beyond such an intention.... In light of this distinction, we can see that an act of self-defense may have two effects: the saving of one's own life and the killing of the attacker. Now, such an act of self-defense is *not* illegitimate just because the agent intends to save his own life, because it is natural for anything to want to preserve itself in being as far as it can.[22]

In this instance, Aquinas breaks from Augustine by permitting an individual legitimately to kill an unjust aggressor in self-defense and not simply in defending an innocent.

Doing war justly, *jus in bello*, requires consideration of the two-pronged principle of double effect—discrimination and proportionality—with both prongs needing to be satisfied for a given act to be acceptable. Discrimination pertains to the killing of noncombatants and establishes a clear distinction between killing that directly is intended and directly done and killing that is permitted only if it is in directly done by the same action intended for legitimate targets. "Acts which directly intend and directly effect the death of noncombatants are to be classed morally with murder and are never excusable.... A desired victory, however, justify conduct in warfare that causes the death, and is foreknown to cause the death, of noncombatants indirectly."[23] Discrimination requires that an evil never be an end or means to an

---

[20] Paul Ramsey, *War and the Christian Conscience* (Durham NC: Duke University Press, 1961), 42.
[21] Renick, "Charity Lost: The Secularization of the Principle of Double Effect in the Just-War Tradition," 447.
[22] Thomas Aquinas, *Summa Theologiae* II-II, q.64.
[23] Paul Ramsey, *The Just War* (Savage MD: Littlefield Adams Quality Paperbacks, 1968, 1983), 154.

end, and as such, evil never can be intended. In short, harm to innocents should not be directly intended as either a means or an end.

The second aspect requires us to observe proportionality. Aquinas writes:

> An act that is properly motivated may, nevertheless, become vitiated if it is not proportionate to the end intended. And, this is why somebody who uses more force than is necessary to defend himself will be doing something wrong. On the other hand, the controlled use of counter-violence constitutes legitimate self-defense, for according to the law it is legitimate to answer force with force provided it goes no further than due defense requires.[24]

Although Aquinas considers self-defense as presenting two effects, the first a good effect of saving one's life and the second an evil effect of exacting violence against an aggressor, he also asserts that, for an act to be morally justifiable, an individual cannot intend the evil effect and, the act, itself, must be proportionate. Proportionality embodies a moral obligation to minimize evil and thus, as for Augustine, charity becomes a key element of the just-war tradition. Renick explains, "If one is to be true to the exaction of charity, [proportionality] can entail nothing less. Infused charity demands the perfection of all human acts. If one faces two options, both of which create more good than evil, one must choose that option which creates the most good. To act otherwise is to choose (and hence to intend) the commission of some degree of avoidable evil."[25]

Just war never intends for noncombatants to be immune from indirect injury or death if there is a "proportionate grave reason for doing this."[26] In other words, killing noncombatants may be permitted through justification of one good or evil effect by weighing the greater good or lesser evil of all other effects the act produces. This requires what Ramsey calls "a prudential estimate of the consequences to see whether there is in the good effect sufficiently grave reason for also indirectly producing the evil effect.... While an effect cannot justify any means, one effect can justify another effect because of the greater good or lesser evil in one than in the other."[27] The crucial points and situations where the single intent results in two effects (ends), one intended and the other unintended, are when the intent is singularly good and the resulting good outweighs any resulting evil. From this, a "moral obligation to minimize evil emerges as implicit in the very use of the term proportionate," and using greater force than necessary is always wrong.[28]

---

[24] *Summa Theologiae* II-II, q.64.
[25] Renick, "Charity Lost: The Secularization of the Principle of Double Effect in the Just-war Tradition," 449.
[26] Ramsey, *The Just War,* 189.
[27] Ibid., 155.
[28] Ibid.

Michael Walzer offers a way of reconciling the good and bad of war by establishing conditions that must be met in order for acts with evil consequences, such as the killing of innocents, to be just:

1) The act is good in itself or at least indifferent [and] it is a legitimate action;

2) The direct effect is morally acceptable;

3) The intention of the actor is good ... he aims only at the acceptable effect; the evil effect is not one of his ends nor is it a means to his ends;

4) The good effect is sufficiently good to compensate for the evil effect.[29]

Walzer also argued that the principle of double effect requires double intention. That is, not only must there be some good to be achieved, but there must also be an effort toward seeing "that the foreseeable evil be reduced as far as possible."[30] According to James T. Johnson, Walzer reminds us "that the moral principles governing the use of force to imply a special care to protect innocent parties from 'collateral damage' due to force aimed at the guilty [and] the effort to avoid harm to the innocent may require taking more potential danger onto oneself."[31] The principle of double effect provides a rather simple formula for resolving certain kinds of moral conflict. It requires identifying evil and to redress that evil in such a way that people produce the least harm possible, especially harm to innocents.

Just-war theory provides criteria by which we may judge particular military actions as morally licit or illicit. Proportionality binds decision makers to an inherent standard of fairness considering options that will impact individuals not immediately involved in the encounter. Gerard Bradley notes, "Fairness requires that we treat the people of the other nations with the same consideration we treat our own, not different consideration merely because they differ from us in ways that are irrelevant to moral valuations, such as having different language, and ethnicity, religion or even different political beliefs."[32] Even a just war does not "suspend or negate the principle of equal human dignity ... and to do everything reasonably with in our power to minimize civilian casualties."[33]

War, whether just or unjust, kills and injures combatants and innocents and directly contributes to the collateral damage sustained during military

---

[29]Walzer, *Just and Unjust Wars*, 153.

[30]Ibid., 155.

[31]James Turner Johnson, "In Response to Terror," *First Things, The Journal of Religion and Public Life*, 90 (February, 1999), 12–13.

[32]Gerard Bradley, participant, *Iraq and Just War: A Symposium*. The Carnegie Endowment for International Peace, Washington DC. September 30, 2002. The transcript for the symposium is at http://pewforum.org/events/print.php?EventID=36

[33]David Blankenhorn, et.al., *Pre-emption, Iraq, and Just War: A Statement of Principles*. November 14, 2002. http://www.americanvalues.org

action, damage that extends beyond the immediate strike area, destroying property and services that cannot easily or quickly be replaced. According to Ghobarah, Huth, and Russett, "The destruction and disruption from the fighting means the loss of transportation infrastructure (roads, bridges, where road system; communications and electricity) to distribute clean water, food, medicine, and relief supplies. It also means destruction of hospitals and other health-care facilities, and the departure of medical personnel."[34] War also means interruption of schooling due to fighting itself and because of a government's diversion of resources from health and education needs to its military needs. "Education is strongly associated with the health of both children and adults in both rich and poor countries," and is an included independent variable in the World Health Organization's analysis of a country's health attainment.[35] Medact's 2002 report, *Collateral Damage: The Health and Environmental Costs of War on Iraq,* claims:

[The 1990s saw a decline in (Iraqi)] schooling. Lower literacy, especially among females, has a known negative impact on health. Before 1990, Iraq was among the forefront of Arab countries promoting education and employment for women, but this has reversed ... and contribute[d] to a worse state of health for women and a rise in infant mortality and morbidity.[36]

Education during the 2003 Iraq war halted with many schools suffering from "widespread looting and vandalism, which left [them] without plumbing, lavatories, light fixtures, wiring, desks, windows, and doors."[37] Iraqi forces used some schools to store their munitions, U.S. forces used schools as shelter, and some schools were bombed. The destruction of the schools and disruption of Iraqi children's education joined the list of collateral damage. Carol Bellamy, Executive Director of UNICEF, emphasized the importance of reestablishing schooling as soon as possible, claiming, "Schools are vital not only because of their educational function, but as centers around which communities can begin to heal themselves, serving as entry points for interventions like health education, psychological support, and nutritional assistance."[38] UNICEF developed a "school-in-a-box" kit with each kit containing enough pencils, paper, educational games, and various teaching materials for up to eighty children and two teachers. USAID targeted its efforts to Iraqi

---

[34]Hazem Ghobarah, Paul Huth, Bruce Russett, *Civil Wars Kill and Maim People—Long After the Shooting Stops* (August 2001), 3. Center for Basic Research in Social Sciences. http://www.cbrss.harvard.edu/programs/hsecurity/papers/civilwar

[35]Ibid., 11.

[36]Jane Salvage, *Collateral Damage: The Health and Environmental Costs of War on Iraq* (November 12, 2002), online at <http://www.medact.org>

[37]USAID Fact Sheet: Rehabilitating Iraq's Basic Education System (August 18, 2003) online at <http://www.usaid.gov/press/factsheets/2003/fs030818.html>

[38]*UNICEF Pushes for Iraqi Schools to Reopen* (April 25,2003 press release) online at http://www.unicefusa.org/emergencies/iraq/releases/042503.html

schools for the 2003–2004 school year by awarding $4.2 million to rehabili-
tating schools, beginning countrywide training programs for teachers and
administrative staff, delivering more than 4 million textbooks to the schools,
and awarding grants worth $15 million to strengthen partnerships between
American and Iraqi universities.[39] Bellamy referred to schools as a "familiar
touchstone of stability for parents, children, and society as a whole. It's also a
safe and caring environment for children. And, importantly, it provides a fo-
cal point for the distribution of aid, so that we can be sure that children, who
are most vulnerable in conflicts, are receiving aid that is designated for
them."[40]

Just-war's principle of proportionality requires a sense of fairness of individuals and organizations involved in the rebuilding of Iraq—it requires the
same of those involved in the rebuilding of our own educational system.

EDUCATION REFORM'S COLLATERAL DAMAGE

Just-war theory permits us to discuss the current battle for education reform
in terms of who/what becomes education's collateral damage as well as how
do they achieve this status. In education's war for reform, free-marketeers attack what they consider the evils within public school education with a wide
arsenal of goods and services, promising that their weapons will eradicate
poor student and teacher performance and equip students with information
necessary to keep the United States as the leader of world markets. Commonly deployed weapons are high-stakes testing, standardized curricula,
and conformity in schools. The fallout from these weapons and the collateral
damage they cause bring them into alignment with conventional military
weapons intentionally aimed at intended targets but that destroy much more
than what once sat at ground zero. To protect investments and ensure safe,
orderly learning environments, schools take on a military atmosphere with
many schools being headed by retired military officers.[41] Learning under
military command assumes that rules will be followed and that all will be accountable.

Although many students receive injuries by the indiscriminate corporatization of public schools, Saltman particularly identified "marginalized
segments of the nonwhite population," bifurcating the segments into "marginalized" and "nonwhite" populations.[42] In K–12, we delineate marginalized students not only by race and ethnicity, but also according to physical
and learning ability, socioeconomic status, and gender; the nonwhite seg-

---

[39]USAID: Assistance for Iraq—Accomplishments: Education (12/03).
[40]*UNICEF Lauds Iraqi Common Sense to Return To School* (April 25, 2003 press release) online at
http://www.unicef.org.uk/press/news_detail.asp?news_id=41
[41]Saltman, *Collateral Damage*, 88–92.
[42]Ibid., 86.

ment includes African American, Latina/o, Asian, and Native American students. The corporatization of public schools increasingly recruits students within these segments, placing their futures and potential in the line of "friendly" fire.

HIGH-STAKES TESTING

In *The Book of Learning and Forgetting*, Frank Smith claims that, "Testing, which has become a mania in education, disregards the classic view that you can *see* whether people or learning by observing what they are doing. Instead, it is based on the odd idea that learning can only be uncovered by *probing* with *test instruments*, scientifically designed and rigorously wielded."[43] Students, teachers, administrators, parents, and politicians have come to rely on standardized testing as central and indubitable aspects of public schooling. These tests focus on how well students perform regarding often arbitrarily selected information rather than looking at "*what* tasks the learners have opportunities to engage in and the degree of their interest and comprehension."[44] Students who score high on standardized tests receive awards for their performance, whereas low scores result in discrimination in the classroom. Smith notes,

> Low scorers are frequently segregated, given relatively more difficult tasks to perform and less time to perform them, receive less help from the teacher, and, naturally, have more and repeated experience of "failure." Teachers treat them differently, other students treat them differently, and they treat themselves differently. Low scorers are identified as being "learning disabled" (or impaired, underprivileged, deprived, challenged, or "at risk") and regarded as educational "problems." They are labeled and discussed in terms that would be regarded as socially reprehensible and politically unacceptable if applied to any group outside the classroom.[45]

High-stakes testing also discriminates against a disproportionate number of poor, non-White students and students with disabilities. The 2002 national average SAT (Scholastic Assessment Test) scores for approximately 1.3 million high school seniors revealed that the gap remained between White and non-White and suburban and nonsuburban students. The average scores for specific ethnic and racial groups were as follows: European American, 1060; African American, 857; Native American, 962; Hispanic and Latino, 922; Mexican American, 903; Puerto Rican, 906; and Asian American, 1010. "Suburban students scored far better than those living in

---

[43]Frank Smith, *The Book of Learning and Forgetting* (New York: Teachers College Press, 1998), 61. Emphasis in the original.
[44]Smith, *The Book of Learning and Forgetting*, 64.
[45]Ibid.

other areas, with average scores of 523 for verbal and 536 for math."[46] Georgia ranked 50th with a total average score of 980 (Washington, DC, came in 51st with a score of 953) despite recent education reform laws intended to bolster student performance on such tests. According to James Salzer, "Several factors play into Georgia's low SAT scores. The state has a more diverse group of test takers than many other states. North Carolina has a similar population, a similar number of test takers, and higher overall scorers. But Georgia has a higher percentage of African-American students taking the test, and they tend to score lower."[47]

For many states using high-stakes testing, including Georgia, "curriculum is also a problem.... [In particular,] curriculum is wide but shallow, with teachers expected to cover many subjects but few in-depth."[48] The greater the use of standardized tests, the less control teachers have to determine curriculum content and to assess what their students are learning. Limiting teachers in matters of curricula and assessment creates problems beyond in-classroom decisions. McNeil found that, "test scores generated by centralized, standardized tests and by the test-prep materials which prepare [students] for those tests, are not reliable indicators of learning. It is here where the effects on low-performing students, particular minority students, begin to skew the possibilities for their access to a richer education."[49] Problems also arise for teachers who question the use of test-prep materials. These teachers often are portrayed as not supporting but actually working against their minority students as well as "not being team players."[50] The relationship between classroom curricula and standardized tests has grown more tightly knit with increased reliance on tests.

Smith explains the relationship between classroom curricula and standardized tests: "The official theory of learning and the prejudiced practice of achievement testing have advanced in influence together, both in education and in popular understanding. They have not done this because they have produced any discernible improvement in schools, but because they support each other."[51] Referring to the relationship between official learning and achievement testing as "totally circular," Smith goes on to note that "testing is good because it follows the precepts of the official theory of learning, and the official theory of learning must be right because it is the

---

[46]Jeffrey R. Young, "SAT Scores Hold Steady; Test's Owner Announces Steps to Encourage Better Writing Skills," *The Chronicle of Higher Education* (28 August 2002), online at <http://chronicle.com/daily/2002/08/2002082803n.htm>

[47]James Salzer, "SAT Scores Land Georgia in 50th Place," *The Atlanta Journal-Constitution* (28 August 2002): A1.

[48]Salzer, "SAT Scores Land Georgia in 50th Place."

[49]Linda M. McNeil, *Contradictions of School Reform: Educational Costs of Standardized Testing* (New York: Routledge, 2000), 237.

[50]Ibid.

[51]Smith, *The Book of Learning and Forgetting*, 65.

basis of all the testing."[52] Good testing and right learning translate into teachers devoting class time to skill-and-drill practices for analogies and prepping students for questions that may appear on high-stakes standardized tests. As testing dominates the classroom, teachers and students become puppets of the marketeers, "manipulated by authorities outside the classroom, who prepare and impose the learning materials and tests to which those in the classroom must adapt."[53]

Adaptation means that when "the fate of individual students, whole schools, teachers, and principals is tied to the results on a single, high-stakes test, that test becomes the center of teaching and learning."[54] Standardized reforms, including standardized curricula and tests, hurt teachers by forcing them to "dumb down" course material and present it in such a way that testing on the material is computer gradable. "Dumbing down" material to meet proficiency requirements may mean deleting courses or units not covered by standardized testing, or teaching information required for high-stakes tests that is disjointed, noncontextual, or in other ways, fragmented. Linda McNeil found teachers in Houston schools teaching two different lessons in order to comply with the required standards. "This 'double-entry' approach," notes McNeil, "included presenting the official proficiency-based material and then doing lessons around the 'real' curriculum."[55] Teachers intentionally compromised higher academic quality to meet standardization requirements. Some Houston teachers reported "unteaching" their students some previously taught information and offering them proficiency drills prior to high-stakes tests. One history teacher in McNeil's study mixed proficiency questions with his own so that students would learn the difference between the types of questions. He told students, "If you see a question that cannot be discussed, that does not invite higher level questioning, then you know that's 'their question,' not mine."[56]

Pauline Lipman, in her comments about Bush's education plan, writes, "While education geared to standardized tests degrades the work of the best teachers, it is little help to the weakest teachers, because it does not increase their knowledge, skill, or commitment to richer teaching and learning. Nor do high-stakes tests address the huge inequalities between affluent schools and low-income and urban schools."[57] As test-prep drills replace the curriculum in many low-income and minority schools, teachers report, "many more students are passing TAAS 'reading,' [however] few of their students are actually readers. Few of them can use reading for assignments in literature, science, or his-

[52] Ibid.
[53] Ibid.
[54] Lipman, "Bush's Education Plan, Globalization, and the Politics of Race," 6.
[55] McNeil, *Contradictions of School Reform*, 211.
[56] Ibid., 215.
[57] Lipman, "Bush's Education Plan, Globalization, and the Politics of Race," 6.

tory classes; few of them choose to read; few of them can make meaning of literature or connect writing and discussing to reading."[58] Testing proponents point to rising test scores to support their position of skill-and-drill learning, thereby justifying continued and increased replacement of regular curricula with test-prep materials. According to McNeil:

> Students in these urban schools are doubly penalized, first for losing out on the [curricula] that their peers in suburban high schools are learning. Secondly, they are penalized by having to spend extra periods on low-level, disjointed drills—[material] divorced from both the applications and the conceptual understandings they will need if they are to hold their own later in upper-level classes with middle-class students. It is unlikely that the middle-class students have been doing "math" from commercial test-prep booklets, rather than from math books, manipulatives, calculators, computers, and peer study groups. The TAAS, then, lowers the quality and quantity of even subjects not being tested in those schools were students have traditionally not tested well, the students who are poor and the minority.[59]

Restructuring classes for test preparation is not the only time that teachers exchange teaching curriculum for something less. Efficiency demands from principals and school districts also lead to changes in classroom learning, not necessarily in the form of test-prep materials but in prepackaged course materials and supplies.

MRES GO TO SCHOOL

The military's meals-ready-to-eat (MREs) have come to school in the form of prepackaged curriculum and hermetically sealed lab packets. Corporate material appears as education-enhancing supplies, equipment, and "teacher-proof" course materials. Consumers Union claims, "Schools' chronic shortage of funding for learning materials has led teachers to welcome free education materials. Teachers are continually looking for new and interesting materials to motivate students, but they have little money."[60] The amount or lack of money raises equity issues among schools, often in the same district, and "exacerbates the resource divide between schools and school districts. In recent years, advertisers who offer free curriculum materials, as well as those who offer small amounts of money in exchange for student access, have been successfully pursuing lower-income communities that are the most desper-

---

[58] McNeil, *Contradictions of School Reform*, 237.
[59] Ibid., 243.
[60] Consumers Union, *Selling America's Kids: Commercial Pressures on Kids of the '90s* (Washington, D.C.: Consumer's Union, 1998), 11.

ate for school resources."[61] According to Giroux, schools are "Seduced by the lure of free equipment and money, [and] curricular materials designed to build brand loyalty among members of a captive school audience."[62] Andrea Bell reports that corporations take advantage of schools and students through indirect advertising "by tying their product or name to school activities or educational material. These include: corporate-sponsored educational materials, including lesson plans and curriculum, that typically correlate to the industry the corporation works in; teacher training (usually related to new software and computer programs); contests, activities, and scholarship programs; and corporate grants and gifts."[63]

Education-enhancing materials provide corporations opportunities to advertise their goods while supposedly offering students a "good," perhaps health and nutrition information or the latest environmentally friendly technology. Regarding the latter, General Motors (GM) provides in-class material and posts a link on the *Weekly Reader* Web site with a byline: "Let GM show you how pollution-free fuel cell vehicles work." The GM site has an animated explanation of how such vehicles work using GM's *HydroGen 1* fuel cell vehicle as the model. Although GM identifies the site as Advanced Technology Vehicles/Fuel Cell Animation/GM Technology Tour/For Kids, the site also provides links to GM's Owner Center/BuyPower/Dealer Locator/Vehicle Adviser/Careers. Colgate-Palmolive entertains children while offering "unique oral health education." Visitors to Colgate's children's oral-health education site are welcomed by cartooned children and animals flying in a hot-air balloon sporting the banner, "Welcome to Colgate: Bright Smiles, Bright Futures and a voice-over by Dr. Rabbit, the world's only rabbit dentist." Colgate's dental-health program also offers a poster, teaching guide, and info-packets for first and second graders each bearing the company's name. Dole Foods and the U.S. Rice Producers Association (USRPA) offer nutrition lessons while, at the same time, promoting their products. Dole Food Company provides "everything you need to get your students excited about eating fruits and vegetables," in its *5 A Day* classroom program conducted in Dole's virtual classroom September 23–28, 2002, including classroom nutrition charts, a Kids Cookbook, lesson plans, and online activities. Dole has everything—and everything bears Dole's logo and brand-named products. The USRPA sponsors www.RiceRomp with links for teachers and students that take visitors to lessons in math, social studies, science, and health, and a link for games, all having to do with rice. USRPA assembles lessons by Grades 4–10 with ques-

---

[61]Arnold F. Fege and Andrew Hagelshaw, "Beware of 'Creeping Corporatization,'" *NAESP Principal Online* (November 2000), 2. Online at <http://www.naesp.org/comm/p1100d.htm>.
[62]Giroux, "Education Incorporated?" 3.
[63]Andrea Bell, "Putting Kids before School: Commercialism," *Education Digest*, 67, issue 9 (May 2002), 32.

tions regarding the history, sociology, geography, and economics of rice for each level. Even though many of the situations and questions USRPA suggests students consider lead to critical thinking and further exploration, the bottom line remains the industry's commodity, its product. BIC Corporation sponsors *Quality Comes in Writing*, a program created by Lifetime Learning Systems "to help students in grades four through six develop strong writing skills that will benefit them throughout their lives.... Students will practice writing skills to decode and create rebus stories, plan and write their own stories, study and write ballads and keep a hypothetical journal for a famous person."[64] The Activity Masters, Teachers Guide, full-color poster of writing hints for the classroom, take-home booklets, and teacher response cards all carry the BIC character and corporate logo.

The aforementioned "indirect" advertising examples illustrate how corporations and industries gain access to a large market and how they are able to deliver their messages of consumerism directly to students. Perhaps a more insidious element of corporatization in the classroom is the adoption of commodification packets or prepackaged courses. Fege and Hagelshaw claim that direct advertisement raises, "education quality and integrity issues.... By shifting the emphasis from teaching students how to think to teaching students what to think, company advertising often directly contradicts the schools' educational messages."[65] The message sounds uncomfortably familiar as it is similar to Paulo Freire's explanation of how "dominant elites" control the oppressed masses: "The dominant elites utilize the banking concept to encourage passivity in the oppressed, corresponding with the latter's 'submerged' state of consciousness, and take advantage of that passivity to 'fill' that consciousness with slogans which create even more fear of freedom."[66]

One basic question educators might ask of a corporate provider is, "will this course material help teachers or will it work against what teachers want to do?" Do these packets promote critical thinking and engage students and teachers in dialogic learning or do they simply promote isolated facts and consumer development? "More worksheets won't help teachers get their students to read more. Novel kits won't help students read deeply," responds Patrick Shannon. Rather, "Good pedagogical choices require knowledgeable teachers who are free to act on their convictions. It might be wise for these teachers to look to pedagogy and not commodities to support students' reading more deeply."[67] Such examination requires us to as-

---

[64] Katy Dobbs, *Quality Comes in Writing* (BIC Corp., 1997), cover letter to educators with BIC pen-man cartoon and logo written by the editorial director of Lifetime Learning Systems, Inc.

[65] Fege and Hagelshaw, "Beware of 'Creeping Corporatization,'" 1.

[66] Paulo Freire, *Pedagogy of the Oppressed* (New York: Continuum, 1970), 84.

[67] Peggy Albers, "Interview with Patrick Shannon," *Talking Points*, 13, no. 2 (April/May 2002), 9.

sess the value of the commodified material and to determine its direct and indirect effects on the teachers and students.

The June 1998 Southern Regional Education Board (SREB) report *Raising the Bar in the Middle Grades: Readiness for Success* identifies various factors that contribute to or deter student preparedness for high school in its 16 member states:

> [Although] educators talk about the importance of aligning curriculum, construction and assessment [and] they say that they want to determine content topics, plan experiences necessary to learn the content, and check to see whether students know the content and how to use it, [e]ight very different middle schools in five states visited by SREB staff all have the same commercial reading program—a "quick fix" to low reading scores.[68]

The SREB staff also noticed a different pedagogy in place in "quick fix" classrooms; "teachers assign worksheets with vocabulary lists and drilled students on sample items from the state assessment test. [The] teacher emphasized isolated bits of information that may be forgotten quickly."[69] The report quotes one Texas middle school principal as saying "We have a whole quick-fix culture that says, 'Get your test scores up if you buy this program.'"[70] Are these programs "fixing" anything? Or are they exploiting schools and turning them into markets?

By commodifying and corporatizing public education, schools miss out on "the creativity and innovation of teachers," and are limited in the ways in which teachers respond to diverse needs and learning styles of students.[71] Giroux addresses "the current assault on educators at all levels of schooling [encouraging educators to] struggle against the ongoing trend to reduce teachers to the role of technicians who simply implement prepackaged curriculums and standardized tests as part of the efficiency-based relations of market democracy and consumer pedagogy."[72] Because prepackaged course materials reduce teachers' "power and autonomy to function as intellectuals," Giroux recommends that teachers be given "time to produce curriculums, engage in dialogues with students, use the resources of surrounding communities, and participate in the organizational decisions that affect their work."[73]

Linda McNeil's case study of four, primarily middle-class, high schools offers a glimpse of school structure, school knowledge, and school control

---

[68] Sondra Cooney, *Raising the Bar in the Middle Grades: Readiness for Success* (Atlanta, Georgia: Southern Regional Education Board, June 1998), 9.

[69] Cooney, *Raising the Bar in the Middle Grades: Readiness for Success*, 9.

[70] Ibid., 10.

[71] David Elkind, *The Hurried Child: Growing up Too Fast Too Soon* (Reading, MA: Perseus, 1988), 47.

[72] Giroux, "Education Incorporated?" 5.

[73] Ibid.

from within the schools themselves. McNeil notes, "When the school's organization becomes centered on managing and controlling, teachers and students take school less seriously. They fall into a ritual of learning that tends toward minimal standards and minimum effort."[74] Teachers often alter classroom structure, materials, and teaching to accommodate mandates for standardization and order. "By reducing course content to its most manageable and measurable fragments," writes McNeil, "the teachers [are] splitting the learning process into means and ends and reinforcing a concern for extrinsic rewards (teacher pay and student credentials, for example."[75] McNeil argues that, at the elementary school level:

> External forces have more directly shaped curricula by de-skilling teachers through the adoption of "teacher-proofed" materials.... Packaged materials, produced by commercial publishers, adopted by state and local school systems under the direction of experts such as child psychologists and reading specialists, have the purpose of reducing teacher discretion and variation. The "teacher-proof" materials contain pre-tests, instructional techniques, sets of content reduced to measurable items, and post-tests for mastery.[76]

Saltman claims, "These prefab curricula take advantage of teachers who are hard-pressed by bureaucratic constraints and heavy workloads. Ultimately, the curricula take advantage of children by depriving them of meaningful education and by not only often promoting unhealthy products and misinformation but by also pushing crass consumerism."[77]

The observed high school teachers in McNeil's study did not experience de-skilling from using such commodified materials but because:

> Their assessment of their effectiveness or even survival within the institution had led them to split their personal knowledge from their classroom teaching in much the same way as pre-packaged materials divorce elementary teachers' ideas from instruction and evaluation.... [W]ithin their classrooms they reinforced these goals of order with the justification that doing so was the only way they could protect themselves from institutional pressures. They got no reward for holding discussions, but felt sanctions for not "covering the material."[78]

Teachers are not alone in these de-skilling experiences. "The teachers' splitting of their personal knowledge from the institutional in attempts to gain minimal compliance may be seen as a kind of de-skilling of students as

---

[74] McNeil, *Contradictions of Control*, xviii.
[75] Ibid., 185.
[76] Ibid., 186.
[77] Saltman, *Collateral Damage*, 59.
[78] McNeil, *Contradictions of Control*, 186.

well."[79] McNeil found students alienated from teachers and from learning in those classrooms where prepackaged materials and tight adherence to standards controlled the knowledge. De-skilling and the resulting alienation leave students unable to rely on in-the-box knowledge to explain or interpret their own experiences and concerns; de-skilling and alienation leave students unable to critically evaluate the provided information or to find alternative information on their own. "Controlling teaching transforms the subject content from 'real world' knowledge into 'school knowledge,' an artificial set of facts and generalizations whose credibility lies no longer in its authenticity as a cultural selection but in its instrumental value in meeting the obligations teachers and students have within the institution of schooling."[80] "School knowledge" becomes something to be "mastered, traded for a grade and, as some students have said, deliberately forgotten afterward."[81] Controlled, deliberate teaching transforms students into the empty vessels often referred to in critiques of essentialist classrooms. Rather than promoting mastery of content and understanding through critical thinking, controlled teaching promotes school knowledge as minimal information to fill in blanks on standardized test forms. "The nature of defensive [controlled] teaching," according to McNeil, "is to transform the role of student into client or consumer rather than an active learner."[82] Thus, students become clients and consumers where knowledge is simply of instrumental value and students its passive receivers.

Clients and consumers belong not in the classroom but in the corporate world where top-down controls coincide with uniformity and quality. "When public education and the private interests become synonymous, a process has begun where the most important mediating influence on the school is not the public interest, but the negotiations between school officials and the businesses with which they contract."[83] Furthermore, as corporations increase their control over educational information and corporate means become education's ends, there is a danger of reduced public discourse to address how corporatization of public schools undermines the democratic principles of justice and freedom, principles that should be at the center of any discussions regarding educational reform.

MILITARIZATION OF SCHOOLS

"The militarization of the public schools is both a material and a cultural project," claims Kenneth Saltman.[84] "As federal responsibility for such public goods as social service provision and public schooling shifts to private corpo-

---

[79] Ibid., 188.
[80] Ibid., 191.
[81] Ibid.
[82] Ibid., 192.
[83] Fege and Hagelshaw, "Beware of 'Creeping Corporatization,'" 2.
[84] Saltman, *Collateral Damage*, 84.

rations and state control, the federal government is increasingly rendered a disciplinary entity concerned primarily with military, policing, prisons, and courts. The new social logic can be seen clearly in the ways that youth become both casualties and commodities in the war on the public."[85] It manifests itself through increased requirements for school uniforms; increased use of metal detectors, surveillance equipment, and armed and unarmed security personnel; and zero-tolerance policies that posit schools as prisons or boot camps rather than places where educating children occurs. It also manifests itself through increased military presence through the Junior Reserve Officer Training Corps (JROTC), Troops to Teachers, and retired military personnel turning school CEOs (chief executive officers).

Uniforms creep into schools under the guise of "foster[ing] greater equality by homogenizing students' appearance."[86] Solid-colored shirts and pants/skirts erase students' class, race, and ethnic differences, replacing individual preferences and realities for one reality created by a school district and the low-bid uniform supplier. Adoption of uniforms happens because, according to Nadine Strossen, president of the American Civil Liberties Union, "Throughout society, there is popular support for any measure that sounds like it supports greater law and order, even if there's no evidence that it actually has any effect."[87] Accepting the myth that unregulated student clothing interferes with instruction and the educational process or threatens the health and safety of others, allows school officials to violate student expressions of free speech, to violate parents' rights to make decisions for/with their child, to violate certain religious/ethnic beliefs and practices, and to create an atmosphere that tolerates only conformity to sameness and rules. Strossen addresses how schools should treat students saying, "We do our best job by treating them [students] as autonomous individuals who deserve to express their own ideas, as long as they equally respect other people's ideas. We should not dress them like prison inmates any more than we should treat them like prison inmates."[88]

The fear of lack of order due to differences leads schools to adopt uniform policies under which many students face new challenges and potential harm from their institution. One such anecdote comes from a charter middle school near Atlanta concerning students who forget to wear or resist wearing the prescribed unembellished, solid-color golf shirt. On the second day of the school year, a young lad wore a golf shirt with a small crest on the chest for which he found himself in the school's main office. The mistake cost him no

---

[85] Ibid., xvii.
[86] Ibid., 95.
[87] Nadine Strossen, "Public Schools Adopting Dress Codes," *ACLU News Wire* (30 September 1997), 1.
[88] CNN.com, *Nadine Strossen: Why the ACLU Opposes School Dress Codes* (CNN chat room interview 8 August 1991), online at <http://wwww..cnn.com/2001/COMMUITY/08/28/strossen.cnna>.

money but, going about school the remainder of the day wearing the loaned bright red shirt with the word "Rental" printed in bold white letters on the back, caused him humiliation by the taunting of classmates and the unwanted attention that the shirt drew to him. The poor fellow also received a warning that students who borrowed a rental shirt four times would no longer be able to attend this particular school.[89] Although this anecdote comes from a charter school with a high percentage of White, middle- and upper-middle-class students, many public schools around the country are enforcing prescribed clothing requirements. Regarding violators, Strossen says, "as with so many disciplinary measures in schools, enforcement of dress codes fall disproportionately on minority students, raising equality violations as well."[90]

Uniforms are only part of a military-like presence in public school. Ron Scapp writes, "Schooling becomes a matter of strategies of social containment, rather than an effort toward social investment."[91] George W. Bush's extensive education plan calls for tougher discipline and penalties for disruptive students. "These measures," claims Pauline Lipman, "are very serious institutionalized escalation of the demonization of use and the criminalization of African-American and Latino use in particular."[92] In a letter dated May 17, 2001, Rod Paige, the U.S. Secretary of Education, informs Senator Robert Byrd:

> *No Child Left Behind* would hold States accountable for school safety. It would require States, as a condition of receiving Federal Safe and Drug-free Schools funds, to: 1) developed definition for a "persistently dangerous school" and to report on safety on a school-by-school basis; 2) provide victims of serious, school-based crimes and students trapped in persistently dangerous schools the option to transfer to a safe alternative; and 3) adopt a "zero-tolerance" policy that empowers teachers to remove violent or persistently disruptive students from the classroom.[93]

---

[89]Personal conversation with the student and his parent, August, 2002. Families that cannot afford the required clothing can apply for clothing assistance from the school. Interestingly, the school strongly objects to the term "uniform," opting instead for "dress code," although the intent of enforced uniformity is apparent. The Violations section of the 2002–2003 Dress Code reads, in part:

> Parents will be notified and a violation will be recorded. At the fourth violation, students will be assigned After-School Detention. If violations continue, the student and parent/guardian will be asked to appear before the Family and Student Accountability Action Team. Parents should be aware that continued non-compliance with the dress policy may result in immediate withdrawal from Peachtree Charter Middle School. Transportation to the alternate school will NOT be provided.

One last note, a tag line under the sectional heading reads: "Help Peachtree earn money by purchasing your dress code clothing through *Lands End.* Click for more information."

[90]Strossen, "Public Schools Adopting Dress Codes," 2.

[91]Ron Scapp, "For Democracy: Why Corporatizing Public Schools Puts a Nation at Risk," *Educational Researcher* (December 2001), 34.

[92]Lipman, "Bush's Education Plan, Globalization, and the Politics of Race," 2.

[93]Rod Paige, May 17, 2001-Letter to Sen. Robert Byrd regarding the Administration's FY 2002 budget request for education, online at <http://www.ed.gov/News/Letters/ 010517.html>.

Under H.R.1, the *No Child Left Behind Act*, subsection Safe Schools for the 21st Century, "the Federal Education Rights and Privacy Act (FERPA) also will be amended to allow public school districts and local law enforcement authorities to share information regarding disciplinary actions and misconduct by students. Project Sentry, a new federal–state partnership will be established to identify, prosecute, punish, and supervised juveniles who violate state and federal firearm laws."[94] These amendments, although purporting to protect and benefit schools and communities, call into question the few guaranteed rights and protections students have at school. The depth and breadth of Bush's education plan not only leaves *no child left behind*, it also leaves no child untouched.

To aid states in their regulatory endeavors various software companies offer their expertise via school administrative software. Rediker Software offers *Discipline Plus*, a program that not only simplifies "the difficult and time-consuming task of tracking student discipline [but that also] helps improve student discipline by ensuring that students are held accountable for their actions."[95] The program not only permits administrators to analyze school disciplinary practices but also generates "customized letters following each incident to inform parents of the incident involving their child."[96] Harts Systems offers the Parent-WISE program that "gives parents timely information about their child's progress in school. With the click of a mouse parents have access to grades, attendance, assignments, discipline, and even their child's teacher."[97] Harts Systems also has an administrator's interface that monitors disciplinary incidents and integrates the information on an as-needed basis. Where security guards walk the hallways as visible code enforcers, computer programs are the silent sentries of America's public schools.

Admittedly, schools should be safe places and the appropriate means taken to address school violence. However, according to the National Center for Education Statistics/Bureau of Justice Statistics study, *Indicators of School Crime and Safety: 2001*, national data reveal, "more serious victimizations happen away from school than at school ... [and that] students were more than two times as likely to be victims of serious violent crime away from school as at

---

[94] *H.R.1, No Child Left Behind, Safe Schools for the 21st Century (Title 5) Part A: Supporting Drug and Violence Prevention and Education for Students and Communities*, as approved by the House, May 23, 2001. Online at <http://www.house.gov/boehlert/hr1.htm> and <http://whitehouse.gov/news/usbudget/blueprint/bud03.html> and <http://www.edworkforce.house.gov/press/press/07/hr1ph52301.htm>.

[95] Rediker Software, "School Administrative Software—For Educators by Educators," online at <http://www.rediker.com/discipline.html>.

[96] Ibid.

[97] Harts Systems, LTD, "School Administration Software, Parent-WISE," online at <http://www.hart.com/PwiseIndex.htm>.

school."[98] Less than 1 percent of violent deaths among school-age children from July 1, 1998, through June 30, 1999, were school associated; during this time period there were 47 school associated violent deaths compared to 2,407 non-school-associated deaths of children ages 5 through 19.[99] The overall school environment improved between 1995 and 1999 with a decrease in the percentage of students who felt unsafe while they were at school or traveling to and from school; from 1993 to 1999, a 42 percent reduction in students Grades 9–12 carrying weapons; 1995–1999, a 12 percent decrease in student-reported gang presence; and between 1995 and 1999, a 4 percent decrease for students aged 12–18 to avoid in places at school for fear of their own safety.[100] Remaining constant was the percentage (7–8 percent) of students in Grades 9–12 who were threatened or injured with a weapon on school property between 1993 and 1999. Marijuana use for 9th through 12th graders remains at about 27 percent between 1995 and 1999. There was an 8 percent increase (to between 30 and 32 percent), however, of students reporting having been offered, sold, or given an illegal drug on school property.[101]

Unfortunately, data also suggest that middle schools and high schools, especially larger schools, are at greater risk for serious violence. Students in urban schools with higher percentages of minority enrollment and students eligible for free or reduced school lunches are twice as likely to experience violence as students in suburban, small-town, or rural areas. Similarly, the "teachers were differently victimized by violent crimes at school according to where they taught.... [During the period] 1995–1999, urban teachers were more likely to be victims of violent crimes than suburban and rural teachers (39 versus 22 and 20, respectively, for 1,000 teachers)."[102]

School Crime and Safety: 2001 also highlights school practices and policies related to safety and discipline. From 1996 to 1997, most public schools reported having zero-tolerance policies for various serious student offenses with "zero-tolerance policy" defined as a "school or district policy that mandates predetermined consequences or punishments for specific offenses."[103] Ninety-four percent of the schools reported zero-tolerance policies for firearms, 91 percent for weapons other than firearms, 87 percent for alcohol, 88 percent for drugs, 79 percent for violence, and 79 percent for tobacco. Of the reporting schools, urban schools in the Southeast and West with a minority enrollment of 50 percent or more and greater than 20 percent of students eligible for free or

---

[98]Phillip Kaufman, Xianglei Chen, Susan P. Choy, Katharin Peter, et al., *Indicators of School Crime and Safety: 2001* (Washington D.C.: U.S. Department of Education, National Center for Education Statistics and U.S. Department of Justice, Bureau of Justice Statistics, 2001), v.
[99]Ibid., vii.
[100]Ibid., ix–x.
[101]Ibid., v–vi.
[102]Ibid., ix.
[103]Ibid., 129.

reduced school lunches also have the greatest number of zero-tolerance policies. City schools, particularly schools in the Northeast and Southeast, have policies where visitors must sign in, closed campuses during lunch, and controlled access to school building and grounds; schools in the Southeast have higher percentages of one or more drug sweeps, use metal detectors to randomly check on students, and use metal detectors for students to pass through each day. Schools with greater than 50 percent minority enrollment or 35 percent of students eligible for free or reduced school lunches demonstrate a greater use of security measures particularly in controlling access to buildings and grounds, using one or more drug sweeps, and regularly and randomly using metal detectors on students. Although school uniforms were not particularly popular between 1996 and 1997, they were more popular in Southeast and West elementary and middle schools, particularly city schools with 50 percent or more minority enrollment. Ten percent of public schools reported having police or some form of law enforcement official from 1 to 30 hours per week, 12 percent did not have law enforcement officials stationed in their schools but would have them available as needed, and 78 percent of schools reporting have no law enforcement officials in their schools. Schools reporting the highest use of police or other law enforcement representatives were primarily middle and high schools with populations of 1,000 or more students, located in cities in the Northeast and Southeast, and with greater than 50 percent minority enrollment.[104]

The 2001 study data reveal a reduction in violence in most of America's public schools, yet there remains a higher percentage of victims of violence at urban schools with a greater number of lower-SES (socioeconomic status) and minority students. School practices and policies relating to safety and discipline are also more prevalent in city schools with higher representations of minority students and students qualifying for free or reduced school lunches. These findings are important as they indicate that what we do on a daily basis regarding school disciplinary and safety practices and policies may be related to school crime and violence. That victims of school violence, drug use, and gangs, and higher percentages of safety and discipline practices and policies are more prevalent in schools with more minority students and lower-SES students, signals the importance not to ignore these students or their schools and to develop comprehensive programs to address the needs of these students.

Who shall lead the public schools in their bid to decrease the violence and increase safe learning environments? According to Philip E. Geiger, "School boards around the country have been hiring a new breed of superintendent [including] military generals.... [T]he reason, they say is that their skills are

---

[104]Ibid., 129–139.

transferable between the private and public sectors and between the military and schools."[105] Seattle tapped U.S. Army (Ret.) Maj. Gen. John Stanford superintendent of its school system in 1995, Duval County, Florida, hired retired Air Force Maj. Gen. John C. Fryer, Jr., in 1998, and New Orleans called up Marine Col. Alfonse Davis to "save" its schools in 1999. Both Davis and Fryer appear to be part of this new breed of leader. Davis taught young marines when he ran the Officer Candidates School for 1995–1997; Fryer was an instructor pilot and an academic instructor at various military education sites and headed the National War College and National Defense University. Fryer "spent considerable time with John [Stanford] in his school system, meeting teachers and principles and assessing the 'culture' of public education."[106] He also served as vice president and general manager of a public company and built its educational-technologies division. Col. Davis utilizes "Tiger teams," "fast-strike crews that aim to get answers without the standard bureaucratic delay," in lieu of committees for finding ways to improve New Orleans schools.[107] Neither Fryer nor Davis came to their jobs with an education degree. Lack of pedagogy is acceptable, according to Geiger, because school boards hire "a No. 2 person who has an educational background who can compensate for what the CEO lacks in pedagogical knowledge and institutional understanding."[108]

Maj. Gen. Stanford appeared to have the "right stuff" for saving Seattle's children and bringing education reform to the home front. After all, he spent thirty years in the military following and giving orders and was responsible for soldiers under his command. In *Victory in Our Schools,* Stanford reveals his leadership style, a blend of military toughness and personal warmth, while discussing his experience as Seattle's school superintendent and the road to education reform. Stanford's first challenge was to debunk the "inflexible and abrasive Pattonesque" military image parents and school board members had of a career-military taking over the helm of their children's education; he relied on a philosophy of leading and loving the students, the teachers, and the community. He met with teachers and principals, students and parents, school board members and members of the community to learn what people believed about Seattle education and the school children. Stanford received disturbing answers to many questions from which he identified ten myths or "philosophies" that were not in the students' best interests and deterred their academic achievement. For example, he found people throughout the school

---

[105] Philip E. Geiger, "When Superintendents Become the Generals," *The School Administrator* Web edition (February 2002), 1.

[106] Ellen R. Delisio, "Retired Air Force Officer Faces New Challenges as School Superintendent," *Education World* (4 September 2001), 2.

[107] Janet McConnaughey, "New Orleans Led by Marine-CEO-Superintendent," AP wire service, 7 August 1999.

[108] Geiger, "When Superintendents Become the Generals," 1.

district believing that: poor and minority children do not get educational support at home, therefore we should not expect them to achieve in school; poor and minority parents want less for their children than middle-class parents so schools should not expect those parents to participate in their children's education; and that sports, arts, and music are expendable "frills" in an academic curriculum. Stanford does not single out or blame any particular entity for these myths, admitting instead "they were held by people who loved the children they worked with and labored with day and night to help them learn. They were just part of the accepted culture."[109] He used these myths to "re-engineer" Seattle's education system utilizing ten "philosophical shifts" as the basis for reform.[110] Stanford's first philosophical shift removed the focus from the adults and placed it on the children: "Every action and every decision would be measured against a single inviolable yardstick: Is this in the best interest of children? Does this promote academic achievement?"[111] Addressing issues of *who* should educate the district's children, Stanford writes, "Schools cannot educate their children alone.... They need their communities to understand that the 'war' in public education is not a war about test scores or curriculum standards. It is a war about the future of our children and our communities, for nothing shapes the future of a city as much as its children."[112] As to *how* Seattle's children should be taught, Stanford's ninth philosophical shift reads, "We would stop serving children out of the sense of duty and start educating them out of the sense of love. We would love every child entrusted to our care, because children don't learn from adults who don't love them."[113]

The myths and philosophical shifts Stanford discusses carry the mark of an individual familiar with modern rules of war, particularly familiarity with the plight of the innocents. John Stanford died in November 1998—responding to his leadership and vision for creating a world-class, student-focused learning system, student test scores and graduation rates increased, school violence decreased to a 10-year low, and student, teacher, and community morale climbed. By consciously or unconsciously applying the principles of just war, Stanford greatly reduced the number of children left as collateral damage in education's war for reform.

Among the ranks assisting the new education commanders are other retired military personnel serving as teachers in public schools under the Troops to Teachers (TTT) program. Congress established TTT in 1994 under the Department of Defense with program oversight transferred in 2000 to the Department of Education. *No Child Left Behind* continues TTT through fiscal year 2006 with its "primary objective to help qualify teachers for schools

---

[109] John Stanford, *Victory in Our Schools* (New York, NY: Bantam, 1998), xi.
[110] Ibid., xii.
[111] Ibid.
[112] Ibid.
[113] Ibid.

that serve low-income families throughout America ... especially in math, science, special education and other high-needs subject areas."[114] First Lady Laura Bush allows the program to use her name and image in informational and media materials, and she seeks new recruits whenever she visits military bases. "The soldiers, who mostly have no teaching experience, are benefiting from the federal government's continued pouring of cash into military welfare programs."[115] The U.S. Departments of Defense and Education have an $18 million budget to assist "eligible military personnel to transition to a new career as public school teachers."[116] The TTT program provides individuals up to $5,000 for teacher certification costs and bonuses of $10,000 to individuals agreeing to teach for three years in a school serving a high percentage of low-income students. One may wonder, as does Saltman, "why the federal government would turn to retired military personnel for staffing classrooms instead of qualify teachers, certified teachers, retired professors, or the glut of unemployed Ph.D. graduates."[117]

TTT is "hailed as a vehicle for providing positive role models to America's youth."[118] However, critics of the program question military discipline and whether soldiers trained to obey orders without question, including orders to kill, are truly the role models that students in the public schools need. Titus Peachey, a director of peace education for Mennonite Central Committee U.S., wonders if TTT is simply "a way for the military to make itself look attractive to impressionable youth in very subtle ways."[119] More than the military's appearance, what about its view of war? Peachey had concerns about the military's mind-set and he wants to "be sure that in a high school history class that the teacher be open to presenting a variety of perspectives on America's wars [including the concept of non-violence] rather than simply the presumption that whenever there's a conflict that the correct response, or the response that ultimately will work, is using military force."[120] Saltman raises concerns about the bootstrap mentality concluding that, "Ultimately, the military narrative that comes with the installment of military personnel in the schools is that the responsibility for success lies with the individual—success or failure derives strictly from discipline and self-discipline. Such narrative covers over the extent to which social conditions such as inferior defunded schools impose limits on the range of individual agency."[121]

---

[114] *Troops to Teachers, Program Overview* (Washington D.C. Department of Defense/Department of Education), on-line at <http://voled.doded.mil/dantes/ttt>.
[115] Saltman, *Collateral Damage*, 91.
[116] *Troops to Teachers, Program Overview*, 1.
[117] Saltman, *Collateral Damage*, 91.
[118] Michael L. Betsch, "Peaceniks Oppose Veterans as Teachers" (CNSNews.com, 15 June 2002), online at <http://www.newsmax.com>.
[119] Ibid., 2.
[120] Ibid.
[121] Saltman, *Collateral Damage*, 91.

Military instructors and superintendents are reputed to be tougher than civilian teachers and administrators in the amount of academic assignments and disciplinary rules. Col. Davis' plan "calls for students to write regular essays about books he chooses. It also proposes a 'Word of the Month' program that involves essays and discussions about *values-based* words such as 'respect' or 'discipline.' [Davis] says he'll get rid of people who aren't committed to change, even if they have contracts."[122] Maj. Gen. Fryer described his goal "to lead the finest school district in America … Reaching that goal requires establishment of a curriculum that has rigor and coherence; alignment of curriculum, instruction, and assessment; incorporation of internationally benchmarked performance standards …"[123] These are no-nonsense men, trained as leaders with high senses of discipline and loyalty, who expect their subordinates and trainees to dutifully follow their lead. Following them onto the battleground of tougher standards and discipline are students enrolled in the JROTC.

The U.S. Department of Defense started the JROTC program under the National Defense Act of 1916 to increase America's military readiness in the face of World War I. The program "brings retired military personnel into public classrooms, teaches a military curriculum, and puts students in uniform. According to a federal regulation, its goal is to 'create favorable attitudes and impressions toward the Services and toward careers in the Armed Forces.'"[124] Currently, JROTC has programs in approximately 3,000 public schools and "its Pentagon funding is expected to rise more than 50 percent, from $215 million last year [2000] to $326 million by 2004."[125] Students enter JROTC at age 14 and the program covers three to four years of high school. Students receive nonacademic elective credit for classroom work utilizing military-oriented textbooks, military drill or marching, and various optional activities such as rifle training. Students wear JROTC uniforms 1 day a week, "enhancing the visibility of the program and solidifying their own identity as soldiers."[126] In addition to the traditional JROTC programs, at least forty career and partnership academies will "combine a JROTC unit with an occupationally-focused curriculum…. The expansion of JROTC is meant to cultivate a public image for the military as efficacious, reliable, and concerned."[127] But, how concerned can it be when, "at the same time schools and communities are implementing preventive programs which strive to involve

---

[122]McConnaughey, "New Orleans Led by Marine-CEO-Superintendent," 2.

[123]Delisio, "Retired Air Force Officer Faces New Challenges as School Superintendent," 3.

[124]Catherine Lutz and Leslie Bartlett, *Making Soldiers in the Public Schools: An Analysis of the Army JROTC Curriculum* (Philadelphia PA: American Friends Service Committee, 1995), 3.

[125]Ron Stodghill, *Class Warfare* (TIME.com, 24 February 2002), 1. Online at <http://www.time.com/time/education/printout/0,8816,212638,00.html>.

[126]Lutz and Bartlett, *Making Soldiers in the Public Schools: An Analysis of the Army JROTC Curriculum*, 4.

[127]Ibid.

the whole school community and identifying solutions to school violence, to teach social skills to help resolve conflicts nonviolently, and to educate young people about the tremendous cost of gun and other violence," JROTC cadets carry real and dummy weapons during drill and color guard activities, participate in marksmanship training, and study from texts that emphasize violence as effective means of settling conflicts on a global scale.[128]

How concerned can it be when JROTC discriminates against people with disabilities and immigrants who do not have legal documentation of their status? A JROTC fact sheet notes, "All high school students who are U.S. citizens, at least 14 years old, and who are physically fit are eligible to join the JROTC."[129] Physical-fitness requirements discriminate against students and instructors with disabilities, including disabled veterans seeking to become instructors. Although the military may be exempt from the Americans with Disabilities Act (ADA) and Individuals with Disabilities Education Act (IDEA), public schools are exempt from neither. JROTC programs, in keeping with the Department of Defense's position that homosexuality is incompatible with military service, also discriminate against gay male, lesbian, and bisexual students and instructors. Because JROTC is an adjunct of the military, there is no legal protection for young gay male, lesbian, or bisexual students who wish to join the program and be open about their identities. The military's history of homophobia and mistreatment of nonheterosexual soldiers should be an indication of how JROTC instructors and cadets will treat gay students who join, or try to join, their ranks. JROTC's intentional exclusion of certain immigrant students and students with disabilities is violative of federal and state nondiscrimination laws, whereas excluding gay male, lesbian, or bisexual students violates many school district policies that prohibit discrimination based on sexual orientation.

How concerned can it be when JROTC programs "are not randomly distributed around the country's high schools, nor do they appeal to an arbitrary selection of students within a selected schools.... Programs are heavily clustered in Southern high schools (65 percent of all JROTC units are in 14 Southern states) and in schools with a high proportion of minority students."[130] Colin Powell was a ROTC cadet at City College of New York and supports the Junior ROTC program, believing that it offers "the best prescription for saving lost inner-city youths."[131] Throughout Powell's autobiography, *My American Journey*, there are references to the

---

[128] American Friends Service Committee, "JROTC: Sending the Wrong Message about Weapons and Violence," *Y&M Magazine* (December 2000/January 2 001), 1.

[129] JROTC Fact Sheet (Washington D.C.: Department of Defense, Public Affairs Office).

[130] Lutz and Bartlett, *Making Soldiers in the Public Schools*, 6.

[131] Stodghill, *Class Warfare*, 1.

positive effects JROTC has on these youths including this oft-quoted statement, "JROTC is a social bargain. Students get a taste of discipline and the work ethic, and experience pride in membership."[132] In 1999, then Secretary of the Army Louis Caldera addressed an assembly celebrating JROTC's expansion plans stating, "This is an investment in our youth. It develops confidence, leadership and teamwork in our young people. Army JROTC contributes substantially to the fabric of our nation by teaching citizenship and leadership to high school students."[133] JROTC is a big investment, an investment shared by the U.S. government and the school districts involved. Although many "poorer schools take on a JROTC unit in an attempt to gain resources not received through their tax base, the unit in fact drains resources from other educational programs in the district through its cost-sharing requirements."[134] JROTC units can cost school districts about $50,000 per school, per year to cover a portion of instructor salaries (JROTC programs require two military officers assigned to each class and the salary depends on the person's military rank and pension); salary supplements including housing allowances; and 100 percent of civilian benefits received by the instructors including health insurance, disability, retirement, prescription plans, and any other benefits provided to regular school district teaching staff. School districts also are responsible for costly modifications to school facilities, which may include the addition of a firing range. Finally, the standard contracts schools sign with the military require schools to cover other costs such as field trips and bonding.[135] Many school districts face budgetary problems and cutbacks, yet participating in the Pentagon's youth investment program leaves JROTC units draining badly needed resources from the schools.

According to Lutz and Barlett, "public schools aim to provide safe, democratic schools to promote respect for others, critical thinking, and basic academic skills. [However,] JROTC does not provide safety, but rather introduces guns into the schools; that it promotes authoritarian values instead of democratic ones; and that it uses rote learning methods and drill in lieu of critical thinking and problem solving skills."[136] The JROTC program claims to provide students with discipline and leadership training, and that it is an investment in our youth. Left unchallenged, "the acceptance of JROTC in the public schools presumes that military institutions are superior in several respects to civilian ones; that military solutions are best suited to respond to contemporary social problems; and that the military's

---

[132] Sergeant 1st Class Connie E. Dickie, "Fifty High Schools Join Army's Junior Reserve Officers Training Corps," *ArmyLINK News* (Washington D.C.: Army News Service, 30 July 1999), 2.
[133] Dickie, "Fifty High Schools Join Army's Junior Reserve Officers Training Corps," 1.
[134] Lutz and Barlett, *Making Soldiers in the Public Schools*, 13.
[135] Ibid., 14.
[136] Ibid., 3.

interests are synonymous with the interests of the American people."[137] However, the military's interests are its own interests, often maintained at the expense of the rest of society. Schools need effective violence prevention programs not programs such as the JROTC that glorify violence as means to justified ends. Schools need teachers to develop students' problem-solving and critical-thinking skills rather than retired sergeants drilling students into thinking and acting like soldiers who dutifully give and take orders. Public schooling is about democracy and fellowship rather than the military's rule of followership; it is about difference and tolerance, not uniformity and conformity. Public education is about children as students not children as collateral damage.

CONCLUSION

Thinking about education reform in just-war terms requires us to take certain concerns into account, specifically: Is the good accomplished proportional to the means used? Are there any other means of handling the problem that have a reasonable prospect of succeeding? Is there a reasonable hope of success? Because education's war for reform arguably produces a series of collateral damages that include students, teachers, administrators, and our communities, we must also ask, "How does the corporatization of public schools lend itself to harming innocents?" and "How do we protect them?" These criteria and questions can aptly guide any discussion of education reform, particularly the role and effects corporatization has on our public schools, our students and teachers, and our communities.

Various education reform strategies exist and many more are yet to be thought of. According to the Center for Commercial-Free Public Education, "every school district in the country should adopt policies that assure positive public school–private sector relationships, and guard against commercial partnerships that requires school districts to advertise is a condition for receiving funds, products, materials or equipment."[138] The Center recognizes that "school-business relationships based on sound principles and community input can contribute to high quality education. However, compulsory attendance confers on educators and obligation to protect the welfare of their students and the integrity of the learning environment."[139] Samples of the Center's policy recommendations permit us a glimpse of how some school districts resolve corporatization efforts in their schools while maintaining the integrity of their schools and protecting their stu-

---

[137]Ibid.

[138]Center for Commercial-free Public Education, *A Citizen's Guide to Adopting Commercial-free School Board Policies in Your Community*, 1–13, online at <http://www.commercialfree.org/policies>. (Downloaded 7 September 2002)

[139]Ibid., 5–6.

dents. Districts use specific policies to restrict the use of sponsor logos in school hallways and classrooms, on informational equipment such as scoreboards, on required student clothing, and in or on school buses. They also restrict the use of advertising in classrooms with regard to electronic media and computer software; restrict the purchase of curriculum materials containing identifiable brand names and limit teacher use of such materials to only those necessary for a particular lesson; and prohibit exclusive vendor contracts from their campuses. At the forefront of the Center's position and those of the sampled school districts, is the student for whom "schools and businesses must ensure that educational values are not distorted.... [and that] selling or providing access to a captive audience in the classroom for commercial purposes is a violation of the public trust."[140] The *Citizen's Guide* contains portions of policy statements from school districts in California, New York, Pennsylvania, Wisconsin, and British Columbia. Although the recommendations are not exhaustive and do not mention just-war tradition or anything about proportionality, they keep them in spirit, offering suggestions for reforming current policies and solutions for maintaining a high-quality public education without sacrificing students, teachers, or curricula.

Austin Interfaith and its Alliance Schools recognize that their work is not "just about improving the existing system of public education, but is instead about changing the culture of schools and entire neighborhoods."[141]

> Furthermore: The theory of change includes a network of partnerships and relationships within and across communities, as well as with school district, civic, and elected officials.... Increased community participation and strong relationships together broaden accountability for improving public education for children of low- to moderate-income families. Public accountability creates the political will to forward equity and school/community connection, thereby improving school climate, curriculum, and instruction making the more responsive to communities, laying the basis for improved student learning and achievement. Stronger schools, in turn, contribute to strengthening community capacity.[142]

Austin Interfaith and the Alliance Schools encourage parents, business and community members, educators, and religious and political leaders to engage in conversation about schools and the community:

---

[140] Ibid., 6.
[141] Elaine Simon, Eva Gold, and Chris Brown, *Strong Neighborhoods, Strong Schools: The Indicators Project on Education Organizing* (Chicago IL: Cross City Campaign for Urban School Reform, 2002), 9.
[142] Ibid., 6.

[Such] conversation creates the conditions for high-quality curriculum and instruction by encouraging reflection on classroom practice, clarifying in raising both teacher and parent expectations for student learning, and drawing attention to the quality and appropriateness of curriculum.... When parents and community members participate in the conversation about schools and children's experiences, they have a clear picture of what is happening in the classroom [and] as a result, they are more likely to hold schools accountable for enabling their children to compete with a strong the students from the best schools and the system.[143]

This spirit of collaboration works to bring about a community vision of public education to "ensure that schools reach and challenge all children, regardless of race and language fluency.... [And, and education that] guarantees that all children, regardless of socioeconomic status, race, or ethnicity, have the resources opportunities they need to become strong learners, to achieve in school, and to succeed in the work world."[144] Austin Interfaith's model stresses networks and partnerships as means to promote individual, family, and community empowerment where such relationships are bound by trust and reciprocity. Creating public conversation about public education and student achievement offers opportunities not only for parents, teachers, and students to take joint ownership of children's education but for all parties to the "we feel mutually accountable for students' school success."[145] Rather than a school simply being a community adjunct, Austin Interfaith's model transforms the school into the community's center. The communitarian nature of this model permits all parties involved to develop a vision that includes a cultural change from "bureaucratic to collaborative" and locates the question of educational reform squarely with the educational success of all community children.

The war for education reform is not being fought with conventional weapons although many of the tactics and monetary costs make it seem otherwise. It is a battle where "it is not possible to offer empirical or quantitative evidence that a democratic school system is somehow superior to one based on market models. Rather it is a choice of values that leads one in one direction or another—after all, these are competing ideologies."[146] The competition is fierce and the stakes are high, necessitating the invocation of rules of engagement. That children are the innocents of education's war for reform allows us to employ rules intended in battles to protect the innocent and reduce the incidence of collateral damage. Education reform, in keeping with the rules concerning double-effect and in the spirit of the just-war tradition, must neces-

---

[143] Ibid., 18.
[144] Ibid., 29–30.
[145] Ibid., 35.
[146] Engel, *The Struggle for Control of Public Education*, 65.

sarily consider various options and not be undertaken until after careful consideration of the aforementioned criteria and questions, especially those pertaining to the current corporatization of public schools. Reforms to recapture market-free education will need to meet the standards of proportionality and ensure that any effect will be sufficiently good as to compensate for and minimize any evil effect. Lastly, any reform must directly and intentionally target only specific identified problems and the means used must be such as to avoid harm to others, especially the innocent.

REFERENCES

Albers, Peggy. 2002. Interview with Patrick Shannon. *Talking Points*, 13, no. 2 (April/May).

American Friends Service Committee. 2000/2001. JROTC: Sending the Wrong Message about Weapons and Violence. *Y&M Magazine* (December 2000/January 2001).

Anscombe, G. E. M. 1981. "Mr. Truman's Decision" and "War and Murder," in *Ethics, Religion and Politics*. Minneapolis MN: University of Minnesota.

Aquinas, Thomas. *Summa Theologiae*, II-II q.40, q.64

Augustine. 1940. *The City of God, XIX*. London: Dent.

Augustine. 1947. *De Libero Arbitrio Voluntatis*. Charlottesville VA: University of Virginia.

Bell, Andrea. 2002. Putting Kids before School: Commercialism. *Education Digest* 67, issue 9 (May).

Betsch, Michael L. 2002. Peaceniks Oppose Veterans as Teachers. CNSNews.com. Available at http://www.newsmax.com. (Accessed 15 June 2002).

Blankenhorn, David, et al. 2002. *Pre-emption, Iraq, and Just War: A Statement of Principles*. Available at http://www.americanvalues.org. (Accessed 14 November 14 2002).

Bradley, Gerard. 2002. Iraq and Just War: A Symposium. The Carnegie Endowment for International Peace. Washington, DC. September 30, 2002. The transcript for the symposium is at http://pewforum.org/events/print.php?EventID=36.

Center for Commercial-free Public Education. 2003. *A Citizen's Guide to Adopting Commercial-free School Board Policies in Your Community*, 1–13. Available at http://www.commercialfree.org/policies.

Consumers Union. 1998. *Selling America's Kids: Commercial Pressures on Kids of the '90s*. Washington, DC: Consumer's Union.

Cookson, Peter W. 1994. *School Choice: The Struggle for the Soul of American Education*. New Haven CT: Yale University Press.

Cooney, Sondra. 1998. *Raising the Bar in the Middle Grades: Readiness for Success*. Atlanta, Georgia: Southern Regional Education Board.

Delisio, Ellen R. 2001. Retired Air Force Officer Faces New Challenges as School Superintendent. *Education World* (4 September 2001).

Dickie, Connie E. 1999. "Fifty High Schools Join Army's Junior Reserve Officers Training Corps," *ArmyLINK News*. Washington DC: Army News Service (30 July 1999).

Dobbs, Katy. 1997. *Quality Comes in Writing*. BIC Corp.

Elkind, David. 1988. *The Hurried Child: Growing Up Too Fast Too Soon*. Reading, MA: Perseus.

Engel, Michael. 2000. *The Struggle for Control of Public Education: Market Ideology vs. Democratic Values*. Philadelphia PA: Temple University Press.

Fege, Arnold F., and Hagelshaw, Andrew. 2000. Beware of "Creeping Corporatization." *NAESP Principal Online* (November 2000). Available at http://www.naesp.org/comm/p1100d.htm.

Finn, Chester and Kanstoroom, Marci. 1999. *Better Teachers, Better Schools*. Washington DC: Thomas B. Fordham Foundation.

Freire, Paulo. 1970. *Pedagogy of the Oppressed*. New York: Continuum.

Geiger, Philip E. 2002. When Superintendents Become the Generals. *The School Administrator*, Web edition (February 2002).

Ghobarah, Hazem, Huth, Paul, and Russett, Bruce. 2001. *Civil Wars Kill and Maim People—Long After the Shooting Stops*. Harvard University Center for Basic Research in Social Sciences, August, 2001. Available at http://www.cbrss.harvard.edu/programs/hsecurity/papers/civilwar.

Giroux, Henry. 1998. Education Incorporated? *Educational Leadership* 56, no.2 (October, 1998).

Harts Systems, LTD. 2000. School Administration Software, Parent-WISE. Available at http://www.hart.com/PwiseIndex.htm.

Johnson, James T. 1981. *Just War Tradition and the Restraint of War*. Princeton NJ: Princeton University Press.

Johnson, James T. 1999. In Response to Terror. *First Things: The Journal of Religion and Public Life*, 90 (February, 1999).

Johnson, James T. and George Weigle. 1991. *Just War and the Gulf War*. Lanham MD: Ethics and Public Policy Center.

Kaufman, Phillip, et al. 2001. *Indicators of School Crime and Safety: 2001*. Washington D.C.: U.S. Department of Education, National Center for Education Statistics and U.S. Department of Justice, Bureau of Justice Statistics.

Lipman, Pauline. 2000. Bush's Education Plan, Globalization, and the Politics of Race. *Cultural Logic* 4, no.1 (Fall).

Lutz, Catherine and Bartlett, Leslie. 1995. *Making Soldiers in the Public Schools: An Analysis of the Army JROTC Curriculum*. Philadelphia PA: American Friends Service Committee.

McConnaughey, Janet. 1999. New Orleans Led by Marine-CEO-Superintendent. AP wire service (7 August 1999).

McNeil, Linda M. 1988. *Contradictions of Control: School Structure and School Knowledge*. New York: Routledge.

McNeil, Linda M. 2000. *Contradictions of School Reform: Educational Costs of Standardized Testing*. New York: Routledge.

Paige, Rod. 2001. Letter to Sen. Robert Byrd Regarding the Administration's FY 2002 Budget Request for Education. (17 May 2001). Available at http://www.ed.gov/News/Letters/010517.html.

Ramsey, Paul. 1961. *War and the Christian Conscience*. Durham NC: Duke University Press.

Ramsey, Paul. 1968. *The Just War*. Savage, MD: Littlefield Adams Quality Paperbacks.

Rediker Software. School Administrative Software-For Educators by Educators. Available at http://www.rediker.com/discipline.html.

Renick, Timothy M. 1994. Charity Lost: The Secularization of the Principle of Double Effect in the Just-War Tradition. *Thomist*, 58, issue 3 (July, 1994).

Saffire, William. 2002. Regime Never Good in Politics or Diet. *The Hamilton Spectator.* Online edition (23 March 2002).

Saltman, Kenneth J. 2000. *Collateral Damage.* Lanham, MD: Rowman and Littlefield Publishers.

Salvage, Jane. 2002. *Collateral Damage: The Health and Environmental Costs of War on Iraq* (12 November 2002). Available at http://www.medact.org.

Salzer, James. 2002. SAT Scores Land Georgia in 50th Place. *The Atlanta Journal-Constitution* (28 August 2002).

Sandel, Michael J. 1997. Commercialism in Schools. *New Republic* 217, no. 9 (1 September 1997).

Scapp, Ron. 2001. For Democracy: Why Corporatizing Public Schools Puts a Nation at Risk. *Educational Researcher* (December 2001).

Shannon, Patrick. 2001. *I Shop, You Shop: Raising Questions About Reading Commodities.* Portsmouth NH: Heinemann.

Simon, Elaine, Eva Gold, and Chris Brown. 2002. *Strong Neighborhoods, Strong Schools: The Indicators Project on Education Organizing.* Chicago IL: Cross City Campaign for Urban School Reform.

Smith, Frank. 1998. *The Book of Learning and Forgetting.* New York: Teachers College Press.

Stanford, John. 1998. *Victory in Our Schools.* New York, NY: Bantam.

Troops to Teachers, Program Overview. 2002. Washington D.C. Department of Defense/ Department of Education. Available at http://voled.doded.mil/dantes/ttt.

Stodghill, Ron. 2002. Class Warfare. *Time.com.* Available at http://www.time.com/ time/education/printout/0,8816,212638,00.html. (Accessed 24 February 2002).

Strossen, Nadine. 1997. Public Schools Adopting Dress Codes. *ACLU News Wire* (30 September 1997).

Strossen, Nadine. 1991. Why the ACLU Opposes School Dress Codes. CNN.com, CNN chat room interview 8 August 1991. Available at http://wwww..cnn.com/ 2001/COMMUITY/08/28/strossen.cnna

UNICEF Pushes for Iraqi Schools to Reopen (25 April 2003 press release). Available at http://www.unicefusa.org/emergencies/iraq/releases/042503.html.

UNICEF Lauds Iraqi Common Sense to Return to School. 2003. (25 April 2003 press release).

USAID. 2003. Assistance for Iraq—Accomplishments: Education (December 2003).

USAID Fact Sheet: Rehabilitating Iraq's Basic Education System. 2003. (18 August 2003). Available at http://www.usaid.gov/press/factsheets/2003/ fs030818.html.

Young, Jeffrey R. 2002. SAT Scores Hold Steady; Test's Owner Announces Steps to Encourage Better Writing Skills. *The Chronicle of Higher Education* (28 August 2002).

Walzer, Michael. 1992. *Just and Unjust Wars*, second ed. New York: Basic Books.

Chapter 7

Private Knowledge, Public Domain: The Politics of Intellectual Property in Higher Education

Benjamin Baez

PART I: THE POLITICS OF INTELLECTUAL PROPERTY

Current economic trends make consideration of intellectual property imperative to a broad understanding of social and political forces (re)shaping higher education. Such property has become a vital component of the American Gross National Product, and it is becoming the object of increasing international attention.[1] As Kamil Idris, Director General of the World Intellectual Property Organization, states, "Intellectual property is increasingly a fundamental element of modern economies. In an extremely competitive global environment, more countries are finding tangible benefits in supporting innovation and creativity."[2] The increasing importance of intellectual property is due to fact that the United States, and perhaps all developed countries, have been transformed from industrial societies to "information societies."[3] In the "information age," it seems, "ideas have be-

---

[1] Keith Aoki, "The Stakes of Intellectual Property Law," in *The Politics of Law: A Progressive Critique*, 3rd ed., ed. David Kairys (New York: Basic Books, 1998), 259–278.

[2] World Intellectual Property Organization, *Annual Report 2001* (Geneva: World Intellectual Property Organization, 2002), 2. Available at http://www.wipo.org/ (Retrieved January 24, 2003).

[3] "Information society" refers to economies in which control over knowledge has replaced control over matter as the ultimate source of economic power; see Series editors' preface to Christopher May, *A Global Political Economy of Intellectual Property Rights: The New Enclosures?* (London and New York: Routledge, 2000), ix.

come prized commodities,"[4] and universities and other corporate owners of such commodities are not sharing them, at least not for free.

The way intellectual-property practices proceed may reflect the way globalization proceeds. Slaughter and Leslie explained that beginning in the 1970s, markets became global due in part to increased economic competition from Pacific Rim countries. Industrial countries lost market share, so multinational conglomerates, which became dominant in the global market, invested in new technologies to remain competitive, and they turned to universities for science-based products and processes to market. In due course, these conglomerates (and their academic lackeys) pressured states to invest in technological innovation.[5] Although Slaughter and Leslie situate this transformation in the 1970s, it may be that the transformation began to mature then but started before. Miyoshi argues that because of the phenomenal advances in communication and transportation since World War II, capital circulated with unprecedented ease in search of maximum profit across nations. With the recent rise of transnational corporations, which are accountable solely to their shareholders and have little regard for national controls, the nation-state lost its power to intervene in the market, allowing the gap between rich and poor to increase drastically. The elimination of the public sector and communitarianism in favor of privatization, individualism, and identitarianism was pervasive, resulting in the intensification of competition and the fragmentation of society.[6]

Intellectual property is essential to economies based on information or knowledge.[7] As knowledge gains value in the products and services provided by multinational corporations, they seek to capture such knowledge for their exclusive control. Knowledge, once feeding the productive processes and services of these corporations, now is itself deemed property. Once knowledge has been deemed property, intellectual-property laws become central to the economy.[8] So Boyle seems correct that intellectual property is the legal form of the information age.[9] Yet, as Boyle argues, although intellectual property provides the key to the distribution of wealth, power, and access in the information society, there currently is no "politics of intellectual property" akin to that, say, of the environment, which has a strong theoretical framework and a common interest. There has been, as a

---

[4] Eyal Press and Jennifer Washburn, "The Kept University," *The Atlantic Monthly* (March 2000): 39–54, 54.

[5] Sheila Slaughter and Larry L. Leslie, *Academic Capitalism: Politics, Policies, and the Entrepreneurial University* (Baltimore: The Johns Hopkins University Press, 1997), 6–7.

[6] Masao Miyoshi, "Ivory Tower in Escrow," *boundary*, 2 (2000): 1–50, 15.

[7] Edwin C. Hettinger, "Justifying Intellectual Property," *Philosophy and Public Affairs*, 18 (1989): 31–52, 31.

[8] May, *A Global Political Economy*, 6–7.

[9] James Boyle, "A Politics of Intellectual Property: Environmentalism for the Net?" *Duke Law Journal*, 47 (1997): 87–116, 88–89.

result, an overprotection of intellectual property, amounting to an intellectual "land grab" and an unprecedented privatization of the public domain. All this takes place, Boyle argues, with very little public debate.[10] I try to show later in this chapter, however, that there can be no "public debate" without a *public* and that the intellectual-property regimes make the emergence of such a public difficult.

This information economy, transnational and absorbing, following Miyoshi, has an effect on the university, and the most structural and decisive change has been technology transfer from the university to industry.[11] "Technology transfer" is a term that represents the activities engaged in by universities to move their research to the market. Postindustrial, transnational capitalism uses higher education, therefore, not primarily for training workers—because technology makes workers less necessary—but for research and development.[12] Intellectual property, consequently, has become extremely important to universities because: (a) intellectual property of universities plays a crucial role in transnational capitalism; (b) revenues generated from intellectual property allow universities to rely less directly on government support; and (c) intellectual property is deemed compatible with the assumed purpose of the university as furthering social progress through the production of knowledge. Universities, thereby, have become active producers and claimants of intellectual properties, and thus their transformation from knowledge producers for social progress into intellectual-property producers for themselves and for a few global firms requires reconsideration of their traditional roles and values.

I thought previously that intellectual property is something that we *do*, that is, something we create, take, withhold, give, assign, and use. Now, I think that intellectual property is something that *happens* to us. Every aspect of our lives is being instrumentalized, bought, sold, and, in short, defined and organized entirely in ways subject to intellectual-property regimes. Such organization is justified as serving the "public interest." But such organization destroys that public interest by foreclosing the *public* from expressing itself or, more accurately, *its selves*. It is only through unencumbered access to knowledge and its products that something like a *public* can take place.

I provide in Part II of this chapter a brief discussion of intellectual property and its role in the processes of globalization. In Part III, I explain the universities' technology transfer and its privatization of knowledge. Finally, in Part IV, I discuss the role of the public domain and argue that such domain is foreclosed by intellectual-property regimes.

---

[10] Ibid., 95-98, 112–115.
[11] Miyoshi, "Ivory Tower in Escrow," 18.
[12] Slaughter and Leslie, *Academic Capitalism*, 25.

PART II: THE STAKES OF INTELLECTUAL PROPERTY

Intellectual property has become central to the processes of globalization.[13] I take as axiomatic a notion of globalization that, following Hardt and Negri, reflects a new world order in which there are no fixed boundaries or barriers and that is dominated by a series of national and supranational entities that manage hybrid identities, flexible hierarchies, and plural exchanges. This world order is replacing industrial labor with communicative, cooperative, and affective labor, and its central concern is the bio-political production of social life itself, a production that combines and invests in all that is economic, political, and cultural.[14] This aspect of globalization, therefore, illustrates most explicitly the prevalence of what Foucault calls bio-power. This power makes society and human bodies the subject of rule, not through violence by any one sovereign but by various mechanisms that through the production of knowledge control the world. These mechanisms produce knowledge used for the health and well-being of the social body, which, now that it has become their objective, provides them with the material through and for which they channel wealth. In other words, the biological (and psychological, cultural, etc.) traits of social bodies become relevant factors for economic management, and around them are organized apparatuses that will ensure dominion over them, not just through subjection but also by increasing their utility.[15]

The current global markets have intensified bio-power by transforming the economic bases for it. The economies of industrial societies, Slaughter and Leslie argue, relied on harnessing new sources of energy and producing mechanical inventions for the social body, but postindustrial societies rely on advances in applied sciences and engineering, especially in areas that generate information, process it, and store it. Postindustrial societies must rely, therefore, on universities, which provide the training necessary for increasing the number of professionals employed by corporations to invent, maintain, and innovate sophisti-

---

[13] *Globalization*, as Jameson points out, defies definition. On the one hand the term represents loosely the enlargement of the world communication and world market, the domination by transnational entities, the importance of regional identities, and the consequent de-stabilization of nation-states. But not all aspects of what one calls globalization are oppressive. Regionalism, for example, may allow individuals and groups to form identities around local or international concerns and thus be relieved of the hegemony of oppressive nation-states; see Fredric Jameson, preface to *The Cultures of Globalization*, eds. Fredric Jameson and Masao Miyoshi (Durham: Duke University Press, 1998), xi–xvii.

[14] Michael Hardt and Antonio Negri, *Empire* (Cambridge: Harvard University Press, 2000), xi–xiii.

[15] See Michel Foucault, *The History of Sexuality: An Introduction Volume I*, trans. Robert Hurley (New York: Vintage Books, 1978), 139–150; Michel Foucault, *Power/Knowledge: Selected Interviews & Other Writings 1972–1977*, ed. Colin Gordon, trans. Colin Gordon, Leo Marshall, John Mepham, and Kate Soper (New York: Pantheon, 1980), 168–172.

cated technologies and products.[16] Thus, the intellectual-property regimes must be conceptualized with an understanding of the forces of
globalization, which were transformed by, but now do the transforming
of, economies, putting premiums on products and processes derived
from scientific innovation and on national policies that enable the capi-
talization of knowledge.

International intellectual-property agreements, such as the Berne Convention for the Protection of Literary and Artistic Work[17] and the Agreement
on Trade-Related Aspects of Intellectual Property Rights (TRIPS),[18] further
the imperatives of globalization by diminishing national boundaries and undermining the cultural fabric of other communities. Aoki explains that as
transnational intellectual-property regimes set minimum standards of protection, traditional territorial and political notions of sovereignty are eroded
because the entities holding increasingly large blocks of intellectual-property rights are not nations but private, multinational corporations (universities included).[19] Such agreements, therefore, ensure the enclosure of the
global intellectual commons.[20]

Universities, as producers of knowledge, are implicated in such globalization and consequent enclosure through their intellectual-property regimes.
Not only do universities serve as conduits for the knowledge marketed by
transnational corporations, but they are themselves active participants in the
intellectual-property scene as owners. As intellectual-property producers

---

[16]See Slaughter and Leslie, *Academic Capitalism*, 26.

[17]This agreement ensures the protection of copyrights in contracting countries, specifically
requiring minimum copyright protection of 50 years. Western nations benefit disproportionately under the agreement. For example, North America, which has about 5 percent of the
world's population, produces 13 percent of the world's books. Similarly, papers, journals, magazines, and 80 percent of the world's knowledge industries are based in Western nations, where
their outputs are copyrighted. See Keith Aoki, "Sovereignty and the Globalization of Intellectual
Property: Neocolonialism, Anticommons Property, and Biopiracy in the (Not-So-Brave) New
World Order of International Intellectual Property Protection," *Indiana Journal of Global Legal
Studies*, 6 (1998): 11–58, 25. Western companies already dominate the global market of copyrighted materials, and this Agreement ensures that they will do so for a long time.

[18]TRIPS requires all member nations to rewrite their intellectual-property laws to conform to
a new set of international regulations developed by the World Trade Organization, amounting
essentially to an international intellectual-property regime premised on the United States
model. TRIPS, among other problems, clearly favors the cash-rich but resource-poor "north-
ern" nations over the cash-poor but resource-rich "southern" nations. For example, 25 percent
of prescription drugs in the United States have active ingredients from Indian plants, and for
the European Union, Australia, Canada, and the United States the market value of prescription
and over-the-counter drugs based on Indian plants is $70 billion. See Scott Holwick, "Trade and
the Environment: Developing Nations and the Agreement on Trade-Related Aspects of Intellectual-Property Rights," *Colorado Journal of International Environmental Law and Policy 1999 Yearbook*
(2000): 49–75.

[19]Aoki, "Sovereignty and the Globalization of Intellectual Property," 27–28.

[20]Referring to something as a "commons" means that anyone is free to use its contents without permission; see Lawrence Lessig, "The Law of the Horse: What Cyberlaw Might Teach," *Harvard Law Review*, 113 (1999): 501–549, 527–528.

and owners, therefore, universities are also significant transnational entities in the global marketplace. Before I discuss the universities' intellectual-property regimes, it might be useful now to discuss what intellectual properties are and how they work.

There are two prevailing justifications for supporting the ownership of intellectual property: (a) a utilitarian bargain between the creator and society in which the former is granted a limited monopoly in return for disclosure and circulation of the intellectual work; and (b) a Lockean justification in which property rights inhere to deserving creators entitled to the fruits of their labor.[21] Intellectual-property rights purportedly address what is usually understood as the "public good" problem. That is, given that the cost of creation is high but cost of reproduction is low, and once the work is created it may be reproduced rapaciously without depleting the original, intellectual-property protection is necessary to ensure that the creator has an economic incentive to create works that, at least ultimately, will benefit the public.[22] Consequently, because technology makes creation expensive but expansive and reproduction cheap and easy, the history of intellectual properties in the United States has been one of expansion.

There are four kinds of intellectual property: trade secrets, trademarks, patents, and copyrights.[23] This paper limits itself, however, to copyrights and patents, because although colleges and universities can (and do) assert trade secrets and trademarks, the most commonly asserted intellectual properties in higher education are copyrights and patents.[24] With regard to the latter, the U.S. Constitution states that Congress has legislative power to "promote the Progress of Science and useful Arts, by securing for limited Times to Authors and Inventors the exclusive Right to their respective Writings and Discoveries."[25] Because one is very different from the other, I briefly discuss each of them separately.

Copyrights and the "Commons"

Copyrights give the owner, called the "author," of a creative expression, called a "work of authorship," the right to exclude others from using original

---

[21] Robert L. Ostergard, "Intellectual Property: A Universal Human Right?" *Human Rights Quarterly*, 21 (1998): 156–178, 156–157.

[22] Jessica Litman, "The Public Domain," *Emory Law Journal*, 39 (1990): 965–1023, 970.

[23] Actually, there may be five kinds of intellectual properties. The fifth kind, the "rights of publicity," protect celebrities' interests in their images and identities; William W. Fisher, *The Growth of Intellectual Property: A History of the Ownership of Ideas in the United States* (1999), 2. Available at http://cyber.law.harvard.edu/people/tfisher/iphistory.pdf (Retrieved February 24, 2003).

[24] A trade secret allows an organization to prevent disclosure of information that gives it a competitive edge over others; a trademark protects a distinctive name, design, logo, slogan, etc., that identifies the organization and distinguishes it from others.

[25] U.S. Const. Art. I, § 8, cl. 8.

creative expressions that have been "fixed in a tangible medium of expression."[26] Creative expressions need not be "published" in the traditional sense, as unpublished works are also protected. Unlike patents, copyrights vest automatically when a work is fixed in tangible form, and their existence and ownership are utterly independent of any government office. Copyrights protect the expression of ideas but not the ideas themselves. Copyright includes the exclusive right to reproduce the work, prepare derivatives of such work, transfer ownership (assignment) of it, and perform, display, and record the work. But in essence, a copyright is the right to exclude others from using the work without the owner's permission. The one exception to this rule is "fair use." Copyright laws permit the "fair use" of protected materials if the use is for, among other reasons, teaching and classroom use or public criticism.

As a result of the Sonny Bono Copyright Extension Act of 1998, copyrights, if owned by the author, last for the life of the author plus 70 years, and where an employer (or corporate entity) own it, such rights last between 95 and 120 years, depending on when the work was published.[27] In 1998, Congress also passed the Digital Millennium Copyright Act, which prohibits among other things, the circumvention of any technology that controls copying, and the publishing or distributing of any technology, product, or tool that circumvents copy-control technology.[28] The Act also requires Internet service providers (ISPs) to remove materials from Web sites that appear to violate copyrights, but it limits their liability for simply transmitting information over the Internet. The Act exempts college and university ISPs from liability for copyright violations by faculty members or graduate students.

The author is legally presumed to own the copyright, but employers can obtain the copyrights to their employees' creations under the "work-made-for-hire" doctrine. The work-made-for-hire doctrine in copyright law reverses the legal presumption that the author is the owner of the copyright and allows the employers to capture works authored by employees acting within their scope of employment or when specifically commissioned by employers. In higher education, universities rarely assert copyrights over academic works, such as scholarly publications and traditional course materials.[29] Many universities, however, have modified their copyright policies

---

[26] The Copyright Act of 1976, Title 17 U.S.C. § 102 et seq.

[27] 17 USCS § 302 et seq. The law extends copyright protection to existing works by at least 20 years, an aspect of the law that was upheld by the Supreme Court on January 15, 2003 in *Eldred v. Ashcroft*, 123 S. Ct. 769 (2003).

[28] 17 USCS § 1201 et seq.

[29] See Kimberly B. Kelley, Kimberly Bonner, James S. McMichael, and Neal Pomea, "Intellectual Property, Ownership and Digital Course Materials: A Study of Intellectual Property Policies at Two-and-Four-Year Colleges and Universities," *Portal: Libraries and the Academy*, 2 (2002): 255–266.

to include specific "work-made-for-hire" language, probably because of potential lucrative royalties from software and teaching notes.[30] Indeed, the categories of things that are copyrightable have been expanded. For example, software and test processes are now subject to copyright protection, making it more difficult for scholars and researchers to access and improve on software or tests.[31] But it is the potential of electronic course materials to generate profits that likely has led to the increasing concern over copyrights in higher education.

The concern with electronic materials imbeds the university squarely within the debates over the Internet or "cyberspace." The "propertization" of cyberspace, as well as a great deal of information in "real" space, has resulted essentially in an enclosure of the intellectual commons, much like that of the English Enclosure Movements of the 17th and 18th centuries. As Travis argues, owners of copyright holdings today will rigorously assert absolute rights of exclusion from their informational "estates." Their copyrights amount to an enclosure of the intellectual commons, first by extending the duration of copyright protection, then by revoking access and transformative uses of copyrighted materials.[32] Equally problematic, a legal structure is in place for the wholesale censorship of Internet speech by means of overbroad copyright laws. The anticircumvention aspects of the Digital Millennium Copyright Act and the legality of "shrinkwrap" licensing as a result of legal decisions and the proposed Uniform Computer Information Transactions Act (UCITA), gives copyright owners extensive authority to dictate the contents of speech.[33] Indeed, the law of copyrights should make one rethink traditional ideas about constitutionalism, which suggests that the actions of government are more dangerous than those of private actors. The latter, through copyright regimes, have been granted unprecedented power to constrain freedom of speech and other civil liberties.[34]

---

[30] Gary Rhoades, personal communication, November 23, 2002.

[31] See Benjamin Baez and Sheila Slaughter, "Academic Freedom and Federal Courts in the 1990s: The Legitimation of the Conservative Entrepreneurial State," in *Higher Education: Handbook of Theory and Research* (Vol 16), eds. John Smart and William Tierney (Bronx: Agathon Press, 2001), 73–118, 104–111.

[32] Hannibal Travis, "Pirates of the Information Infrastructure: Blackstonian Copyright and the First Amendment," *Berkeley Technology Law Journal*, 15 (2000): 777–864, 785–790, 808.

[33] UCITA is a model legislation which would restrict consumers from (a) reading licenses before accepting them, (b) suing vendors if the product is defective, and (c) donating the product to others, even to charity. UCITA has been adopted in Maryland and Virginia, and other states have either considered it or are planning to do so; see Edward R. Johnson, "The Law Against Sharing Knowledge," *The Chronicle Review* (February 14, 2003): B14.

[34] See Lawrence Lessig, *The Future of Ideas: The Fate of the Commons in a Connected World* (New York: Random House, 2001).

Patents and Privatization

Patents allow owners to exclude others from making or using their inventions. Patent law protects new inventions reduced to practice, discoveries, and designs, including new uses for existing things. Only the first *person* (institutions cannot file for patents) to invent or file for the patent receives it. Unlike a copyright, which vests immediately upon the fixing of an expression in tangible form, a patent is a document issued by the U.S. Patent and Trademark Office that grants the owner, or the "inventor," a monopoly on the use of an invention for a limited period of time (either 14 or 20 years, depending on the type of patent).[35] Also unlike copyrights, patents cover all matters associated with the invention, including ideas and methods. Furthermore, unlike copyrights, universities successfully claim ownership of patent rights.[36]

The most common patents are called "utility patents."[37] Utility patents are granted for 20 years for "useful," "original," and "nonobvious" inventions involving processes, machines, manufactures, compositions of matter, or improvements of an existing idea that falls into one of the four categories. Patents are not available for mathematical formula or naturally occurring phenomena. Before a patent can be issued, the invention must be "reduced to practice"; that is, one must build and test the invention (to see if it works), although filing an application for a patent is evidence of reduction to practice. The invention cannot be publicly disclosed (other than for experimentation to see whether it works) for more than one year before the formal patent application is filed. Patent rights, like copyrights, include the right to use, license, or transfer the patent. As with a copyright, the essence of patent rights is that they allow the inventor to exclude others from using the invention. There is some question as to whether patent law permits a "research exemption" akin to "fair use" in copyright law. Patent statutes do not explicitly provide such a right, but conventional practice, and scientific norms, have permitted researchers to use patented inventions for research purposes.[38]

The purpose of the patent system is to promote the public welfare through the stimulation and use of inventions. The problem, as Vaughan correctly identified it more than fifty years ago, is that few inventors have the ability to put their inventions into commercial form, and so they must seek a corporate sponsor for their patents. Furthermore, most companies and uni-

---

[35] See The Patent Act, Title 35 § 101 et seq.
[36] Pat K. Chew, "Faculty-Generated Inventions: Who Owns the Golden Egg?" *Wisconsin Law Review*, 1992 (1992): 259–314.
[37] The other two kinds of patents are "design patents," issued for nonfunctional and innovative designs, and "plant patents," issued for sexually or asexually reproducible plants.
[38] Carol Nottenburg, Philip G. Pardey, and Brian D. Wright, "Accessing Other People's Technology for Non-Profit Research," *The Australian Journal of Agricultural and Resource Economics*, 46 (2002): 389–416.

versities require assignment of patent rights. The public welfare underlying patent rights has given way to the private interests of corporations and universities, many of which own so many patents that they control entire markets. Thus, what starts out as a limited-period monopoly of a specific invention turns into an indefinite monopoly of an industry, something that the antitrust laws were supposed to prohibit. And, when these corporations and universities agree to grant cross-licenses to their competitors, an entire market is cornered because the corporations and universities, as the only sellers, hire all the inventors in the area, and then only license to specific others. As Vaughan argues, the patent-owning individual has been displaced by the patent-owning corporation, which then extends the exclusive rights that the patent confers.[39]

Moreover, patent rights have become essential to the privatization of knowledge, and the university is a central component of such privatization. The Bayh–Dole Act of 1980, as I discuss further in the next section, allows universities to patent inventions resulting from federal grants, permitting institutions to exploit their faculty's intellectual work. Patent rights have fundamentally altered the nature of faculty relationships with others. The problem is not just that faculty pursue for-profit research, but that the presentation or publication of a study, thesis, or dissertation "anticipates" a patent and is therefore held up.

Furthermore, patents have become potentially lucrative, especially in biotechnology and computer technology. The potential for lucrative returns has led institutions of higher education to expend a great deal of resources to defend their interests, even if this means suing their own faculty, students, and affiliates. More important, the litigation over intellectual property, especially because it can involve complex, multistate litigation, is very costly and redirects resources away from the purported core mission of the university—teaching, research, and service—and moves intellectual property out of the purview of the faculty. Such activity strengthens administrative offices at the periphery of the university and undermines the legitimacy of faculty as decision makers for the university.[40] Given its significance, further discussion of the universities pursuit of patents follows next.

PART III: TECHNOLOGY TRANSFER
AND THE PRIVATIZATION OF KNOWLEDGE

Much of the profit from university research comes in the area loosely termed "biotechnology." Biotechnology is a group of technologies based on molecu-

---

[39] Floyd L. Vaughan, "Patent Policy," *The American Economic Review,* 38 (1948): 215–234, 215–229.
[40] See Baez and Slaughter, "Academic Freedom and Federal Courts in the 1990s," 96–97, 101.

lar biology that enable scientists to genetically manipulate and replicate living cells.[41] Its economic value is in basic research and the extensive number of applications to which this technology can be put to use (most commonly in medicine, agriculture, food processing, and energy).[42] Biotechnology inventions are a significant part of most major universities' licensing operations, amounting to approximately 60 percent of university licenses. Indeed, the university was the birthplace of biotechnology. The growth of the pharmaceutical industry would not have been possible without university-biotechnological research and subsequent patents.[43] The Cohen–Boyer patents and the Biologically Functional Molecular Chimeras issued to Stanford University and the University of California in the early 1980s epitomize university biotechnological licensing and provided the genesis of the university licensing industry.[44] The profitability of biotechnology, however, leads to an unprecedented university–industry collaboration in research. Biotechnology, therefore, calls into question the public domain of scientific research, which relies on free access to new knowledge.[45]

The pursuit of patents in biotechnology (and other areas) by universities has been sparked by pro-competition legal decisions and public policies. In 1980, the Supreme Court held that living organisms can be patented.[46] But that legal decision, although opening up the patent system to biotechnology, could not remove the most significant barrier to its commercialization: the public ownership of federally sponsored inventions. Thus, more than anything else, the privatization of knowledge and technology transfer by universities was sparked by the Bayh–Dole Act of 1980.[47] The Act was part of a slew of federal initiatives in the 1980s to ensure American dominance in the global marketplace, a dominance that was in question as a result of the economic success of other countries at the time, especially Japan. The Bayh–Dole Act purports to serve the public interest by allowing universities and small busi-

---

[41] As an important example of biotechnology, the Human Genome Project, illustrates bio-power most explicitly. The Project began in 1990 as a projected 15-year effort to identify all of the estimated 100,000 genes found in the human DNA, to determine the sequence of the 3 billion bases that make up the human DNA, to store this information in accessible databases, and to develop tools for analyzing the massive amounts of data generated by this project.

[42] Nicholas S. Argyres and Julia Porter Liebeskind, "Privatizing the Intellectual Commons: Universities and the Commercialization of Biotechnology," *Journal of Economic Behavior & Organization*, 25 (1998): 427–454, 433.

[43] John M. Golden, "Biotechnology, Technology Policy, and Patentability: Natural Products and Invention in the American System," *Emory Law Journal*, 50 (2001): 101–191, 106.

[44] Kenneth Sutherlin Dueker, "Biobusiness on Campus: Commercialization of University-Developed Biomedical Technologies," *Food and Drug Law Journal*, 52 (1997): 453–509, 454–455.

[45] Rebecca S. Eisenberg, "Proprietary Rights and the Norms of Science in Biotechnology," *Yale Law Journal*, 97 (1987): 177–231.

[46] *Diamond v. Chakrabarty*, 447 U.S. 303 (1980). The Court upheld a lower court's decision ordering a patent on a human-made, genetically-engineered bacterium capable of breaking down multiple components of crude oil.

[47] 35 USCS § 200 et seq.

nesses (less than 500 employees) to patent and commercialize inventions developed from federally sponsored research. But as part of a slew of initiatives seeking to spark economic development, as Slaughter explains, the Bayh–Dole Act blurred the boundaries between public and private sectors and pioneered the legal and administrative mechanisms for technology transfer between public and private entities. These initiatives, in increasing intellectual-property protection for federally funded knowledge, ensured the commodification of that knowledge.[48]

Universities aggressively took advantage of the Bayh–Dole Act through technology transfer, which is based primarily on intellectual property and is the most direct form of academic capitalism.[49] Universities themselves rarely sell products to consumers, so their technology transfer is primarily accomplished by establishing technology-transfer offices to promote discovery and inventions, entering into sponsored-research agreements with commercial organizations, developing venture capital endeavors to promote university–industry activities, creating and supporting start-up companies and taking equity positions in them, and establishing "strategic partnerships" with commercial and noncommercial entities, including other universities, to share information regarding their patent portfolios and other intellectual-property inventories.[50] Slaughter adds that technology-transfer offices allow universities to manage and police the intellectual-property faculty and students develop, and to improve their legal capacity to engage in complex, multistate, multiyear litigation to protect their intellectual properties.[51]

These findings clearly illustrate that the fundamental question for economic institutions in the information age[52] is becoming the fundamental question for institutions of higher education: How best to (re)organize scientific and technological resources for commercial innovation and economic growth? This reorganization takes place primarily through technology transfer, and it must be stressed that it is subsidized predominantly by federal and state governments. The federal government subsidizes technology transfer through tax exemptions, tax breaks, low-interest loans, and outright sponsoring of commercial projects. Some funding,

---

[48] Sheila Slaughter, "Federal Policy and Supply-Side Institutional Resource Allocation at Public Research Universities," *The Review of Higher Education*, 21 (1998): 209–244, 216–218.

[49] Slaughter and Leslie, *Academic Capitalism*, 19. Slaughter and Leslie also attribute such phenomenon to decreased public funding of higher education, forcing universities (especially public ones) to resort to entrepreneurial activities in order to generate revenues. See also, Gary Rhoades and Shelia Slaughter, "Academic Capitalism, Managed Professionals, and Supply-Side Higher Education," *Social Text*, 15, no. 2 (1997): 9–38.

[50] Dueker, "Biobusiness on Campus," 469.

[51] Sheila Slaughter, "Professional Values and the Allure of the Market," *Academe: Bulletin of the American Association of University Professors* (September–October 2001): 22–26, 23.

[52] See Maryann P. Feldman and Maryellen R. Kelley, "How States Augment the Capabilities of Technology Pioneering Firms," *Growth and Change*, 33 (2002): 173–195, 173.

however, comes from industry sources, private foundations, and state governments, which do much of the same as the federal government but also provide for public institutions' operating budgets and capital improvement funds for laboratories and research facilities.[53] These activities, moreover, fundamentally alter traditional academic norms, such as pursuing knowledge for its own sake rather than for profit, and disseminating freely the results of research.

Despite these concerns, the Association of University Technology Managers (AUTM) extols the virtues of the Bayh–Dole Act.[54] It reports that since the Act was passed, innovations based on university research have added $40 billion to the U.S. economy, supported 260,000 jobs, spawned numerous new businesses, created industries, and opened new markets. Before the Bayh–Dole Act, universities produced approximately 250 patents a year; since the Act, patent applications have increased dramatically to more than 2,000 per year.[55] According to the annual *AUTM Licensing Survey*, in 2000: (a) institutions issued 4,362 licenses; (b) they had $29.5 billion in sponsored-research expenditures, of which $18.1 billion came from the federal government; (c) industry-funded research amounted to $2.7 billion; (d) academic research led to more than 13,000 disclosures,[56] close to 6,400 patent applications, and 3,700 patents;[57] (e) institutions established 454 new start-up companies; (f) they issued 4,362 licenses; (g) 54 percent of the licenses that went to small businesses (including start-ups) were exclusive, whereas 37 percent of the licenses that went to large companies were exclusive; and (h) 9,059 licenses yielded income. The gross license income was $1.26 billion (compared to $862 million in 1999)—much of this income was due, however, to one-time payments (rather than continuous royalty payments).[58]

The potential income from technology transfer, to be clear, is not great when viewed in light of total university revenues. Its value lies, however, in the fact that such income is unencumbered and free from all the burdens

---

[53]Ibid., 178–179.

[54]AUTM was established in 1974 to professionalize university technology transfer; see Dueker, "Biobusiness on Campus," 476–477. Its member institutions include U.S. universities, hospitals, research institutes, patent management organizations, and similar Canadian institutions. For more information on AUTM, see http://www.autm.net/index_ie.html (Retrieved March 3, 2003).

[55]Association of University Technology Managers, *Surveys -Bayh-Dole Act* (Northbrook: Association of University Technology Managers, 2000). Available at http://www.autm.net/pubs/ survey/facts.html (Retrieved July 23, 2002).

[56]"Disclosures" describe inventions and are filed before the formal patent application. Disclosures are not patent applications themselves, but they can be used to prove the date of conception of the invention should a contrary claim be made.

[57]This brought the total number of patents issued to its members since 1993, the first year AUTM collected data, to over 20,000.

[58]Association of University Technology Managers, *AUTM Licensing Survey: FY 2000 Survey Summary* (Northbrook: Association of University Technology Managers, Inc., 2001). Available at http://www.autm.net/pubs/survey/facts.html (Retrieved July 23, 2002).

and constraints of the other funding sources.[59] Yet, income from technology transfer can be large for some universities. In 1999, for example, Columbia University led all universities in licensing income ($100 million), and it was followed by the University of California ($88 million) and Stanford University ($35 million). Just a year later, however, the University of California led all universities in such revenues (over $261 million), followed by Columbia University (over $138 million), Dartmouth College (over $68 million), Florida State University (over $67 million), and Stanford University (over $34 million). More than 50 colleges and universities made over $2 million in licensing income in 2000.[60] Therefore, the competition among universities for a larger share of research-and-development resources is intense, most of them searching for project grants, license incomes, and the prestige that comes with this activity.

Indeed, it is remarkable what lengths universities will go to generate revenue from technology transfer. Officials at the University of Michigan, for example, lamenting that the university is spending too much money to generate only a few million dollars in patent income, point out that Stanford makes close to $35 million although spending a lot less per project. Universities apparently aim for one disclosure per $1 million spent on research; the University of Michigan, however, gets only 0.3 inventions, ranking it in the bottom third of universities. This technology transfer may constitute a closed market, for the goal of universities is not just to make money but to outdo each other. As Marvin G. Parnes, the University of Michigan's Associate Vice President for Research states, the university's performance "wasn't commensurate with [its] standing." The solution seemed clear: Increase the research budget, bring in more experienced administrators (read as: give them more control over faculty research), and give those administrators more flexibility in making deals with outside companies (read as: they will have little oversight and accountability for the decisions they make). After all, as Nisbet, the University of Michigan's Director of Technology Transfer, states, "It's all part of a new philosophy ... Do more deals, and the money will follow." Nisbet may need to understand, however, that the "problem" for the university is not just administrative but cultural. As Parnes indicates, "the culture of our faculty was not strongly oriented toward commercialization."[61]

Changing faculty culture may not be too difficult, because faculty tend to see intellectual property as a justifiable extension of their work. All universities need to do, according to this logic, is to make faculty entrepreneurs by giving them royalties and other incentives to patent (at many universities,

---

[59] Dueker, "Biobusiness on Campus," 457.

[60] Goldie Blumenstyk, "Income from University Licenses on Patents Exceeded $1-Billion," *The Chronicle of Higher Education* (March 22, 2002): A31.

[61] See Goldie Blumenstyk, "University of Michigan Finds Good Research is Not Enough," *The Chronicle of Higher Education* (July 19, 2002): A24–A26.

faculty can earn up to 50 percent of the net income from royalties). One can also change the culture by punishing faculty who refuse to patent (e.g., by failing to fund their research), though this must be done carefully. Universities have also sued professors and students who seek to commercialize research on their own or to take their inventions elsewhere. The University of Pennsylvania successfully sued one such faculty member in 1990 over royalties from Retin-A (the wrinkle-retardant product).[62] Indeed, the potential profits are so high that universities have become active litigants over intellectual property.[63]

There is a growing fear that as a result of technology transfer, universities will resemble nothing more than commercial-research centers. It also may be the case that the "new-wave" corporations will resemble nothing more than university-research entities. That is, the conjoining of universities and industries is more extensive than it first appears. Many universities form collaborative projects with commercial entities in which they share facilities and knowledge. Also, many of the university spin-off companies are nothing more than commercial/university-research/employment centers; they start off as satellite research-and-development entities, providing students and graduates with jobs and training, while the companies receive information and technology from universities. Furthermore, some university-related labs and companies grow into corporations that then form industrial research parks, such as Silicon Valley in California, Route 128 in Massachusetts, the Research Triangle in North Carolina, the Princeton Corridor in New Jersey, Silicon Hills in Texas, the Medical Mile in Pennsylvania, Optics Valley in Arizona, and the Golden Triangle in San Diego.[64] The point here is that insisting upon a distinction between universities and commercial entities in the information age may become meaningless.

At any rate, what is wrong with technology transfer? Certainly, technology transfer has public benefits. But the conversion of knowledge into intellectual property means that "the public" is excluded from using that knowledge. Thus, the real beneficiaries are not the public but the corporations and entrepreneurs who reap (or can reap, if they hit it big) enormous profits through less-than-equitable pricing.[65] More fundamentally, technology transfer and the intellectual-property regime that supports it, sheds doubt on the viability of the commonsense distinctions that structure our thought, such as university versus corporation and public versus private. Public and private universities are major players in the intellec-

---

[62] See Goldie Blumenstyk, "Universities Try to Keep Inventions From Going 'Out the Back Door'," *The Chronicle of Higher Education* (May 17, 2002): A33–A34.
[63] See Baez and Slaughter, "Academic Freedom and Federal Courts in the 1990s," 96–111.
[64] See Miyoshi, "Ivory Tower in Escrow," 26–27.
[65] Ibid., 28.

tual-property scene, and they compete very well with multinational corporations. One may note again that technology transfer is predominantly publicly subsidized. Universities, therefore, as publicly subsidized entrepreneurs, are active and competitive players in the marketplace. In this way, Readings is correct that universities are not *like* corporations, they *are* corporations.[66]

The corporatization of the university means its globalization, because the crucial corporations are typically transnational. Indeed, as Miyoshi argues, universities are reworked through countless international ties, such as study-abroad programs and international exchanges, and, I might add, the global marketing of their research. Universities are transnational corporations, and the global academic industry that attracts and absorbs students and scholars is a de-territorialized corporation, and its scholars will soon have less to do with their fellow citizens or place of origin or arrival than with the transnational corporate culture of their universities.[67]

Stanford University is a case in point. It recently formed a $225 million research partnership to develop clean-energy research and technology with a number of multinational conglomerates, including ExxonMobil (who plans on donating up to $100 million), General Electric ($50 million), E-ON ($50 million), Schlumberger ($25 million), and Toyota ($25 million), which is expected to come on board. These corporate sponsors will be able to receive exclusive licenses to commercialize inventions without paying anything to the University for the first five years. All this, of course, raises concerns about how independent from those sponsors Stanford University will be, a problem the university says is not really one because it will only consult with the sponsors and the research decisions will be entirely its own. Yet, as Bryan Flannery, manager of ExxonMobil's department of safety, health, and environment science, states, the company chose Stanford University, not only for its "science and engineering expertise and its international connections [, or because] the institution is known for working with industry," but also because "a number of Stanford professors were willing to 'change their career directions' in order to be a part of this project." This co-opting of the university's research is deemed forgivable, because, as Frankin Orr, the Dean of the University's School of Earth Sciences (and director of this endeavor, called G-CEP), stated, "the project will bring resources to research that the entire world needs."[68] So now it seems that it is not just the United States that benefits from the commercialization of knowledge, as supporters of the Bayh–Dole Act envi-

[66] Bill Readings, *The University in Ruins* (Cambridge: Harvard University Press, 1996), 22.

[67] Miyoshi, "Ivory Tower in Escrow," 37.

[68] Goldie Blumenstyk, "Greening the World or 'Greenwashing' a Reputation?" *The Chronicle of Higher Education* (January 10, 2003): A22–A25.

sioned, but the "entire world," ensuring Stanford University's status as an indispensable transnational corporation.[69]

The Bayh–Dole Act, in privatizing knowledge derived from federal research and promoting the kinds of partnerships described previously, reflects a transformation in the public subsidy of knowledge. Bollier argues that after World War II, there was a broad consensus that intellectual property resulting from federal research would remain in the public domain, but beginning in the 1970s, large pharmaceutical, electronic, and chemical industries campaigned to reverse the presumption of public ownership of the products of federally funded research. The Bayh–Dole Act and similar pro-competition policies cause and legitimate the technology transfer of publicly funded research to the private sector, a massive giveaway of taxpayer-sponsored research and development worth billions. The Act did accelerate university research in the applied sciences and sparked important inventions brought to the market, Bollier acknowledges, but there have been significant long-term costs, most notably, the sweeping privatization of publicly funded knowledge, the ceding of research agendas to the private sector, and the erosion of public confidence in the independence of university research. As Bollier argues, huge swaths of knowledge have been fenced off into privately owned plots, destroying the academic commons so essential to scientific advancement.[70] Now, instead of a robust intellectual commons, there are multiple closed domains to be exploited solely by those who own them.

The "mining" of knowledge severely constrains inter- and intrauniversity relationships, privileges those discourses that promote profit at the expense of those that emphasize more altruistic goals, and transforms the societal commitment to universities. As Bollier argues, the public-spirited ethic of the academy has been challenged by a frankly acquisitive ethic that aggressively seeks private ownership and profit from the fruits of university research, and scholarly arenas are then reconceptualized as market resources, to be treated as items in an investment portfolio.[71] Universities, supposedly not-for-profit, now

---

[69] *The Chronicle of Higher Education* reports that other universities have entered into similar million-dollar agreements with other companies, including: (1) Princeton University's $20 million partnership with BP and Ford Motors for research associated with carbon dioxide and global warming; (2) [the notorious] $25 million agreement between the University of California at Berkeley and Syngenta (formerly Norvatis) for research in plant genomics and other things; (3) Washington University's $5 million a year deal (now totaling about $120 million) with Pharmacia for cancer and cardiovascular-disease research; (4) Massachusetts Institute of Technology's $35 million deal with DuPont for research in plastics, high-performance materials, and chemicals; (5) Harvard University's $13 million partnership with Aventis (formerly Hoechst) for research associated with cell cycles and regulation; and (6) the State University of New York at Albany's approximately $400 million agreements with International Sematech and Toyko Electron, Ltd.; see Ibid., A24.

[70] David Bollier, "The Enclosure of the Academic Commons," *Academe: Bulletin of the American Association of University Professors* (September-October 2002): 18–22, 20–21.

[71] Ibid., 19.

seek greater returns on marketable intellectual property benefiting themselves and other businesses, and scholars have been converted into corporate employees and managers.[72] Moreover, the privatization of knowledge has dramatically changed the nature of faculty work: It becomes a commodity in the most direct sense and sold to highest bidder. What matters to and about faculty is transformed. The public dissemination of their work takes a backseat to the potential commercial value of that work. Indeed, the primary value attached to faculty work has been redirected from publications to commercially motivated research. Faculty who do not engage in academic capitalism will become *mere* teachers.[73] The core reason for academic freedom—the protection of higher education—has gotten lost. The universities' missions are now tied to the intellectual-property regimes, undervaluing public goals and being replaced by the inequities of the market. All this is done in the "public interest." But there can be no "public interest" until a *public* exists, a point I elaborate on in the concluding part of this chapter.

PART IV: INTELLECTUAL PROPERTY AND THE PUBLIC DOMAIN

In American law, intellectual-property rights are premised on the belief that the public benefits from the dissemination of intellectual creations, and to encourage such creations the author or inventor is given a limited monopoly on use so as to benefit economically from his or her creations.[74] The right to withhold ideas and creations from public dissemination, however, is *the* intellectual-property right at stake—it is the state-sanctioned monopoly the author gets for creating something that is potentially useful to the public. Yet, when knowledge is alienable, anyone other than the owner can be excluded from using it. When the author or inventor assigns away his or her rights to, say, a university, she or he is also excluded from such use. Indeed, it is often the case that the creator is in the same position as the general public, because intellectual properties usually are owned by corporate entities. Much of the debate about intellectual property in higher education seems to focus on this problem of ownership, so faculty-creators are pitted against university-owners. But, as Rhoades argues, the best path to enhancing faculty's positions in these debates may be less in advancing private claims to ownership than in promoting the public's access to and benefits from their intellectual work.[75]

---

[72] Miyoshi, "Ivory Tower in Escrow," 31–33.
[73] Slaughter and Leslie, *Academic Capitalism*, 211.
[74] See Hettinger, "Justifying Intellectual Property," 36.
[75] Gary Rhoades, "Whose Property Is It? Negotiating with the University," *Academe: Bulletin of the American Association of University Professors* (September/October 2001): 38–43, 40.

To appreciate Rhoades' argument, one must first engage the idea of the "public" to which he referred. His argument echoes those defending the public domain that indicate that creativity and innovation is based on the free access to information, which the intellectual-property regime effectively eliminates. It is important to consider, therefore, how the spatial concept of the public domain structures thought and language in the intellectual-property discourse.[76] How is the public domain deployed in this discourse and what are its effects?

The public domain, as Litman explains with regard to copyrights, is a concept imported from the realm of real property. The term describes a true commons, comprising elements of intellectual property that are ineligible for private ownership. The contents of the public domain may be used by anyone, without seeking permission. Works in the public domain include those whose copyright have expired, those that were ineligible for copyright protection,[77] or those that failed to comply with the requirements for securing it. But these categories of work, Litman argues, are the least important parts of the public domain. The most important aspect of the public domain comprises the parts of copyrighted materials that the law does not protect, those aspects of intellectual creations that cannot be owned by anyone. These aspects include ideas, facts, methods, systems, processes, and so forth (and, specifically with regard to patents, "natural" things).[78] Indeed, as Litman persuasively argues, authorship entails transferring and recombining what is already been said or done, and thus it necessarily relies on a robust public domain. The public domain makes authorship possible, and so one must guard against protecting the rights of authors at the expense of authorship.[79]

The university historically has been conceptualized as a kind of public domain, especially with regard to its research. Rhoades proposes that academe is a distinctive ecology, defined less by short-term commercial payoffs than by long-term educational values—it is a professional public domain—and privatization threatens this.[80] I agree with Rhoades, not because he argues that academe *is* a public domain but because it *should be* that. Yet, it may now be problematic to insist upon the idea of the university as a public domain, because it can work to mask the increasing privatization of the university.

For example, note how the idea of the "public" is deployed by a few major public universities. The University of California's copyright policy states that

---

[76] For discussions of how spacial concepts are deployed and to what effect, see Mike Crang and Nigel Thrift, eds., *Thinking Space* (London and New York: Routledge, 2000).

[77] For example, the United States originally thrust all works created by foreign nationals into the public domain, a practice gone even before the recent international intellectual-property agreements.

[78] Litman, "The Public Domain," 975–977.

[79] Ibid., 966–969.

[80] Rhoades, "Whose Property Is It?" 43.

"The creation of copyrighted works is one of the ways the University fulfills its mission of contributing to the body of knowledge for the *public good*."[81] Its patent policy states that "The University recognizes the need for and desirability of encouraging the broad utilization of the results of University research, not only by scholars but also in practical application for the *general public benefit*."[82] The University of Virginia's patent policy is said to "Provide an incentive to creative intellectual effort and the advancement of knowledge for the *welfare of mankind*."[83] The University of Michigan's patent policy states that "The University of Michigan is a public institution devoted to teaching, research, and service. One aspect of its mission is the application of knowledge to problems of *general public interest*."[84] The University of North Carolina at Chapel Hill's patent and copyright policy states that "The University of North Carolina is dedicated to instruction, research, and extending knowledge to the *public (public service)*."[85] The "public interest" rhetoric is pervasive in university-intellectual-property discourse, but all this rhetoric does is justify the technology transfer of university research to the private sphere, sometimes for extensive profits but mostly for the possibility of profit. The fact that universities use these policies to own knowledge obviously shatters the idea of a university *as a public domain*.

Yet, the belief that the university is a public domain, albeit one that has forgotten its *raison d'etre*, is pervasive; so much so that the most common arguments for protecting this supposed public domain include expanding the concepts of free speech and "fair use" in copyright law [86] and the "research exception" in patent law,[87] limiting the availability of intellectual-property rights in certain areas,[88] and requiring that universities and other research-oriented entities grant compulsory licenses to their intellectual properties.[89] I agree these things should happen, but simply relying on these limits is not enough because they merely put obstacles in the path of the privatization of

---

[81]University of California, *UC Copyright Policy* (Berkeley: University of California, 1992), emphasis added. Available at http://otl.berkeley.edu/inventor/uccopyright.php (Retrieved December 30, 2002).

[82]University of California, *University of California Patent Policy* (Berkeley: University of California, 1997), emphasis added. Available at http://otl.berkeley.edu/inventor/ucpatent.php (Retrieved December 30, 2002).

[83]University of Virginia, *Patent Policy* (Charlottesville: The University of Virginia, 1998), emphasis added. Available at http://www.virginia.edu/finance/polproc/pol/xve2.html (Retrieved December 30, 2002).

[84]University of Michigan, *Revised Policy on Intellectual Properties: Including Their Disclosure, Commercialization, and Distribution of Revenues from Royalties and Sale of Equity Interests* (Ann Arbor: The University of Michigan, 1996). Emphasis added. Available at http://www.research.umich,edu/policies/um/ippolicy.html (Retrieved December 30, 2002).

[85]University of North Carolina, *Patent and Copyright Policies* (Chapel Hill: The University of North Carolina, 2001), emphasis added. Available at http://northcarolina.edu/aa/departments/research/copyright/copyright.cfm (Retrieved December 30, 2002).

[86]See Travis, "Pirates of the Information Infrastructure."

[87]See Nottenburg, Pardey, and Wright, "Accessing Other People's Technology."

[88]Ostergard, "Intellectual Property."

[89]See Golden, "Biotechnology, Technology Policy, and Patentability."

knowledge and enclosure of the public domain. They do not address adequately the very idea of owning knowledge. One must take issue with the logic of the intellectual-property regime itself, and how that regime prevents the formation of a public interest. Jaszi is correct that those of us concerned with the public domain must find new ways of speaking about intellectual property, especially because recent intellectual-property policies and legal decisions have devalued the public domain.[90]

Aoki argues that the intellectual-property regime diminishes the rich public realm of political debate and intellectual exchange.[91] Aoki's argument assumes a public realm, but it does permit us to consider what a "public" might be. A recent editorial in *The Nation*, discussing the *Eldred v. Ashcroft* Supreme Court case upholding the law granting copyright extension to preexisting works, argues that the Court should have overturned the law and reaffirmed that copyright serves the public interest. The editorial also suggests that perhaps *Eldred* can "galvanize a nascent public movement against the expansion of intellectual property."[92] I agree that the "public interest" component should again be given much greater weight in intellectual-property law, although I do not assume, as do the editors of *The Nation*, a preexisting (even if "nascent") *public*. What, then, is or should be the "public" that we are concerned about?

Uncovering the "Public"

The commercialization of university research through intellectual-property regimes sheds doubt on the commonsense distinction between the "public" and "private," and it requires a reconsideration of such ideas in the information age. Habermas allows us to think through this distinction by conceptualizing a separation between the state, society, and the public. Habermas provides in *The Structural Transformation of the Public Sphere* a historical-sociological explanation of the emergence, transformation, and disintegration of the bourgeois public sphere, a sphere between society and the state in which rational-critical debate was institutionally guaranteed and that took shape in the specific historical circumstances of a developing market economy.[94] As economic activity became oriented toward a commodity market that had expanded under state supervision, a "public" of bourgeois people installed itself

---

[90] Peter A. Jaszi, "Goodbye to All That: A Reluctant (and Perhaps Premature) Adieu to a Constitutionally-Grounded Discourse of Public Interest in Copyright Law," *Vanderbilt Journal of Transnational Law*, 29 (1996): 595–611, 596.

[91] Aoki, "The Stakes of Intellectual Property Law," 266–267.

[92] "Copyright Monopolies, *The Nation* (February 17, 2003): 6–7.

[93] I want to acknowledge and thank Deron Boyles for the assistance he gave me in proposing the following ideas about the "public."

[94] Jürgen Habermas, *The Structural Transformation of the Public Sphere: An Inquiry into a Category of Bourgeois Society*, trans. Thomas Burger with Frederick Lawrence (Cambridge: The MIT Press, 1989, c. 1962).

as an opponent of a modern state that exceeded its mercantilist functions and began to concern itself with what had previously been deemed "private" and within the purview of the household economy. The bourgeois public sphere was a sphere of "private people come together as a public" to debate state authority over the rules that governed private commodity exchange and social relations—and the medium of this debate was the people's use of their reason; the venues were institutions set up for public participation (e.g., parliament, the press, journals, coffee houses, salons, etc.).[95]

Habermas explains, however, that the structural contradictions of the public sphere eventually lead to its transformation beginning in the late 19th century: The "public sphere" was egalitarian within itself but "the public" included only those individuals who were educated and owned property—it excluded everyone else. Consequently, the public sphere was transformed to include previously excluded individuals and concerns, and this transformation was accomplished, Habermas argues, by the rise of the welfare state, which emerged when the masses translated economic antagonisms into political conflicts. Since the late 19th century, an intermeshing of society and state has taken place, and so the modern era is characterized by private institutions that have assumed a public character—they became bigger, took on public functions, and formed contracts with public agencies—and the sphere of the public was altered by the influx of private interests that received privileged exposure in it—although these were by no means representatives of the interests of private people as the public but of private people as owners of private property.

The public sphere now, for Habermas, is merely a field of competition among conflicting interests, in which organized representatives of diverse factions of private bureaucracies, special-interest associations, political parties, and public administration, negotiate and compromise among themselves, all the while leaving a majority of people out of the process. The liberal idea of the public sphere is still important, but only because it rationalizes the exercise of state authority and the compromise and negotiation that leads to it. The media, originally an ally in the rational-critical debate of the public sphere, has been co-opted by commercial interests and now merely is a vehicle for propaganda; its object is not relaying information for the purposes of critical debate but for cultural consumption.[96]

---

[95]Ibid., 27.

[96]The mass media have given the public more access to those materials from which they were originally excluded, but Habermas calls this access only a "psychologically-facilitated" one. That is, access to "high" culture for the masses through, say, higher incomes and availability of cheap books, came by lowering the threshold capacity required for appreciation or participation; see Ibid., 166. This may not be quite fair, as Calhoun points out, since Habermas did not consider how access was opened in important ways, such as by the extension of public education and mass literacy. (See Craig Calhoun, "Introduction: Habermas and the Public Sphere," in *Habermas and the Public Sphere*, ed. Craig Calhoun (Cambridge: The MIT Press, 1992, 1–48, 23–24.) Providing education and literacy to all opens up a previously exclusionary public sphere, but if individuals are educated and made literate merely to reproduce consumerist culture, what kind of participation can that be?

Habermas' work has been heavily criticized by those who question the reliability of his historical and sociological evidence, and by those who feel that he romanticizes too much the idea of the bourgeois public sphere.[97] Still, despite these critiques, one can pillage the remains of Habermas' public sphere for those tidbits that allow us to rethink the assumptions behind the public-interest rhetoric in intellectual-property discourse. If Habermas was even remotely correct that a now completely passive public merely consumes culture and whose opinion is "mediatized," can we say that it has any "real" interest of its own? To what "public" do, say, universities refer? There is no real public, according to Habermas, not even a bourgeois one. And there can be no public, as Arendt also points out, until it is given the means to express itself.[98]

We may ask, therefore, with Garnham, what kind of "public" is possible in a world dominated by largely international markets, caused and reinforced by progressive deregulation and privatization of national telecommunication monopolies, the increased penetration of corporate sponsorship into the financing of cultural activities, the move of educational and research institutions toward the private sector under the pressure of public spending cuts, the growing tendency to make profitability the criteria for the provision of public services, and, I would add, the expansion of an international intellectual-property agenda that encloses the entire global world?[99] Habermas sees a public sphere as providing the best possible hope for countering the hegemony of the market (and the power of the authoritarian state). I agree. The competing interests that now dominate the public sphere, however, do not permit consensus on *a* public interest. But Habermas also believes that it is possible to come to an agreement about universal and binding criteria for resolving the divergent claims of these competing interests. And it is here where I part company with Habermas.

Habermas argues that radical democratic change must aim to ensure that the social-integrative power of solidarity (through communicative action) can prevail over the powers of the other two control resources, that is, money and administrative power.[100] This social-integrative power of communicative action is first of all located in intimate and social relationships, but because these relationships engender too many unresolvable convictions, the political public sphere must become the quintessential concept denoting all those condi-

---

[97] For examples of such criticism, see Craig Calhoun, ed., *Habermas and the Public Sphere* (Cambridge: The MIT Press, 1992).

[98] See Hanna Arendt, *The Human Condition*, 2nd ed. (Chicago: University of Chicago Press, 1998, c. 1958).

[99] Nicholas Garnham, "The Media and the Public Sphere," in *Habermas and the Public Sphere*, ed. Craig Calhoun (Cambridge: The MIT Press, 1992), 359–376, 362.

[100] Jürgen Habermas, "Further Reflections on the Public Sphere," in *Habermas and the Public Sphere* (trans. Thomas Burger), ed. Craig Calhoun (Cambridge: The MIT Press, 1992), 421–461.

tions of communication under which can form a discursive opinion and will on the part of a public composed of the citizens of a state. Habermas believes that a universalization of interests and appropriate application of norms embodying such interests are possible, a possibility that comes from a discourse-centered approach to ethics that views the exchange of arguments and counterarguments as the most suitable procedure for resolving moral-practical questions. Such an approach, for Habermas, may lead to the redemption of normative validity claims, "for it anchors the validity of norms in the possibility of a rationally founded agreement on the part of all those who might be affected, in so far as they take on *the role of participants in a rational debate.*"[101] The settling of political questions, therefore, depends on the institutionalization of practices of rational public debate.

In an era of competing and conflicting discourses, is such communicative action possible or even desirable? Butler seems correct when she argues that the ideal of consensus undergirding such communicative action makes sense only to the degree that the terms in question submit to a consensually established meaning. For Habermas, such consensus can come only when one agrees to univocal meanings. Equivocal meanings, consequently, pose a threat to the ideal of consensus. But who, Butler asks, stands above the interpretive fray in a position to assign the same utterances the same meanings? And why is it that the threat posed by such an authority is deemed less serious than the one posed by equivocal interpretation left unconstrained? One may note here that hegemony maintains its internal cohesion, and thus its domination, because it enforces a common way of viewing the world. There seems more emancipatory possibility in equivocality, as Butler suggests, than in univocality. That there is no consensus on understanding might allow hegemonic discourses to be turned or derailed in some significant way and, most important, that the very discourses that dominate might well miss their mark and produce an effect counter to the one intended, as when corporate brands are parodied.[102]

I believe, with Habermas, however, that something like the idea of a public domain is indispensable to democratic political practice. But like Fraser, I think that the presence of multiple counterpublics appropriately expand the public "discursive space." The existence of these publics reflects not only an inevitability but a desirability for progressive politics. They provide a contestatory function that may allow them to offset the unjust participatory privileges employed by dominant social groups in stratified societies.[103] Yet no counterpublic, no matter how contestatory, is possible without knowl-

---

[101] Ibid., 447, emphasis in original.

[102] Judith Butler, *Excitable Speech: A Politics of the Performative* (London and New York: Routledge, 1997), 86–87.

[103] Nancy Fraser, "Rethinking the Public Sphere: A Contribution to the Critique of Actually Existing Democracy," in *Habermas and the Public Sphere*, ed. Craig Calhoun (Cambridge: The MIT Press, 1992), 109–142, 111, 123–125.

edge and its products, something that the intellectual-property regimes increasingly make subject to private ownership.

Cultural products, increasingly subject to intellectual-property regimes, form the basis for expanding the public discursive space. One of the most significant aspects of the postmodern age is the acknowledgment of the centrality of intertextuality in the creation of social meanings and practice. That is, a text's meaning, as intended by the creator and as experienced by the reader, can be understood only in relation to other texts. The idea of intertextuality can be applied to culture, and as a result the existence of multiple texts in the public domain is crucial to the evolution and transformation of the meanings of culture.[104]

Coombe proposes that intellectual properties play a constitutive role in the creation of contemporary cultures and in the social life of interpretive practice. The images of commerce, she argues, are a rich source of expressive activity, yet most pictures, texts, motifs, labels, logos, trade names, designs, tunes, jingles, and even some colors and scents are governed, if not controlled, by regimes of intellectual property. These regimes, Coombe argues, enable the production and reproduction of cultural forms, while paradoxically prohibiting and inviting their interpretive appropriation for contrary interests and agendas.[105] In other words, for Coombe, the "texts" protected by intellectual-property laws convey and generate meanings in the lives of those who incorporate them; they provide symbolic resources for the construction of identity, community, subaltern appropriations, parodic interventions, and counterhegemonic narratives. Ideas of self, society, and identity, Coombe argues, are realized only through the expressive cultural activity that reworks cultural forms that occupy the space of the social imaginary.[106] What intellectual-property regimes attempt to do, unfortunately, is to freeze the play of significations, giving extensive authority over those significations to those who "own" the cultural texts.[107]

Indeed, bio-power in the information age controls even the most fundamental aspects of human bodies: DNA sequences are subject to knowledge regimes and ownership. Thus, intellectual-property regimes of bio-power prevent in a sense what Foucault calls the "technologies of the self," or those techniques or operations that individuals use to effect their bodies, souls, thoughts, conduct, and ways of being, so as to transform themselves in order to attain a certain state of happiness, purity, wisdom, perfection, immortality.[108] These technologies are

---

[104]See Ashley Packard, "Copyright Term Extensions, the Public Domain and Intertextuality Intertwined," *Journal of Intellectual Property Law*, 10 (2002): 1–32.

[105]Rosemary J. Coombe, *The Cultural Life of Intellectual Properties: Authorship, Appropriation, and the Law* (Durham: Duke University Press, 1998), 6.

[106]Ibid., 270–271.

[107]Ibid., 8.

[108]Michel Foucault, "Technologies of the Self," in *Technologies of the Self: A Seminar with Michel Foucault*, eds. Luther H. Martin, Huck Gutman, and Patrick H. Hutton (Amherst: The University of Massachusetts Press, 1988), 16–49, 19.

different from what Foucault has elaborated as the discursive regimes of truth, or the "technologies of power," which control individuals through the production of knowledge about them. Intellectual-property regimes permit the "technologies of power" to govern human bodies and social life while foreclosing the contestatory function of the "technologies of the self," which necessarily utilize cultural forms to elaborate alternative conceptions of self.

All this means is that the *public*, as Habermas understands it, has been reworked in texts that privilege certain things over others, namely commodity over other possible meanings. But this commodified public, when understood through intertextuality, is vulnerable to reappropriation, an appropriation that may be foreclosed by intellectual-property regimes. *It is the increasing removal of texts, therefore, not their commercialization per se, that is the most serious threat posed by the privatization of the public domain.* As Coombe argues, for subjects in contemporary consumerist societies, political action must involve a critical engagement with commodified cultural forms. But in the current climate, intellectual-property regimes operate to stifle dialogic practice in the public spheres of the world, preventing individuals and groups from using the most powerful, prevalent, and accessible cultural forms (the technologies of the self) to express alternative visions of those spheres (and even of their own bodies).[109]

The intellectual-property regimes, it should be noted, are currently being resisted, if only at the boundaries. Indeed, the World Wide Web represents a challenge to the traditional media, as almost anyone with a computer can attest, and some of its information transcends the banality of the programs offered by the traditional media and becomes crucial to the creation of counterpublics that, as Habermas envisions, question the hegemony of the market and authoritarian state.[110] In this way, the World Wide Web has usurped the role that traditional media played in the bourgeois public sphere. But now this public domain is also being enclosed through copyright protection.[111] Only some of this enclosure, however, is economically motivated; other motivations exist for certain prohibitions, such as the restrictions on cyberporn. One wonders, then, whether the enclosure of the public domain is necessarily pecuniarily driven. What other possible reasons are there? Could it be that the imperatives of transnational capitalism fear the emergence of counterpublics that will challenge it? Do the copyright and patent owners, mostly multinational corporations and universities, fear the public's awakening?

I believe that intellectuals play a crucial role in creating counterpublics. Bourdieu argues that there can be no genuine democracy without opposing

---

[109]Coombe, *The Cultural Life of Intellectual Property*, 42.
[110]Of course, it has also permitted publics that further the imperatives of the market and authoritarian state. But that is the risk that one takes with a public domain.
[111]Travis, "Pirates of the Information Infrastructure," 851–857.

critical powers. He urges writers, artists, philosophers, and scientists to make their voices heard directly in all the areas of public life in which they are competent.[112] The global market is powerful not only because it is reinforced by a slew of institutional arrangements, but also because it dominates and restricts the "marketplace of ideas." In the work of inventing the public in the face of an unprecedented privatization and enclosure, intellectuals have a decisive role to play. They must, following Bourdieu, engage in a battle over ideas. This battle, as Rhoades suggests, should not be over ownership of those ideas but over the ability to generate and disseminate them freely.[113] Given globalization, these battles must be international; that is, intellectual workers must pursue international mobilization, as everyone is affected by the few but dominant global firms and universities.

To enable such counterpublics, however, intellectuals must be able to create, use, and disseminate their texts freely, texts that give meaning to people's lives, texts that are increasingly owned by the firms and universities that dominate the global market by controlling those texts. But those firms and universities are not disembodied things; they require the actions of individuals to remain effective as such. As central components of the knowledge industry, they rely on the products created by intellectuals and others. Intellectuals, consequently, play a critical role in both the emergence and foreclosure of publics, even if they do not wish it. Critical intellectuals, especially those in the public domains that universities are supposed to be, therefore, must resist the lure of intellectual property. They must also refuse to patent and, although they cannot avoid creating copyrights because they exist when ideas are fixed in tangible forms, ensure that their copyrighted work is freely available. If they are truly interested in countering what Bourdieu calls the "tyranny of the market," they must forego personal gain and not just assert but actually work for the creation of something like a public interest.

REFERENCES

Aoki, Keith. 1998. Sovereignty and the Globalization of Intellectual Property: Neocolonialism, Anticommons Property, and Biopiracy in the (Not-So-Brave) New World Order of International Intellectual Property Protection. *Indiana Journal of Global Legal Studies* 6: 11–58.

Aoki, Keith. 1998. "The Stakes of Intellectual Property Law." In *The Politics of Law: A Progressive Critique*, 3rd ed., ed. David Kairys, 259–278. New York: Basic Books.

Arendt, Hanna. 1998. *The Human Condition*, 2nd ed. Chicago: University of Chicago Press.

---

[112]Pierre Bourdieu, *Acts of Resistance: Against the Tyranny of the Market*, trans. Richard Nice (New York: The New Press, 1998), 8–9.

[113]See Rhoades, "Whose Property Is It?"

Argyres, Nicholas S., and Julia Porter Liebeskind. 1998. Privatizing the Intellectual Commons: Universities and the Commercialization of Biotechnology. *Journal of Economic Behavior & Organization* 25: 427–454.

Association of University Technology Managers. 2000. *Surveys—Bayh–Dole Act.* Northbrook: Association of University Technology Managers. Available at http://www.autm.net/pubs/survey/facts.html (Accessed 23 July 2002).

Association of University Technology Managers. 2001. *AUTM Licensing Survey: FY 2000 Survey Summary.* Northbrook: Association of University Technology Managers. Available at http://www.autm.net/pubs/survey/facts.html (Accessed 23 July 2002).

Baez, Benjamin, and Sheila Slaughter. 2001. "Academic Freedom and Federal Courts in the 1990s: The Legitimation of the Conservative Entrepreneurial State," In *Higher Education: Handbook of Theory and Research* (Vol 16), eds. John Smart and William Tierney, 73–118. Bronx: Agathon Press.

Blumenstyk, Goldie. 2002. University of Michigan Finds Good Research is Not Enough. *The Chronicle of Higher Education* (July 19): A24–A26.

Blumenstyk, Goldie. 2002. Universities Try to Keep Inventions From Going "Out the Back Door." *The Chronicle of Higher Education* (May 17): A33–A34.

Blumenstyk, Goldie. 2002. Income from University Licenses on Patents Exceeded $1-Billion. *The Chronicle of Higher Education* (March 22): A31.

Blumenstyk, Goldie. 2003. Greening the World or "Greenwashing" a Reputation? *The Chronicle of Higher Education* (January 10): A22–A25.

Bollier, David. 2002. The Enclosure of the Academic Commons. *Academe: Bulletin of the American Association of University Professors* (September–October): 18–22.

Bourdieu, Pierre. 1998. *Acts of Resistance: Against the Tyranny of the Market,* trans. Richard Nice. New York: The New Press.

Boyle, James. 1997. A Politics of Intellectual Property: Environmentalism for the Net? *Duke Law Journal* 47: 87–116.

Butler, Judith. 1997. *Excitable Speech: A Politics of the Performative.* London and New York: Routledge.

Craig Calhoun, ed. 1992. *Habermas and the Public Sphere.* Cambridge: The MIT Press.

Chew, Pat K. 1992. Faculty-Generated Inventions: Who Owns the Golden Egg? *Wisconsin Law Review* 1992: 259–314.

Coombe, Rosemary J. 1998. *The Cultural Life of Intellectual Properties: Authorship, Appropriation, and the Law.* Durham: Duke University Press.

Crang, Mike, and Nigel Thrift, eds. 2000. *Thinking Space.* London and New York: Routledge.

Dueker, Kenneth Sutherlin. 1997. Biobusiness on Campus: Commercialization of University-Developed Biomedical Technologies. *Food and Drug Law Journal* 52: 453–509.

Eisenberg, Rebecca S. 1987. Proprietary Rights and the Norms of Science in Biotechnology. *Yale Law Journal* 97: 177–231.

Feldman, Maryann P., and Maryellen R. Kelley. 2002. How States Augment the Capabilities of Technology Pioneering Firms. *Growth and Change* 33: 173–195.

Fisher, William W. 1999. *The Growth of Intellectual Property: A History of the Ownership of Ideas in the United States.* Available at http://cyber.law.harvard.edu/people/tfisher/ iphistory.pdf (Accessed 24 February 2003).

Foucault, Michel. 1978. *The History of Sexuality: An Introduction Volume I*, trans. Robert Hurley. New York: Vintage Books.

Foucault, Michel. 1980. *Power/Knowledge: Selected Interviews & Other Writings 1972–1977*, ed. Colin Gordon, trans. Colin Gordon, Leo Marshall, John Mepham, and Kate Soper. New York: Pantheon.

Foucault, Michel. 1988. "Technologies of the Self." In *Technologies of the Self: A Seminar with Michel Foucault*, eds. Luther H. Martin, Huck Gutman, and Patrick H. Hutton, 16–49. Amherst: The University of Massachusetts Press.

Fraser, Nancy. 1992. "Rethinking the Public Sphere: A Contribution to the Critique of Actually Existing Democracy." In *Habermas and the Public Sphere*, ed. Craig Calhoun, 109–142. Cambridge: The MIT Press.

Garnham, Nicholas. 1992. "The Media and the Public Sphere." In *Habermas and the Public Sphere*, ed. Craig Calhoun, 359–376. Cambridge: The MIT Press.

Golden, John M. 2001. Biotechnology, Technology Policy, and Patentability: Natural Products and Invention in the American System. *Emory Law Journal* 50: 101–191.

Habermas, Jürgen. 1992. "Further Reflections on the Public Sphere." In *Habermas and the Public Sphere* (trans. Thomas Burger), ed. Craig Calhoun, 421–461. Cambridge: The MIT Press.

Habermas, Jürgen. 1989. *The Structural Transformation of the Public Sphere: An Inquiry into a Category of Bourgeois Society*, trans. Thomas Burger with Frederick Lawrence. Cambridge: The MIT Press.

Hardt, Michael, and Antonio Negri. 2000. *Empire*. Cambridge: Harvard University Press.

Hettinger, Edwin C. 1989. Justifying Intellectual Property. *Philosophy and Public Affairs* 18: 31–52.

Holwick, Scott. 2000. Trade and the Environment: Developing Nations and the Agreement on Trade-Related Aspects of Intellectual-property rights. *Colorado Journal of International Environmental Law and Policy 1999 Yearbook* (2000): 49–75.

Jameson, Fredric, and Masao Miyoshi, eds. 1998. *The Cultures of Globalization*. Durham: Duke University Press.

Jaszi, Peter A. 1996. Goodbye to All That: A Reluctant (and Perhaps Premature) Adieu to a Constitutionally-Grounded Discourse of Public Interest in Copyright Law. *Vanderbilt Journal of Transnational Law* 29: 595–611.

Johnson, Edward R. 2003. The Law Against Sharing Knowledge. *The Chronicle Review* (February 14): B14.

Kelley, Kimberly B., Kimberly Bonner, James S. McMichael, and Neal Pomea. 2002. Intellectual Property, Ownership and Digital Course Materials: A Study of Intellectual Property Policies at Two-and-Four-Year Colleges and Universities. *Portal: Libraries and the Academy* 2: 255–266.

Lessig, Lawrence. 1999. The Law of the Horse: What Cyberlaw Might Teach. *Harvard Law Review* 113: 501–549.

Lessig, Lawrence. 2001. *The Future of Ideas: The Fate of the Commons in a Connected World.* New York: Random House.

Litman, Jessica. 1990. The Public Domain. *Emory Law Journal* 39: 965–1023.

May, Christopher. 2000. *A Global Political Economy of Intellectual-property rights: The New Enclosures?* London and New York: Routledge.

Miyoshi, Masao. 2000. Ivory Tower in Escrow. *boundary* 2: 1–50, 15.

The Nation. 2003. Copyright Monopolies. (February 17): 6–7.

Nottenburg, Carol, Philip G. Pardey, and Brian D. Wright. 2002. Accessing Other People's Technology for Non-profit Research. *The Australian Journal of Agricultural and Resource Economics* 46: 389–416.

Ostergard, Robert L. 1998. Intellectual Property: A Universal Human Right? *Human Rights Quarterly* 21: 156–178.

Packard, Ashley. 2002. Copyright Term Extensions, the Public Domain and Intertextuality Intertwined. *Journal of Intellectual Property Law* 10: 1–32.

Press, Eyal, and Jennifer Washburn. 2000. The Kept University. *The Atlantic Monthly* (March): 39–54.

Readings, Bill. 1996. *The University in Ruins.* Cambridge: Harvard University Press.

Rhoades, Gary. 2001. Whose Property Is It? Negotiating with the University. *Academe: Bulletin of the American Association of University Professors* (September/October): 38–43.

Rhoades, Gary, and Shelia Slaughter. 1997. Academic Capitalism, Managed Professionals, and Supply-Side Higher Education. *Social Text* 15: 9–38.

Slaughter, Sheila. 2001. Professional Values and the Allure of the Market. *Academe: Bulletin of the American Association of University Professors* (September–October): 22–26.

Slaughter, Sheila. 1998. Federal Policy and Supply-Side Institutional Resource Allocation at Public Research Universities. *The Review of Higher Education* 21: 209–244.

Slaughter, Sheila, and Larry L. Leslie. 1997. *Academic Capitalism: Politics, Policies, and the Entrepreneurial University.* Baltimore: The Johns Hopkins University Press.

University of California. 1992. *UC Copyright Policy.* Berkeley: University of California. Available at http://otl.berkeley.edu/inventor/uccopyright.php (Accessed 30 December 2002).

University of California. 1997. *University of California Patent Policy.* Berkeley: University of California. Available at http://otl.berkeley.edu/inventor/ucpatent.php (Accessed 30 December 2002).

University of Michigan. 1996. *Revised Policy on Intellectual Properties: Including Their Disclosure, Commercialization, and Distribution of Revenues from Royalties and Sale of Equity Interests.* Ann Arbor: The University of Michigan. Available at http://www.research.umich,edu/policies/um/ippolicy.html (Accessed 30 December 2002).

University of North Carolina. 2001. *Patent and Copyright Policies.* Chapel Hill: The University of North Carolina. Available at http://northcarolina.edu/aa/departments/research/copyright/copyright.cfm (Accessed 30 December 2002).

University of Virginia. 1998. *Patent Policy.* Charlottesville: The University of Virginia, 1998. Available at http://www.virginia.edu/finance/polproc/pol/xve2.html (Accessed 30 December 2002).

Travis, Hannibal. 2000. Pirates of the Information Infrastructure: Blackstonian Copyright and the First Amendment. *Berkeley Technology Law Journal* 15: 777–864.

Vaughan, Floyd L. 1948. Patent Policy. *The American Economic Review* 38: 215–234.

World Intellectual Property Organization. 2002. *Annual Report 2001.* Geneva: World Intellectual Property Organization.

Chapter 8

The Two-Way Street of Higher Education Commodification

Gary A. Miller

Since World War II and the inception of the Serviceman's Readjustment Act (also known as the G.I. Bill of Rights), there have been dramatic increases in the number of students pursuing postsecondary education.[1] Aronowitz interpreted 1997 data from the National Bureau of Higher Education Statistics to suggest that about half of America's 18-year-olds are enrolling in colleges and universities.[2] With such a large proportion of students opting for postsecondary education, it is no surprise that disagreements over the purposes of higher education continue to be part of our public, political, and institution-specific discourses. Although a variety of perspectives and influences inform those debates, the rise in corporate culture has been among the most pervasive.

In many ways corporate culture and American culture are synonymous. Components as far ranging as popular culture, religious life, the arts, and language are teeming with corporate influence. Tom Pendergast noted that consumption and consumerism are "the very things with which most of those outside the United States identify the nation."[3] This identification is closely tied with the hatred directed toward America from many fundamentalist groups, who view such widespread materialism as an affront to religious beliefs and regional cultures. The Americanization of the global

---

[1] Margaret Barr, Mary K. Desler, and Associates, *The Handbook of Student Affairs Administration* (San Francisco: Josey-Bass Publishers, 2000).

[2] Stanley Aronowitz, *The Knowledge Factory* (Boston: Beacon Press, 2000).

[3] Tom Pendergast, "Consuming Questions: Scholarship on Consumerism in America to 1940," *American Studies International* Vol. 36, No. 2 (1998): 23–44.

culture has understandably lead to backlash. The attacks on the World Trade Center and the Pentagon of September 11, 2001, demonstrate just how extreme the response can be. American materialism, resulting from a corporate culture that seeks to define and redefine individuals and groups as markets, continues to spread throughout the world. A culture of consumerism broadens to other parts of the planet, having already saturated America.

From this perspective, it is not surprising that such materialism can be correlated to an intensified consumerist and careerist perspective informing the purposes of higher education. Whereas Rob Leffel noted that it is not new for universities to respond to the needs of the corporate world,[4] there are clearly valid missions of postsecondary institutions beyond the needs of the market and corporations. Regrettably, institutions of higher education reinforce corporate culture and consumerist viewpoints in numerous ways, including marketing and recruitment strategies, privatization of services and sponsorships, an emphasis on occupational curricula, and market-driven faculty research. The focus on these aspects is often to the detriment of other aspects of the university. It is my intention in this chapter to underscore the relationship between corporate culture and the lives of today's college-age individuals by discussing its effect on college choice, and exploring higher education's complicity in the commodification of higher education.

CORPORATE CULTURE AND THE LIVES OF STUDENTS

Teenagers have a wealth of influences from which they can draw. Family life, religious beliefs, peer groups, schooling, and popular culture are examples, and there is a great deal of interplay in how these components shape attitudes and perceptions. However, an argument can be made that each of these components is heavily predisposed toward a corporate perspective and, when combined, support a process of "consumer socialization."[5] Henry Giroux summarized this experience from another angle in stating, "The only type of citizenship that adult society offers to children is that of consumerism."[6]

Perhaps most subtle, if incompletely defined, is the corporate influence on language. So pervasive is corporate culture and commodification in our society that we typically take for granted the degree to which we use a market vernacular in everyday conversation. If someone tells a story we think false, we might say, "I don't buy that." If we are presented an idea we choose to be-

---

[4]Rob R. Leffel, "Public Policy and the Academy in an Era of Change," *ERIC Documents*, ED432 171 (1999).
[5]Scott Ward, Daniel B. Wackman, and Ellen Wartella, *How Children Learn to Buy* (Beverly Hills: Sage Publications, 1977).
[6]Henry Giroux, *Stealing Innocence* (New York : St. Martin's Press, 2000), 19.

lieve, we say, "I'm sold." We are "taking stock" during contemplative mo-
ments in life. At times we define our very lives as enterprise, telling others to
"mind their *own* business" if they offer unwelcome inquiries into our activities. Phrases such as "thinking outside of the box" seep from the boardroom
to the dining room. Yet, seemingly little research has been dedicated to the
spread of corporate and market language into popular discourse. Although
the topic is valuable and worthy of greater exploration, for our purposes here
it suffices to say such language is both a reflection and a reinforcement of a
consumerist approach to daily life.

Of the many influences an individual may have, chief among them is family life. Parents are typically charged with passing on the values of the family,
which, in the case of American families, are typically the values of a
consumerist society. Ward, Wackman, and Wartella stated that families have
the most notable impact on the consumer behavior development in children
and state that the rampant presence of consumer socialization in families
leads children to "select and interpret various parent behaviors as a basis for
learning" how to be consumers.[7] But, in addition to providing for an environment in which children mirror parental buying strategies, home life itself
can be very businesslike. For example, Charlotte Baecher reports that about
half of nine- to fourteen-year-olds receive some type of allowance. She also
notes that over three fourths of those children are required to perform
household chores as a stipulation of the allowance.[8] Although allowances are
often given under the guise of "responsibility training," Vonda Doss suggested the actual result is often "premature affluence."[9] I might argue with
Doss that in American/corporate culture the term *premature affluence* is
oxymoronic. However, I believe the concept at the heart of her claim, that allowances typically serve not to instill responsibility but rather are effectively
training children to be consumers, is on target. Taking it a step further, I
would suggest that the forms of "responsibility" that parents seek to instill are
actually the corporate definitions thereof. In this context, "responsibility"
means doing your job, following authority, not questioning the power structure, and in doing so, being rewarded financially.

Family systems often share structure with corporations, as well. Roy Kern
and Paul Peluso paralleled families and corporations along a number of
lines.[10] They noted that the corporate chief and head of the household share
similar duties of leadership, tone, and agenda setting. Other family members
take on the role of subordinates and middle managers. The values of the or-

---

[7]Ward, Wackman, and Wartella, 98.
[8]Charlotte Baecher, "Allowances," *Zillions* (1991): 5–7.
[9]Vonda S. Doss, "Middle School Children's Uses of Money," *Journal of Consumer Affairs* 29, no.
1 (1995): 219–241.
[10]Roy M. Kern and Paul Peluso, "Using Individual Psychology Concepts to Compare Family
Systems Process and Organizational Behavior," *Family Journal* 7, no. 3 (1999): 236–245.

ganization are transmitted via company/family atmosphere and rules. Family meetings can mirror staff meetings, and "child training" is correlated to the training of employees. It can subsequently be argued that corporate training begins at home, and then logically continues through the process of schooling and into the workforce.

An individual's spiritual life is not untouched by corporate culture, either. Certainly the rise of so-called mega churches can be correlated to the rise of monolithic corporations that control large segments of a given industry, such as media conglomerates. In 1991 there were six American churches that could claim weekly attendance to Sunday services topping 10,000.[11] In an article published ten years later, *Ebony* details twice that number.[12] Although my line of research does not lead down this path, it would be worthwhile to consider if the influx of mega churches triggers smaller churches to cease operations in the same way that the arrival of a Wal-Mart often means death for many small-business owners. A microlevel example of corporate life infecting the spiritual realm can be found at Brentwood Baptist Church in Houston, Texas. In May 1999, the church installed a McDonald's fast-food restaurant in its new $7 million Joe Ratliff Lifelong Learning Center, and have gone so far as to include drive-through service. The action was defended as an example of the church's outreach and service to the community.[13]

There are other examples of organized religion's similarities to the corporate world that bear mention here. The commercialization of religious holidays, most obviously Christmas, clearly supports the assertion that spirituality and consumerism can be closely tied. The frequency with which we read reports concerning fraud and embezzlement in religious organizations can be aptly compared to corporate scandals of the same nature. Indeed, Brian Kluth, president of the Christian Stewardship Association, pointed out "there are 2,350 passages in the Bible dealing with money and material possessions."[14]

Just as many religious texts speak of an afterlife, Peter Stromberg spoke of Elvis Presley's symbolic life after death. Stromberg argued that Elvis worship typifies a consumerism-as-escapism ideology offered by popular culture. The central tenet of this ideology is "the belief that the mundane existence of the day-to-day life of the believer is not the ultimate reality.... The believer encounters evidence of this second world countless time each day: in advertisements, in movies, in television programs, and in magazines."[15] Although popular culture's allure might be tied to escapism, there is no escaping that

---

[11]"Counting the Congregation," *The Economist* 319, no. 7711 (1991): 27.
[12]"The New Mega Churches," *Ebony* 57, no. 2 (2001): 148.
[13]Lloyd Gite, "McDonald's Goes to Church," *Black Enterprise* 32, no. 2 (2001), 24.
[14]Melynda Wilcox, "On a Shoestring and a Prayer," *Kiplinger's Personal Finance Magazine* (1999), 99.
[15]Peter Stromberg, "Elvis Alive? The Ideology of American Consumerism," *Journal of Popular Culture* 24, no. 3 (1990), 11.

American popular culture offers little that cannot be tied to consumerism, commodification, and corporate culture. As such, I do not belabor the point here. But, by sheer volume of influence through television, toys, music, movies, and more, popular culture trains our citizens that consumerism, choices, and daily life are inextricably linked. Leming noted that "nearly half of the adolescent's waking hours involve music or visual media as either foreground or background."[16] This means corporations have a direct pipeline to adolescents through which marketing messages can be funneled for a significant portion of each day.

Similarly, compulsory education occupies large portions of adolescents' waking hours. Experience in the K–12 education system is an obvious influence on college choice and expectations of postsecondary education, and I submit the K–12 experience supports a consumerist and careerist approach to life. Deron Boyles noted that too often within the educational system the purpose of schooling is defined by the need to "prepare students to compete in the world marketplace" and "supply businesses with qualified workers."[17] Boyles suggested that the corporate approach to education with its emphasis on discipline and accountability can actually have the opposite outcome, leading to passivity, which leaves students underprepared for life outside of the classroom. Democratic schooling, he argued, is more likely to bring about classroom participation, which can contribute to innovative thinking and authentic participation in both the workplace and the larger society. Corporate schooling, lacking such authentic participation, endangers democracy.[18]

Kenneth Saltman's book *Collateral Damage* distills that sentiment in its subtitle, "Corporatizing Public Schools—A Threat to Democracy." In this text, Saltman contended conservatives and neoliberals have successfully redefined the common good as synonymous with corporate good. Under this rubric, schooling is useful only as it benefits economic prosperity.[19] According to Saltman, the K–12 educational system serves to support an "upward redistribution of wealth" and attacks democracy by redefining the roles of the individual, the school system, and knowledge itself. He said:

> Citizenship becomes defined by an anticritical following of authority, knowledge becomes mistakenly presented as value-free units to be deposited, schooling models the new social logic that emphasizes social mobility rather than social transformation—namely it perceives society as a flawed yet unchangeable situation into which individuals should seek assimilation.[20]

---

[16] James S. Leming, "Rock Music and the Socialization of Moral Values in Early Adolescence," *Youth and Society* 18, no. 4 (1987): 363–383.

[17] Deron R. Boyles, "The Corporate Takeover of American Schools," *The Humanist* (1995), 20 and 23.

[18] *Ibid.*

[19] Kenneth J. Saltman, *Collateral Damage* (Lanham, MD: Rowman and Littlefield Publishers, Inc., 2000).

[20] *Ibid*, 82.

For however true we may have believed it previously, primary and secondary schools are no longer a place meant to develop a democratic citizenry. Too often schools serve as a factory to produce workers or as just another marketing or investment opportunity. From advertisements on buses and the installation of fast-food restaurants in school cafeterias to "Coke in Education Day," "Nike Week," and teaching materials sponsored by Exxon and Dow Chemicals, students from pre-kindergarten to postsecondary are bombarded with a directive to consume.[21]

It is not my intention here to argue that the sole purpose of schooling, either K–12 or postsecondary, is to foster democratic citizenry. Debates on the purposes of schooling are varied, numerous, and as urgent as ever. But, such debates, although certainly connected to the thesis of this chapter, are too lengthy in scope to be dealt with in detail here. However, Boyles, Saltman, Giroux and others correctly record that corporate culture presides over American educational systems. It is this point I carry into the following arguments.

COLLEGE CHOICE AS A CONSUMER

Given the full immersion in consumer culture experienced by American students, a careerist/consumerist approach to the decision to pursue postsecondary education should come as no surprise. A study by Jane Hemsley-Brown indicates that students display standard characteristics of consumer behavior when researching and making college choices, and those behaviors are heavily influenced by social and cultural factors. Her research shows that, by the age of fourteen, most students have developed bias toward or against certain schooling options and that these predispositions were formed "within the context of the family and among peers."[22]

In describing the careerist/consumerist approach, John W. Moore noted that students, as well as parents and administrators, view higher education as follows:

> [Higher education is] merely a way to enhance personal prosperity. How often have you heard the statistic that a college education pays for itself through increased earning power, even if it costs $20,000–$30,000 per year? Investing in education pays off just as investing in the stock market does, provided you wait long enough. Attending a better school gets you a better job and a better income. In other words, a certified level of education is a commodity—something that is useful and can be turned into commercial advantage.[23]

[21]Henry A. Giroux, "Education Incorporated," *Educational Leadership* 56, no. 2 (1998): 12–17.

[22]Jane Hemsley-Brown, "College Choice: Perceptions and Priorities," *Educational Management and Administration* 27, no. 1 (1999): 85–98.

[23]John W. Moore, "Education: Commodity, Come-On, or Commitment?," *Journal of Chemical Education* 77, no. 7 (2000), 805.

Family members interviewed by Patricia McDonough expressed this sentiment repeatedly. Parents articulated a desire for their children to "do better than we did" and "be successful," and those interviewed also used a more veiled language regarding applying to schools with high levels of "prestige."[24] This prestige factor is connected to what James Hearn described as "institutional stratification" in American postsecondary education in which status and resources are inversely proportional to the schools' "level of openness to the masses."[25] Hearn pointed to studies by Sewell and Solomon to suggest the strata in which a school lays helps determine the socioeconomic attainments of students attending, and used works by Trow to note this creates a system in which "advantage begets advantage."[26] The college applicant-as-consumer literally hopes to "buy into" this system of advantage.

From the perspective of a consumer, choosing a college is a major purchase. When making major purchases, like buying a home, individuals typically require some form of professional assistance. So, it is no surprise that a cottage industry has developed around college choice and admissions. The combination of college recruitment and marketing efforts and increased competition to enroll in the "right" college has prompted students, primarily those of a higher socioeconomic standing, to seek assistance beyond the services offered by their high school guidance counselor. From college guidebooks and SAT preparation to essay-writing assistance and private counselors, for many businesses and entrepreneurs a new market has been created. Patricia McDonough described this new market as populated with a new social construct called "the college applicant."[27] Perhaps most notable among the different products and services being offered to this market are those of admissions/educational consultants. In the late 1980s, the *Wall Street Journal* called such consultants the "new growth industry of higher education."[28] These consultants complete the analogy of "college choice-as-home buying" by taking on the role of realtor, providing information, guiding expectations, assisting with paperwork, and eventually helping "close the deal" for another consumer hoping to purchase part of the American dream.

---

[24] Patricia M. McDonough, *Choosing Colleges* (New York: State University of New York Press, 1997).

[25] James C. Hearn, "Academic and Nonacademic Influences on the College Destinations of 1980 High School Graduates," *Sociology of Education* 64, no. 3 (July, 1991) pp. 158–171. See also W. H. Sewell, "Inequality of Opportunity for Higher Education," *American Sociological Review* 36 (1971): 793–809; L. Solomon, "The Definition of College Quality and Its Impact on Earnings," *Explorations in Economic Research* 2 (1975): 537–587; and M. A. Trow, "The Analysis of Status," in *Perspectives on Higher Education: Eight Disciplinary and Comparative Views* edited by Burton Clark (Berkeley: University of California Press, 1984).

[26] *Ibid.*

[27] Patricia M. McDonough, "Buying and Selling Higher Education," *Journal of Higher Education* 65, no. 4 (1994) Electronic document retrieved via JStor Database 7/17/2002.

[28] E. G. Gottschalk, "Better Odds? Parents Hire Advisers to Help Children Get Into College," *Wall Street Journal* (7 November 1986), 33.

But, in addition to the social-mobility expectations of the average college "shopper," newer consumerist demands are appearing. John Sutter, residence hall director at Purdue University, said parents are suggesting, "if they're going to spend big bucks, they want to see what they're going to get for their money."[29] But, it's not libraries, classrooms, or research facilities that are of particular concern to the parents in Sutter's experience. Fast-food outlets, cable television, indoor pools, gyms, and in-room movies are the amenities sought.

"For a lot of students, the academic program is not their top priority," said Peg Layton, another housing officer.[30] But fingers cannot wag solely at the students and parents who seek these amenities. Universities and colleges have gone beyond simply "caving in" to consumer demands and are actively providing and promoting such conveniences as an intrinsic part of campus, and some have seemingly lost sight of common sense in the process. For example, Kenyon College, which requires all students to purchase a university meal plan, apparently sees no rupture in logic when spending $100,000 to add kitchens to three of its residence halls.[31] It is from this point that we move into discussion of the ways in which institutions of higher education play active roles in fostering consumerism and the commodification of education.

HIGHER EDUCATION'S COMPLICITY IN COMMODIFICATION: MARKETING AND RECRUITING

Sheila Slaughter and Larry Leslie described market-related activities in higher education as *academic capitalism*.[32] Their use of this term encompasses an array of activities such as market-driven research, corporate partnerships, spin-off companies, endowments, service privatization, and similar dealings. Here I have chosen to focus on the areas of academic capitalism that relate most closely to students and college choice, primarily marketing and recruitment strategies, playing the "rankings game," privatization of services, and the vocationalization of the curriculum (and market-related research as it relates to the curriculum). Certainly in-depth work could be done on each of these topics. Length dictates they be given a survey treatment, with the focus on connecting these activities to higher education's complicity in its own commodification.

Admissions officers use the term *admissions funnel* to describe the process by which prospective students become inquiries, inquiries become applicants, applicants become accepted students, and accepted students become

[29]"Colleges Lure Students with Post Amenities," *Christian Science Monitor* 87, no. 191 (1995), 13.
[30]*Ibid.*
[31]*Ibid.*
[32]Sheila Slaughter and Larry Leslie, *Academic Capitalism* (Baltimore, MD: Johns Hopkins University Press, 1997).

enrolled students. This is not a new concept. However, what has changed is the growth in use of marketing programs to increase the number of students going through the funnel, and the way in which these efforts reinforce the consumer/careerist approach that students bring to the process of choosing a college.

Interwoven with this new reliance on marketing is the redefinition of students as customers and education as a product.[33] But rather than redefining with reluctance, schools have accepted this change with aplomb, undertaking market research, branding, and positioning themselves against competitors. Berger and Wallingford, who are in favor of institutions honing their marketing skills toward this end, summarized the willingness of postsecondary education to undertake such marketing. They note, "institutions have finally recognized that different colleges and universities have different target markets."[34] Others have noted that, "it has long been considered improper to think of an institution of higher education as a business, but the cold hard facts are that this has become a necessity" and thusly called for seizing the "opportunity to sell to the customer" through marketing strategy.[35]

Studies have shown that university promotional materials rank high among influencing factors in the choosing of colleges,[36] which leads one author to note "there appears to be a great need to influence students' choice by improving the promotional materials they and their parents receive."[37] Although attempts to attract students are not intrinsically corporate, the manner by which large numbers of institutions have carried out this effort is cause for concern. Focus groups, for example, are used by marketers to identify trends and learn about consumer viewpoints. Armstrong and Lumsden argue that more work of this nature should be done in directing college recruitment materials.[38] However, given the careerist/consumerist perspective that students bring to the process of choosing a college, the use of focus groups to alter recruitment materials would likely lead to further reinforcing the commodification of higher education.

---

[33] Karen A. Berger and Harlan P. Wallingford, "Developing Advertising and Promotion Strategies for Higher Education," *Journal of Marketing for Higher Education* 7, no. 4 (1996): 61–72.

[34] *Ibid*, 63.

[35] Deborah E. Rosen, James. M. Curran, and Timothy B. Greenlee, "College Choice in a Brand Elimination Framework: The Administrator's Perspective," *Journal of Marketing for Higher Education* 8, no. 4 (1998): 67–81.

[36] Studies include those by the Carnegie Foundation for the Advancement of Teaching as reported in the January/February 1986 edition of *Change*, C. Anderson in *College and University* Vol. 70, No. 38.

[37] Jami Armstrong and D. Barry Lumsden, "Impact of Universities' Promotional Materials on College Choice," *Journal of Marketing for Higher Education* 9, no. 2 (1999): 83–91.

[38] *Ibid*, 85.

THE RANKINGS GAME

University rankings, such as those done by *U.S. News and World Report*, the *Princeton Review*, and others, are frequently part of a school's recruitment efforts. For some, such as Yale and Harvard, the rankings serve to reinforce the prestige associated with the school. For others, the strain to increase rankings can drive not only marketing efforts, but actual admissions criteria for the institution. Even those who profess disdain for the rankings still find themselves playing the rankings game. A case in point involves Michael McPherson, president of Macalester College, which is affiliated with the Presbyterian Church. When Macalester College was ranked by the *Princeton Review* as the number one institution "where students ignore God on a regular basis," McPherson sent an e-mail to a school dean suggesting they encourage some of their more-devout students to fill out the *Princeton Review*'s survey.[39] The plan backfired when word of his request spread across campus and accusations of impropriety were made. In response to the accusations, McPherson retracted the idea and stated his actions were hastily undertaken. However, his post-retraction comments show signs of sour grapes. "The survey is nonsense," he said. "The idea that they can tell exactly which school is the fifth-least religious or the seventh-least religious is completely absurd, and they should be ashamed."[40]

Although there are certainly ethical considerations involved, my point is not to argue that McPherson was morally wrong in his attempt to alter the ranking of Macalester College. To do so would give legitimacy to what I feel is already a problematic and hollow rankings industry. Rather, McPherson's example shows us that even those who may reject the systems still find themselves playing the game, as the rankings are prominent in the eyes of many potential students and their families. Bill McClintock, vice president of the National Association for College Admissions counselors, noted that he "probably spends as much time debunking the rankings as I do on quality family counseling."[41] The popularity of these rankings is reflected in the high sales of the *U.S. News and World Reports* rankings issue and the expanded college-ranking supplement section.[42] But, for an example of just how meaningless such listings can be, consider the *U.S. News and World Report*'s pattern of ranking of the undergraduate e-commerce program at Georgia State University. The farce here is that Georgia State University does not have, nor have they ever had, an under-

---

[39] Dana Mulhauser, "Thou Shalt Not Manipulate Data," *Chronicle of Higher Education* 48, no. 16 (14 December 2001): A8.
[40] *Ibid.*
[41] Jeanne Ponessa, "College Rankings Rankle Counselors, admissions officers," *Education Week* 15, no. 12 (1995), 5.
[42] James Monks and Ronald G. Ehrenberg, "U.S. News and World Report's College Rankings. Why Do They Matter?" *Change* 31, no. 6 (1999): 42–52.

graduate e-commerce program. This has not, however, kept said program from being highly ranked for the past several years. Nor has it kept the institution from including the ranking in their promotional materials.

Studies on just how much power such rankings hold have not been conclusive. Some have reflected the rankings as "very helpful" in assisting students in evaluating prospective colleges. Others have found they hold less influence over college choice.[43] Regardless of how much they are relied on or disregarded by future college students, one must question the degree to which universities are willing to support what is essentially a means to sell magazines, reports, and guide books.

PRIVATIZATION AND COMMERCIALIZATION OF CAMPUS

Rankings, of course, are not the only "selling point" used by higher education to lure students. Increasingly, schools are focusing on amenities not related to education to appeal to the student-as-consumer. As noted earlier in the chapter, prospective students are not simply looking for the best match for their academic interests when searching for a college, and for the most part they are finding that schools are trying to meet their demands. Non-academic services and conveniences ranging from the addition of cable television to dorm rooms up to on-campus restaurants with room service are being added and lauded as meeting the "needs" of the customer. Frequently universities promote these luxuries in attempts to differentiate from other schools. Ashland University, for example, after winning a national prize for best college food service in 1992, sent approximately 20,000 chocolate-chip cookies to high school seniors and invited them to tour campus and take in a free lunch.[44] In that they are both forms of marketing, it is a philosophically short distance from enticing students by sending cookies to offering coupons and discounts. Perhaps future college students can look forward to receiving university junk mail advertising 20 percent off all liberal arts programs or promising that the first 100 callers to enroll will also receive a free super-shammy. As exaggerated as these examples are, they help shed light on the larger issues surrounding the perceptions that marketing and recruitment materials can foster. Using such amenities as selling points might draw the attention of students to a given school. But, it does so in a manner that supports the commodification of higher education and the devaluing of other aspects of the institution.

Going beyond the marketing of consumer-driven services, the outsourcing of various segments of the university to private corporations con-

---

[43] *Ibid.* Referencing a study by the Art and Science Group and a nationwide poll by the *New York Times*.

[44] H. Collingwood, "A Syllabus You Can Sink Your Teeth Into," *Business Week* No. 3256 (1992): 48.

tributes to what I have chosen to call the "strip malling" of postsecondary campuses. The Ivory Tower, it would seem, is being bulldozed to make room for the Ivory Foodcourt, Ivory Gameroom, and Ivory Giftshop. From food services to campus bookstores to maintenance and janitorial services, universities are increasingly contracting out services and departments.

The privatization of bookstores is one of the most rapidly growing examples of corporate outsourcing on college campuses. In 1998 there were 915 contract-managed campus bookstores in the United States. One year later, there were 1,250.[45] Citing a need for increased revenues due to budget restrictions, campus bookstores changed motive from "break even" to "make profit" in the 1970s, noted Kenneth Bowers, director of the university-run bookstore at the University of California at Santa Barbara.[46] So, whereas proponents say partnering with large corporations such as Barnes and Noble and Follett generates revenue and allows the store to be run by a "specialist," others correctly note that the goals of a private corporation typically do not match the traditional goals many have for higher education.

Food services are perhaps the most visible area on American campuses that are succumbing to the trend of corporate outsourcing. Although it can be difficult to argue that universities are better able to provide food services than corporations such as Marriot International or Versa Services, the greater issue is the perception that the university campus shares as many similarities as differences with the average shopping center. As our campuses "grow" to include national restaurant chains such as Pizza Hut and Subway, the quads and student centers become just one more "branded" location for students to consume food of questionable nutritional value.

Soft-drink partnerships in higher education are a closely related concern. The recent landslide of campus "pouring rights" has large numbers of universities choosing their poison: Pepsi or Coke. These deals typically involve exclusive rights for the drink manufacturer in all campus restaurants, vending machines, and snack bars, and include large sums of money for the institutions. For instance, in 1998 the University of Maryland signed a fifteen-year deal with Pepsi that procured $58 million for the university.[47] Public Enterprise, Inc. is a company that helps broker such deals. Their president, Steve Hudson, stated, "It's a win-win for both parties. Domestically, Coke and Pepsi face a marketplace that is not growing from a new-user standpoint. Their objective is to help solidify their brand with students. Meanwhile, what the university is looking for is an opportunity to create some revenue."[48] Of course,

---

[45] John L. Pulley, "Whose Bookstore Is it, Anyway?," *Chronicle of Higher Education* 46, no. 22 (4 February 2000): A41–A42.
[46] *Ibid.*
[47] Jon Marcus, "Coke or Pepsi? U.S. Universities Choose Their Sponsor," *Times Higher Education Supplement* Issue 1386 (28 May 1999): 12–17.
[48] *Ibid.*

as an advocate, Hudson did not comment on the negative factors that have been associated with such deals. These factors include reports of notable price increases, cries regarding loss of choice, and most important, blatant commercialism on campus.[49]

When it comes to fostering brand loyalty, cola companies do not begin with higher education, however. A well-publicized commotion developed around an incident in 1998 called "Coke in Education Day." Pitted in competition against other schools in their district for a $500 prize, Greenbrier High School in Georgia became a Coca-Cola propaganda machine for a day. Activities included discussing the chemical composition of the beverage in science classes, speeches from company administrators, and a giant Coke pep rally that involved the entire student body forming letters to spell the company name for a photograph.[50] The media uproar surrounding this situation was not in regard to the level of distaste related to such an obvious corporate invasion of a public school, but rather centered on two students who chose to wear T-shirts with the logo of another soda manufacturer. Unsettling is the notion that the rebelling students thought only to promote a competing corporation as means of defiance and expression of individualism. More unsettling is the response by school administrators-come-corporate pawns. The students were suspended.

That the large majority of students at Greenbrier High School did not rebel against Coke Day would be more unsettling were it not for the fact that their lives, like the lives of the large majority of adolescents in America, are replete with such corporate mingling. As such, the transition from high school "Coke in Education Day" programs to exclusive pouring rights on university campuses does not seem odd or inappropriate to most students. It is simply a continuation of the corporate presence in their lives. It also indicates that the students' experiences in all facets of higher education can be reified toward consumerism. They move easily from consuming in campus bookstores and restaurants to consuming in the classroom. So, although the addition of corporate brands to campus may not seem illogical to students, the addition of these businesses to our landscape reinforces the student-as-consumer pattern.

CURRICULUM ISSUES AND MARKET-RELATED RESEARCH

In a primarily pro-privatization article in the *Chronicle of Higher Education*, Joyce Mercer reported an unnamed higher education official to say the "day is coming that there will be almost no limit to what a campus will con-

---

[49] *Ibid.*
[50] Saltman, 57.

sider privatizing."[51] One does wonder if that lack of limit extends to faculty, research, and curricula, and that thought is perhaps not as rhetorical as many would prefer. Scientific research performed at universities has historically been somewhat reflective of the needs and interests of society. For instance, the mid-twentieth century "race to the moon" focused large numbers of researchers on that goal and concerted efforts were made to steer students toward the study of mathematics and science. And, in the last quarter of the twentieth century university research was increasingly commercialized "in response to pressures from globalization of the political economy, changes in national higher education policy, and resource dependence."[52]

In the 1980s, for example, government and industry sought public–private partnerships to aid in restoring the lagging economy.[53] In particular, Lynton and Elman point out that university research was viewed as a commodity that should be actively circulated outside the walls of higher education and put to use in the marketplace.[54] Market-oriented research is clearly a topic that has considerable breadth and depth. For the purposes of this chapter, I prefer to connect it only to curriculum issues and program emphases, as they most strongly correlate to students' college choice and the careerist perspective therein.

The focus of research efforts on those areas that most benefit economic prosperity typically includes applying greater resources toward that end. If the purpose of this increase in focus is to boost economic development related to a given discipline, then it follows that opportunities and growth in the job market associated with that discipline can occur. Case in point is the rise of the "dot com" industry in the 1990s. That decade saw rapid expansion in the technology related to computing and the Internet, with much of this growth emanating from college campuses across the globe. This fueled not only the private industries connected to the technology, but also the degree programs offered and emphasized by institutions. Computer science and computer information systems programs multiplied and universities began to offer coursework and degrees in electronic commerce, which attracted, and still draws, notable numbers of students.[55] An increase in students pursuing such programs equates to an increase in department credit hours, which typically increases funding. A cycle is created that serves to re-

---

[51] Joyce Mercer, "Contracting Out," *Chronicle of Higher Education* 41, no. 43 (7 July 1995), A37–A38.

[52] Slaughter and Leslie, 1997.

[53] James Fairweather, "Academic Research and Instruction: The Industrial Connection," *Journal of Higher Education* 60, no. 4 (1989): 388–407.

[54] Earnest A. Lynton and Sandra E. Elman, *New Priorities for the University* (San Francisco: Jossey-Bass, 1987).

[55] Much of this commentary is based on my own experiences as an academic advisor in a college of business during the latter portion of the dot-com boom.

inforce the commodification of higher education in the minds of students. Higher education institutions assist in the growth of an industry; programs develop and expand related to the field; institutions promote and market those programs; and ultimately schools shoulder responsibility of training individuals to staff the growing industry.

Business programs, of course, are perhaps the easiest to connect to a careerist perspective on higher education. One would be hard-pressed to locate an undergraduate business student who had chosen such a program for purposes other than career development. But, the so-called "executive education" programs are among the most blatant examples of institution-led careerism in higher education and have risen in popularity. Executive MBA (master of business administration) programs shape their business curriculum to corporate executives' schedules and training needs, but do so for a hefty price tag. For example, in 1999 *Business Week* reported tuition for the executive MBA at the Wharton School at Pennsylvania at $92,400. In that same report, the twenty schools featured cost on average $57,270.[56] The Graduate Management Admissions Council reported that "over half (56 percent) of the Executive programs indicated an increase in enrollment over last year."[57] Rotating 180 philosophical degrees from executive programs, the development of business courses at liberal arts colleges since the 1980s shows just how widespread the call for business education has become. Wesleyan University, for example, introduced its first accounting course in 1985 after 153 years of maintaining a pure liberal arts focus.[58]

I do not mean to suggest that students attending higher education should do so without merging their higher education experiences into their career. Clearly, higher education provides an opportunity for individuals to guide themselves into future occupations. As stated by Linda Ray Pratt, "Of course students need to be prepared for employment, and the United States needs to compete in a world market. From the earliest founding of our universities, vocation and civic instruction was *part* of the mission" (emphasis added).[59] However, suggested here is the commodification of higher education as primarily a means to a careerist end, has devalued other aspects of the institution. As Aronowitz noted, "There is not much evidence of real learning taking place at most postsecondary institutions, if by that we mean the pro-

---

[56] Retrieved from <http://www.businessweek.com/1999/99_42/b3651032.htm> on August 10, 2002.
[57] Retrieved from <http://www.gmac.com/research/Surveys/enrollment/enrollment_trends_survey_2001.shtml#Executive> on August 10, 2002 .
[58] Barbara Ann Scott, "The 'New Practicality' Revisited: Changes in the American College Curriculum," *Journal of Education* 174, no. 1 (1992): 87-104.
[59] Linda Ray Pratt, "Giving Higher Education 'the Business'," *Education Digest* 60, no. 5 (1995), 18.

cess by which a student is motivated to participate in, even challenge, established intellectual authority."[60]

CLOSING

Although those words by Aronowitz brutalize the efforts of many in higher education, it is neither his argument nor mine that redemption is unattainable. He notes,

> Notwithstanding their anxiety about the future, students are ill-served by educational regimes that tailor their learning to a rapidly changing workplace whose technological shifts belie the assumptions driving many specialist curricula. Ironically, the best preparation for the work of the future might be to cultivate knowledge of the broadest possible kind to make learning a way of life that in the first place is pleasurable and then rigorously critical. For it is only when the learner loves literature, enjoys puzzling out the meaning of art works and those of philosophy, is intrigued by social and cultural theory, or becomes an indefatigable researcher that she acquires intellectual habits that are the precondition for further learning. The learner who really understands the economy knows how fragile is the concept of career.[61]

Here Aronowitz argued against a specialized vocational approach to higher education. However, by offering a different approach but still relying on its relationship to work and career, the argument appears to be weakened. Although we might better persuade those with a careerist outlook to consider different perspectives by using the vernacular of occupation, I posit that an additional step needs to be taken—moving beyond the language of economics in defining higher education simply as it relates to the world of work.[62]

As noted at the beginning of this chapter, the debates on the purpose of higher education are ongoing, although as argued, the consumer approach is deeply entrenched. Gerald Bracey accurately summarized this argument by noting that the debates on purpose have been "overwhelmed by a recent shift to a single-minded view about education: Education is about jobs."[63] I have described here some of the ways institutions of higher education reinforce student consumerism, which supports a view of postsecondary education as a product to be bought and sold for purposes of procuring a job. I

---

[60] Aronowitz, 2000, 143.

[61] *Ibid.*, 161.

[62] By using Aronowitz here, I mean only to demonstrate how even those who argue against a careerist approach to higher education are sometimes tied to vocationalist language. I do not mean to imply that Aronowitz himself never moves beyond such career-based arguments.

[63] Gerald W. Bracey, *The War Against American's Public Schools. Privatizing Schools, Commercializing Education* (Boston: Allyn and Bacon, 2002).

argue, however, that higher education can and should exist for reasons other than career training. Furthermore, I claim it already does.

The challenge for higher education is to champion those "other reasons" in the face of vast numbers of opposing views. Michael McPherson addressed this challenge when he stated, "Educators may feel sure that the value of education cannot be reduced to financial calculations alone, but if they are to make a convincing case ... of the 'non-economic' dimensions of higher education in this environment, they will need to be unusually persuasive."[64] However difficult it may be, undertaking this challenge is necessary for what Frank Newman called "saving higher education's soul."[65] Newman noted that the changes that have taken place in higher education have put the institution in danger of losing important characteristics, including taking a long-term view of student needs rather than simply serving immediate career goals, and emphasizing "learning and scholarship apart from maximizing revenue streams."[66]

In 1966, Raths, Harmin, and Simon outlined three stages of the valuing process: choosing values, prizing them, and acting on them.[67] Consider some of those "important characteristics." Although they are numerous, I would like to highlight three areas in particular: service to the community, providing a setting for personal development, and offering a forum for critical thinking and debating ideas.

Edward Zlotkowski defined service learning as "meaningful community service that is linked to students' academic experience through related course materials and reflective activities" and notes that service learning "creates a bridge to knowledge as civic responsibility and public work."[68] Service learning can assist in engaging students in the problems of their immediate community as active participants.[69] Service learning should be undertaken with the goal to give students insights into current social problems, "the contribution they, as individuals, might make to solving those problems and their responsibilities as citizens."[70]

Service learning can also help students to place themselves in context with the local community and can lead to healthy efforts to work with the commu-

---

[64]Michael McPherson, "Value Conflicts in American Higher Education: A Survey," *Journal of Higher Education* 54, no. 3 (1983), 244–245.

[65]Frank Newman, "Saving Higher Education's Soul," *Change* 33, no. 5 (2000), 16.

[66]*Ibid.*, 16.

[67]Louis E. Raths, Merril Harmin, and Sidney B. Simon, *Values and Teaching: Working with Values in the Classroom* (Columbus, OH: Merrill, 1966).

[68]Edward Zlotkowski, from *A New Model of Excellence*, as quoted in Maureen Burrows, Sheila Chauvin, Cathy Lazarus, and Peggy Chehardy, "Required Service Learning for Medical Students: Program Description and Student Response," *Teaching and Learning in Medicine* 11, no. 4 (1999), 9.

[69]John Mohan, "Thinking Local: Service-Learning, Education for Citizenship and Geography," *Journal of Geography in Higher Education* 19, no. 2 (1995): 129–143.

[70]*Ibid.*, 129.

nity to address issues of concern. Service-learning programs should carefully consider their approach to such interaction and strive to avoid playing the role of "community savior." Doing so is condescending to community members and alters student participants' vision of themselves in the related context. As noted earlier, a careerist approach to education can lead to passivity. Stewart Page pointed out that "vocationalism emphasizes the general value system of competition, but in the process de-emphasizes the general value system of cooperation. It emphasizes values devoted large to me-ism and caring about one's self, and de-emphasizes values devoted largely to caring about others."[71] Service learning can help alter this vision. "As a place of thought, the university would re-articulate the relation between educational practice and the social life of our communities, particularly so as to enhance the prospects for such ideals as democracy."[72]

However, higher education can also be a place of self-discovery, and providing opportunity for growth and development is another aspect of higher education that should be lauded in these times of careerism. In reviewing empirical research from 1973 through 1987 on student development, Frederick Thrasher and Paul Bloland found that students who participate in campus programs designed to foster personal development scored higher on self-concept, autonomy, mature lifestyle plans, interdependence, and college satisfaction scales. They also note that students participating in such courses of similar design showed increases in cognitive complexity and increased in sense of purpose and educational plans.[73] The challenge for postsecondary institutions is to better integrate programs intended to foster student development into the core of the higher education experience and coordinate efforts to provide a more coherent plan for these activities.

Critical thinking is a concept often bandied about during arguments surrounding the purpose of higher education and is lacking singular definition. For the purposes of this chapter, I use the term corresponding to what Aronowitz calls *critical appropriation*. By this he meant "the process by which students acquire the means to challenge—if not reverse—the technical divisions that fragment society as well as the higher learning, and perhaps most important, by which they are encouraged to become critical intellectuals prepared to swim against the current."[74] Preparing students not only to un-

---

[71] Stewart Page, "Students and Humane Values in a Competitive World," *Guidance and Counseling* 12, no. 1 (1996), 15.

[72] Roger I. Simon, "The University: A Place to Think?" in Henry A. Giroux and Kostas Myrsiades (Eds.) *Beyond the Corporate University* (Lanham, MD: Rowman and Littlefield Publishers, Inc., 2001).

[73] Frederick Thrasher and Paul Bloland, "Student Development Studies: A Review of Published Empirical Research, 1973–1987," *Journal of Counseling and Development* 67 (1989): 547–554.

[74] Aronowitz, 126.

derstand a given concept, but also to synthesize, challenge, and debate concepts should be a primary goal of higher education.

The free and open debate of ideas is, for me, perhaps the primary function of higher education. Such debate is the wellspring of democracy. The goal of higher education should not simply be to train workers to fill the halls of corporate America, but rather to educate individuals to critique and change not only corporate America, but society itself. Saltman put it this way: "Rather than teaching students to be citizens concerned with the well-being of others and the development of radically democratic communities" our educational systems train students to be consumers.[75] Although I am not confident, as Saltman appears to imply, that our educational systems have ever actually functioned under his preferred rubric, I concur with his sentiment that corporate-driven education systems present students with "a singular vision of the future and a singular set of values—namely, faith in capitalism. When this happens, there is nothing left to discuss. Authority becomes unquestionable, and dissent, the lifeblood of democracy, appears as disruption and threat."[76]

Higher education must strive to reduce complicity in the commodification of education. It is not my argument that there is no place in higher education for students to parlay educational experience into a career, and it is not my contention that postsecondary education should function only as an Ivory Tower cut off from greater society. Rather, the converse is being suggested. Leaders in higher education must take steps to avoid becoming passive participants in the corporatizing of schooling. Those in university life must redefine the role of the institution in society. Let the debates continue and the struggles over purpose rage, because the struggle for education is, indeed, part of the struggle to define and improve culture.

REFERENCES

Armstrong, Jamiand Lumsden, D. Barry. 1999. Impact of Universities' Promotional Materials on College Choice. *Journal of Marketing for Higher Education* 9, no. 2: 83–91.

Aronowitz, Stanley. 2000. *The Knowledge Factory.* Boston: Beacon Press.

Baecher, Charlotte. 1991. Allowances. *Zillions:* 5–7.

Barr, Margaret, Mary K. Desler, and Associates. 2000. *The Handbook of Student Affairs Administration.* San Francisco: Jossey-Bass Publishers.

Berger, Karen A., and Harlan P. Wallingford. 1996. Developing Advertising and Promotion Strategies for Higher Education. *Journal of Marketing for Higher Education* 7, no. 4: 61–72.

---

[75] Saltman, x.
[76] *Ibid.*, ix.

Boyles, Deron R. The Corporate Takeover of American Schools. *The Humanist* (1995): 20–24.

Bracey, Gerald W. 2002. *The War Against American's Public Schools. Privatizing Schools, Commercializing Education.* Boston: Allyn and Bacon.

Collingwood, H. 1992. A Syllabus You Can Sink Your Teeth Into. *Business Week* No. 3256: 48.

Doss, Vonda S. 1995. Middle School Children's Uses of Money. *Journal of Consumer Affairs* 29, no. 1: 219–241.

Fairweather, James. 1989. Academic Research and Instruction: The Industrial Connection. *Journal of Higher Education* 60, no. 4: 388–407.

Giroux, Henry A. 1998. Education Incorporated. *Educational Leadership* 56, no. 2: 12–17.

Giroux, Henry. 2000. *Stealing Innocence.* New York: St. Martin's Press.

Gite, Lloyd. 2001. McDonald's Goes to Church. *Black Enterprise* 32, no. 2: 24.

Gottschalk, E. G. 1986. Better Odds? Parents Hire Advisers to Help Children Get Into College. *Wall Street Journal* (7 November): 33.

Hearn, James C. 1991. Academic and Nonacademic Influences on the College Destinations of 1980 High School Graduates. *Sociology of Education* 64, no. 3 (July): 158–171.

Hemsley-Brown, Jane. 1999. College Choice: Perceptions and Priorities. *Educational Management and Administration* 27, no. 1: 85–98.

Kern, Roy M. and Paul Peluso. 1999. Using Individual Psychology Concepts to Compare Family Systems Process and Organizational Behavior. *Family Journal* 7, no. 3: 236–245.

Leffel, Rob R. 1999. Public Policy and the Academy in an Era of Change. *ERIC Documents,* ED432 171.

Leming, James S. 1987. Rock Music and the Socialization of Moral Values in Early Adolescence. *Youth and Society* 18, no. 4: 363–383.

Lynton, Earnest A. and Sandra E. Elman. 1987. *New Priorities for the University.* San Francisco: Jossey-Bass.

Marcus, Jon. 1999. Coke or Pepsi? U.S. Universities Choose Their Sponsor. *Times Higher Education Supplement* Issue 1386 (28 May): 12–17.

McDonough, Patricia M. 1994. Buying and Selling Higher Education. *Journal of Higher Education* 65, no. 4. Electronic document retrieved via JStor Database 17 July 2002.

McDonough, Patricia M. 1997. *Choosing Colleges.* New York: State University of New York Press.

McPherson, Michael. 1983. Value Conflicts in American Higher Education: A Survey. *Journal of Higher Education* 54, no. 3: 244–245.

Mercer, Joyce. 1995. Contracting Out. *Chronicle of Higher Education* 41, no. 43 (7 July): A37–A38.

Mohan, John. 1995. Thinking Local: Service-Learning, Education for Citizenship and Geography. *Journal of Geography in Higher Education* 19, no. 2: 129–143.

Monks, James and Ronald G. Ehrenberg. 1999. *U.S. News and World Report's* College Rankings. Why Do They Matter? *Change* 31, no. 6: 42–52.

Moore, John W. 2000. Education: Commodity, Come-On, or Commitment? *Journal of Chemical Education* 77, no. 7: 805.

Mulhauser, Dana. 2001. Thou Shalt Not Manipulate Data *Chronicle of Higher Education* 48, no. 16 (14 December): A8.

Newman, Frank. 2000. Saving Higher Education's Soul *Change* 33, no. 5: 16.

Page, Stewart. 1996. Students and Humane Values in a Competitive World. *Guidance and Counseling* 12, no. 1: 15.

Pendergast, Tom. 1998. Consuming Questions: Scholarship on Consumerism in America to 1940 *American Studies International* Vol. 36, No. 2: 23–44.

Ponessa, Jeanne. 1995. College Rankings Rankle Counselors, Admissions Officers *Education Week* 15, no. 12: 5.

Pratt, Linda Ray. 1995. Giving Higher Education "the Business." *Education Digest* 60, no. 5: 18.

Pulley, John L. 2000. Whose Bookstore Is it, Anyway? *Chronicle of Higher Education* 46, no. 22 (4 February): A41–A42.

Raths, Louis E., Merril Harmin, and Sidney B. Simon. 1966. *Values and Teaching: Working with Values in the Classroom.* Columbus, OH: Merrill.

Rosen, Deborah E., James M. Curran, and Timothy B. Greenlee. 1998. College Choice in a Brand Elimination Framework: The Administrator's Perspective. *Journal of Marketing for Higher Education* 8, no. 4: 67–81.

Saltman, Kenneth J. 2000. *Collateral Damage.* Lanham, MD: Rowman and Littlefield Publishers, Inc.

Scott, Barbara Ann. 1992. The "New Practicality" Revisited: Changes in the American College Curriculum. *Journal of Education* 174, no. 1: 87–104.

Sewell, W. H. 1971. Inequality of Opportunity for Higher Education *American Sociological Review* 36: 793–809

Simon, Roger I. 2001. "The University: A Place to Think?" In Henry A. Giroux and Kostas Myrsiades, eds., *Beyond the Corporate University.* Lanham, MD: Rowman and Littlefield Publishers, Inc.

Slaughter, Sheila and Larry L. Leslie. 1997. *Academic Capitalism: Politics, Policies, and the Entrepreneurial University.* Baltimore, MD: The Johns Hopkins University Press.

Solomon, L. 1975. The Definition of College Quality and Its Impact on Earnings. *Explorations in Economic Research* 2: 537–587

Stromberg, Peter. 1990. Elvis Alive? The Ideology of American Consumerism. *Journal of Popular Culture* 24, no. 3: 11.

Thrasher, Frederick and Paul Bloland. 1989. Student Development Studies: A Review of Published Empirical Research, 1973–1987. *Journal of Counseling and Development* 67: 547–554.

Trow, M. A. 1984. "The Analysis of Status." In *Perspectives on Higher Education: Eight Disciplinary and Comparative Views,* Burton Clark, ed. Berkeley: University of California Press.

Ward, Scott, Daniel B. Wackman, and Ellen Wartella. 1977. *How Children Learn to Buy.* Beverly Hills: Sage Publications.

Wilcox, Melynda. 1999. On a Shoestring and a Prayer. *Kiplinger's Personal Finance Magazine.* 99.

Zlotkowski, Edward. From *A New Model of Excellence,* as quoted in Maureen Burrows, Sheila Chauvin, Cathy Lazarus, and Peggy Chehardy. 1999. Required Service Learning for Medical Students: Program Description and Student Response. *Teaching and Learning in Medicine* 11, no. 4: 9.

Chapter 9

Egocentrism in Professional Arts Education: Toward a Discipline-Based View of Work and World

Larry Stultz

As curricula in higher education become more specialized toward preparing graduates for professional careers, and as students become less tolerant of program content that appears to them to be off-task, significant cultural change in academia is a source of much angst and debate. Concurrently, the market and those individuals who hire the graduating products of professional programs are seeking to exert influence upon the curriculum content and the skills and technological development, thereby contributing to the turmoil. We have a dilemma, well known to us as the professional arts versus the liberal arts.

Cultural change in the interface between a workview and a worldview is inevitable and constant, but useful and intelligent change must be managed, perhaps negotiated, with a Janus head.[1] When the market, the professions,

---

[1] The head of the god, Janus, had two faces, each looking in an opposite direction. Janus' significance of vigilance calls us to continually remain open to what has been marginalized, split off, or left out of the dialogue. This writing accepts that there is more than one discourse for opening a workable path to professional education that remains socially and cognitively preparatory for its graduates. Ref: *Janus Head: Journal of Interdisciplinary Studies in Literature, Continental Philosophy, Phenomenological Psychology, and the Arts* (July 1998), E-Journal on-line. Available from <http://www.janushead.org> [August 1, 2002]. Professional education appears to have a Janus face, looking in two directions at once—toward a student's personal (skills) development and toward social (market) integration—which might actually not be two separate directions. What I propose is much more realistically defined as the liberal arts' worldview and the practical arts' workview. The vision required to meld the two views into a useful educational program requires the head and the eyes of Janus.

and the industries of society become involved in the education of our young, problems will arise. The cultural change we are seeing is in the corporate model with market values and practices. Commercial spheres are replacing public and academic spheres, and we feel a sense of loss of democracy, to whatever degree democracy ever existed. From many sides we are asked to believe in the goodness of the market's effect on higher education, because it is in the best interest of our students, and ultimately that it is in the best interest of our colleges and programs. Corporate culture functions largely to cancel out the democratic impulses of civil society by either devaluing them or absorbing them into market logic.[2] In this chapter I explore how we might accommodate and negotiate reasonable cultural change in higher education. In order to highlight the larger point, I point to some professional arts programs that are arguably getting it wrong.

Programs in higher education that are purposefully, methodically, and skillfully generating graduates in areas we call the professional arts[3] seem to be following very nontraditional guidelines in curriculum planning and exit-competency measurement. In fact, measurement is most often taken of student success (persistence, retention) and jobs attained (placement), the latter tracked and publicized in terms of employer status and the timeframe within which gainful employment is secured. Employer satisfaction is also often surveyed to measure postcurricular success and to serve as a litmus test for further program adjustment. These programs seem to be finding rationalizations and redefinitions of previously normative educational practices to accommodate the requirements of the market and the expectations of the students. Even what was once normative contained a hidden curriculum that is not so hidden today. What Giroux calls "the creeping vocationalization and subordination of learning to the dictates of the market"[4] has become an open and defining principle of professional education.

Of course, the demands of the market would be quite self-serving, seeking highly skilled, work environment–disciplined, and loyal problem solvers who understand customer service and employer demands on their time. Contemporary student culture expects a curriculum that will get them where they want to go, when they want to be there, and at a predictable and maximum return on their investment in terms of credits per tuition dollar, and with little or nothing philosophical or otherwise confusing to take them off

---

[2] Henry A. Giroux, "Vocationalizing Higher Education: Schooling and the Politics of Corporate Culture" in *Beyond the Corporate University: Culture and Pedagogy in the New Millennium,* ed. Henry Giroux and Kostas Myrsiades (Lanham, MD: Rowman & Littlefield Publishers, Inc., 2001), 30–31.

[3] The professional arts include, but are not limited to, all the professions for which there are higher education programs, such as engineering, law, medicine, dentistry, accounting, architecture, chiropractic, and all the applied arts such as graphic design, interior design, industrial design, the emerging multimedia-web design field, and culinary arts.

[4] Giroux, *Beyond the Corporate University,* 34.

course in their marketable skills development. They are migrating to high-end professional colleges and institutes or to preprofessional programs for law and medicine. No longer do they come to study under distinguished scholars to gain knowledge for its own sake.[5] Marilee Jones, dean of admissions at MIT, observes that students are "idealistically pragmatic." They know what they want, they want the world to be a better place, and they have a plan. They are not likely to study subjects for pure pleasure. They prefer relevance and purpose. They are "savvy consumers."[6]

The professional arts and applied arts schools in higher education are catering to corporate influence, a workview, often to the exclusion of a liberal arts education toward a worldview and the purposeful, thoughtful development of social and cognitive intelligences. Professional degree programs tend to have curricula written by, advised by, and taught by experienced industry members so that graduates may be recruited with assurance of productivity and performance. The programs are packaging themselves not only to attract students as consumers, but also to attract industry members to a productive recruiting table.[7] Corporate influence is ubiquitous and persistent. Public universities, and more so the private and for-profit higher education organizations,[8] are quick to accommodate market values, needs, and suggestions. Students are myopically focused on the quick acquisition of skills and a job attendant to their future position as college graduate.

There is a proliferation of professional program/industry coalitions that is contributing to the development and expansion of a management versus skilled worker hegemony. The quality of the skilled workers turned out is varied, whereas the quantity of quickly trained graduates is not.

Their numbers are growing, but jobs are not becoming more prolific. Gerald Bracey believes the call by business and industry for higher and higher levels of skills and more dutiful response to industry demands by higher education is a blatant attempt by corporate America to drive down wages.[9] The combination of enhanced technology in nearly every professional field and the higher availability of highly skilled applicants has a net effect of driving wages down for even the most highly capable graduates. The most significant risk to these graduating skilled workers is their sheer number. More candi-

---

[5] Sheila Slaughter, "Professional Values and the Allure of the Market," *ACADEME* (Sept/Oct 2001). E-Journal on-line. Available from <http://www.aaup.org/publications/Academe/01SO/so01sla.htm> [August 16, 2002].

[6] Marilee Jones, "There's a New Kid in Town: Observations on the Newest Generation of MIT Students," *MIT Technology Review* (April 2002): 13–14.

[7] Slaughter, op. cit.

[8] The use of the term, "organizations," is necessary due to the prolific variety of professional certificate and degree programs where one will find universities, colleges, institutes, programs, and centers. "Organization" is necessary as a defensive means to not elevate the academic status of any one institution to a place it should not be.

[9] Gerald Bracey, *The War on America's Public Schools* (Boston: Allyn and Bacon, 2002), 40–43.

dates mean more choices for the employer. Newer high-skilled graduates put older, higher-paid workers on the firing line. Industry continues to serve itself, and education is victimized by the shell game.[10]

But students maintain a self-view as consumers, owed something by their schools, purchasing a future job with no desire for the development of a worldview. Are graduates becoming undereducated and less adaptive? If the skills development in professional education is exclusionary regarding liberal arts and humanities study, can the graduates expect lives of practicality? Liberal education versus professional training and technical practicality is a much-debated dualism. Call it liberal arts versus practical arts or professional arts. Call it a worldview versus a workview. Call it knowing a hawk from a handsaw.[11]

Professional and technical training is presumed by employers, students, and especially parents to be a practical education, and a liberal arts education carries an imputed impracticality. Marshall Gregory calls the dichotomy pitting practical arts against liberal arts "intellectually incoherent and politically duplicitous."[12] The two concepts cannot be disconnected in a socially, cognitively, and productively intelligent life, and the opposing of skills and scholarship gratuitously serves the interests of the market. Gregory asks, "In what job, career, or profession, for example, do issues of fairness, community, language, emotion, and morality not play important roles—determinatively important roles—in how the worker or the professional develops his skills and performs her job? Doing a job well is never just a matter of skills."[13]

My claim could, of course, be that a wholly educative and life-preparatory environment could use far less professional influence and a renewed focus on liberal arts material. It is not a hard argument to make, not an obtuse concept to absorb and adopt as foundational and an imperative change. But I think there is more to see embedded in the reasons, the actions, the problems, and the solutions.

The professional arts are very egocentric, and there is a lot of money to be made for those who walk the walk, talk the talk, and uphold the myths of their

---

[10] Ibid.

[11] Marshall Gregory, "Liberal Learning vs. Professional Training, or Liberal Education Knows a Hawk from a Handsaw," Conference paper, Butler University, 1997 and William Shakespeare, *Hamlet* (II, ii, 366–370). Hamlet speaks as a man who wants to know the truth as opposed to nearly all around him, "when the wind is southerly [he] know[s] a hawk from a handsaw." Gregory invokes this passage to remind us that philosophers of liberal arts are asked to ignore the difference between a hawk and a handsaw by expediency masters. The hawk must be considered representative of the liberal arts, and the handsaw, the professional arts. The market and those who direct the response of the professional programs that serve industry so faithfully must certainly be the expediency masters.

[12] Ibid.

[13] Ibid.

professional artistry. In the industry case I draw upon, the visual arts,[14] the egocentrism becomes more accurately solipsism, and it is pervasive, extending through industry professionals, academic administrators and instructors, and students like the web of a conceptual mind map.[15] Whether stemming from the industry's unique, or at least mythical, problem solutions, the anxious service to the industry by the schools, or the mimicry of impressionable students (if not their professors), the solipsism is created and enhanced by all concerned. Or could it be for the money? Perhaps so, and perhaps we can find our way out of this dilemma with a binocular look at the worldview and the workview.

As educators we must recognize and investigate evolving societal needs and cultural changes, and occasionally we are presented with questions that might suggest a reevaluation of our academic beliefs and practices. Must we, and how should we, allow for and respond to cultural change even if it is antithetical to a liberal educational construct and places limitations on an academically defined worldview?

Culture is not static. Not for society, not for professions, and not for academia. People were appalled when the Renaissance gave way to Impressionism, and they were appalled when Beethoven reinvented symphonic structure. New ideas like Bob Marley take time to accept. When students wanted to focus on postmodernism over classic knowledge, perhaps mature academicians were equally appalled. A study solely in the classic and traditional would disallow culture change and mind expansion. In the case of an academic view conflicting with a corporate view, the values that once marked a sacred boundary between the two seem quaint and naive.[16] Change and reinvention must constantly be investigated and, possibly, accommodated, but the cost to society and the worldview must be considered.

I can point to several changes and reinventions that have been enculturated into and embraced by society at an arguable cost. Debate has arisen over the value of distance education from educative, socialization, and even marginalization points of view. Applications of the Internet as a whole have also been charged with an assault on societal values. Certainly, religious and political changes have their costs and deleterious effects on some worldviews. The dutiful service of industry by educational organizations stand at the forefront

---

[14]For the purposes of illustration, I will utilize graphic design as the basis of example, because it is the professional art that is best known to me. I will often compare or refer to other professional arts programs.

[15]A mind map is a conceptual thinking tool known to many in the areas of psychology and the applied arts. It is a self-expanding diagram of thoughts, randomly drawn and ever growing as the thought stream progresses. It can be called starbursting or flapdoodling, and was originally defined by German psychiatrist, Tony Buzan. Information is available at <http://www.cityscape.co.uk/buzan>.

[16]Slaughter, op. cit.

of the debate I undertake here. It is when the change serves itself and its originators to the exclusion of the worldview that we must take issue with its value.

No culture change with any chance of being long lasting can afford to be solipsistic. The service of expediency masters[17] must be turned into a cohort relationship, and it is apparent that the schools must take the first steps. Vermont College's interdisciplinary art and design program is demonstrative of positive change, engaging the field as cultural practice, and addressing issues of authenticity and morality. The program director, G. Roy Levin, believes that:

> [Students are] radicalized in a fundamental sense of having gained a more complex and confident view of the world as artists and as people … and perhaps, most crucially, they recognize that art is not simply about art, and artists are not lone geniuses, but both exist and take on their significance through a relationship to the world. They recognize that art and artists are part of the social, cultural, political, and economic contexts that they influence and help define and that define them.[18]

If we as educators agree to a neo-logical academic culture change, we must insist that the path of corporate culture also be altered, that the path the market is insisting we all walk be resisted. The social construct of our cooperation must not be based solely on productivity, efficiency, dependable skilled workers, technological prowess, or the service of market values and economic imperialism. We must insist that institutions like the family, the school, and the state be guided by goals that are not economic.[19]

Something might still be missing in the plot to change the dynamic between education and business, between liberal arts and professional/practical arts. Borrowing from the earlier reference to Marilee Jones' idealistically pragmatic students, I suggest that we maintain an idealistic pragmatism in any evolving school culture. I am drawn to Richard Rorty's urging that we combine the Eye of the Mind (thought, intellect, and insight) with the knowledge of realities and truths outside the mind. The pragmatic blending of knowledge, conceptual and critical thinking, and reasonable action can contribute to a positive and humane culture creation.[20]

So, through what lens, eyes, or ideology can we see the worldview and the workview most pragmatically? How can we maintain the pragmatic view without falling into an entirely new type of solipsistic rationalization, an example of which soon follows?

---

[17] Gregory, op. cit.
[18] G. Roy Levin, "Art as Cultural Practice," *Art Journal* 58, no. 1 (Spring 1999): 17–20.
[19] Barry Schwartz, *The Battle for Human Nature: Science, Morality, and Modern Life* (New York: W.W. Norton & Company, 1987), 322.
[20] Richard Rorty, "Pragmatism, Relativism, and Irrationalism" in *Epistemology: The Big Questions*, ed. Linda Alcoff (Malden, MA: Blackwell Publishers Inc. 1998), 336–348.

Nearly all curriculum theory utilizes a hybrid, remix, new rationale, or different emphasis of the same three educational objectives: subject matter, student needs, and societal expectations.[21] A subject matter driven curriculum is, or stands a good chance of being, academically pure. Higher education faculty most likely have independent authority and disciplinary tradition. Student needs in curriculum can vary, but are quite subject to societal influence, much more than to subject matter influence. Students might now consider themselves sovereign consumers, but many tend to be quite passive, going quietly from one requirement to another. Societal expectations will most often effect curricular change. If the influences of society are material values and success, then capitalism becomes the driving force in curriculum theory. When universities were charged with failing to produce a viable labor force for the twenty-first century in *A Nation at Risk*,[22] they fell into line with the "resurgent managerial ethos. They began to behave more like corporations."[23]

If education is a social construct, then is the market also integrated into our social construct? Shall we take the market for granted, or go beyond common sense and into personal subjectivity and consciousness? Maxine Greene points to what she calls a "situated freedom" which sees free activity as grounded in the acceptance of our defined situation.[24] I think there is more to freedom in education than service to a defined situation. Taking the market for granted is what has put education in the service of industry, and educators continue to believe it makes sense. The thinking about personal subjectivity and consciousness is the opening of professional education to liberal arts concepts and the maintaining of a worldview in the social construct of the workview. Karl Mannheim wants curriculum to be a negotiated knowledge, which students and teachers create, while he also believes the main educative agent to be the community. Because the community includes family, social, and market culture, we must not be intent upon the sole goal of skill-based professional training. Rather than self-serving purposes, any educational construct must remain concerned about values and the human condition.[25]

I am left, then, with a need to find a methodology that considers all three elements of subject matter, student need, and societal expectation. I also

---

[21] Herbert Kliebard, "The Tyler Rationale," *Forging the American Curriculum: Essays in Curriculum History and Theory* (New York: Routledge, 1992), 153–164.

[22] United States, National Commission on Excellence in Education, *A Nation at Risk* (Washington, DC: Government Printing Office, 1983).

[23] Jackson Lears, "The Radicalism of Tradition: Teaching the Liberal Arts in a Managerial Age," *The Hedgehog Review* 2, no. 3 (Fall 2000), University of Virginia: Institute for Advanced Studies in Culture.

[24] Maxine Greene, *The Dialectic of Freedom* (New York: Teachers College Press, 1988), 7.

[25] Karl Mannheim, *From Karl Mannheim*, ed. Kurt H. Wolff (New York: Oxford University Press, 1971).

see a need for presenting a reasonable and complete, life-preparatory education in a manner that includes production ability, a perspective on knowledge, an ability to think critically, and a sense of ethics. Directly applicable to this ideology is the work of Elliot Eisner in art education and his concepts in discipline-based art education (DBAE). Proponents of DBAE claim that social and cognitive intelligence is developed hand-in-hand with professional skills when an equal focus is put on production, criticism, history, and aesthetics/ethics.[26] Eisner makes a clear distinction between the practice of art and the intellectual and cognition-building value of art experience. The four major aims central to the concept of DBAE relate directly to what one can do within the arts. One can create art (production); one can perceive and respond to its qualities (criticism); one can understand the arts' place in history and culture (art history); and one can make reasoned judgments about art and understand the grounds upon which those judgments rest (aesthetics).[27]

Concurrent with Eisner's work in DBAE has been the rapid growth of the marketing and communication industry's need for skilled graphic designers. DBAE was intended to be equally applicable to the fine arts and the applied arts. Interestingly, these seemingly similar disciplines more closely approximate the debate at hand: liberal arts versus professional arts. The two arenas, fine arts and applied arts, have become divergent. The traditional fine arts, including painting, sculpture, music, and theater, have found that they fit easily into DBAE's prescription. Graphic design and similar industries do not fit so neatly. As I demonstrate later in this chapter, postsecondary applied arts education has tended to become vocational, skills based, and psychomotor driven, and many schools seem to have abandoned the DBAE construct in an effort to get graduates employed quickly and efficiently at the highest profit and the lowest pedagogical investment. Where are the weaknesses in DBAE that have allowed, perhaps encouraged, its variants and even its abandonment? Was it conceived to encompass the applied arts in the first place?

Eisner presents a credible, four-part equity argument on behalf of DBAE. The first and second arguments relate to the teaching of art in schools. First, the arts represent the highest form of human achievements to which students should have access; and second, the school is the primary public institution that can make such access possible for the vast majority of students in the United States.

---

[26] Elliot Eisner, *The Role of Discipline-Based Art Education in America's Schools* (Los Angeles: The J. Paul Getty Trust, 1988). I use the terms "aesthetics" and "ethics" relatively interchangeably. Roughly speaking, aesthetics is to such values as artistic beauty, meaning, and impression as ethics is to values of fairness, rightness, and appropriateness. Both are value-laden and normative. Both are representative of what is good.

[27] Ibid.

The third and fourth arguments can be globalized in reference to all professional education programs. Third, work in the arts develops unique and important mental skills, including both social and cognitive intelligence; and fourth, the inclusion of art production, art criticism, art history, and aesthetics in curriculum encourages the development and understanding of multiple forms of literacy.[28]

Read these two again in an altered form: Third, work in ergonomics develops unique and important mental skills, including both social and cognitive intelligence, and fourth, the inclusion of ergonomic production, human factors criticism, history of human environments, and ethics and aesthetics in curriculum encourages the development and understanding of multiple forms of literacy.

Or, further altered: Third, work in prelaw develops unique and important mental skills, including both social and cognitive intelligence; and fourth, the inclusion of legal production, legal criticism, judicial history, and ethics in curriculum encourages the development and understanding of multiple forms of literacy.

Not only would I answer that yes the applied arts must reacquaint themselves and attach themselves to the concept of discipline-based education (DBE), I also suggest that professional education programs investigate and adopt the ideology.[29] Although the DBE concept has been known and acclaimed for more than thirty years, the majority of production-oriented, career-focused professional education programs are not following through. I suggest that the problems we see with market control in higher education and with student-as-consumer attitudes among administrators and faculty might be avoided if a way is found to integrate and blend the experiences and concepts in production, history, criticism, and aesthetics/ethics as well as liberal education methodologies in all curricula and courses.

The DBE argument suggests a far-reaching curriculum theory that should be viewed as a unifying pedagogy, providing a lens through which one views world events, popular culture, personal production, and aesthetics/ethics as a whole, an interdependent web of perception, knowing, and cultural existence. The kind of environment in which a student lives and goes to school affects the kinds of aptitudes he or she forms, the mental skills he develops, and the cognitive structures through which she perceives and interprets the world. Students should be given the opportunity to understand the relation-

---

[28]Elliot Eisner, "Beyond Creating: The Place for Art in America's Schools, " *ArtsEdNet*, 1999. E-Journal on-line. Available from <http://www.artsednet.getty.edu/ArtsEdNet/Read/Beyond/whyart.html> [Accessed April 20, 2002].

[29]The concept of discipline based art education (DBAE) is applicable to nearly any field or course of study, and it is reasonable to expand the discussion of these concepts by eliminating the word "art." Throughout this chapter I will occasionally refer to discipline based education, or DBE, as an indication that art and design are not the only fields that can benefit from this writing.

ship between their profession and culture, the interaction between technology and ideology. Students must be able to participate in the dialogue and meaning making that stems from their work, their basis for cultural appraisal, and to have faith in their own reasoned judgment. Their approach to their world of work might remain in the skills-based arena, but their understanding and perception of the reasons and values of their work cannot help but have a refining effect on the work itself. Their value to themselves, to their employers, and to society as a whole will be enhanced. The possibility also exists that they will grow to industry leadership, thereby more dramatically spreading their worldview and benefiting the conscience of the market.

Defining more specifically the potential contributions of DBE to society and the cognitive skills necessary for living and working productively, I apply Eisner's summary of his major ideas to an expanded and random list of professional arts:[30]

- Social work makes a unique contribution to human experience and understanding. Though it is the case that social work can be used for the attainment of nonsocietal ends, we might be more beneficially concerned with educating human vision so that the world man encounters can be seen as social.
- Computer systems education as a field of practice has not been isolated from the mainstream of human society. Instead, programmers have had to be responsive to various pressures and expectations that society has brought to bear on the schools, not surprising because schools are social institutions and political structures.
- Most adults, including many teachers and administrators, consider culinary arts to be marginal in school curricula. Parents want schools to attend to the business of developing skills necessary for meeting the demands of the socioeconomic system, assigning educational priorities to sanctioned skills.
- Scientific development is not a simple unfolding of a preprogrammed genetic constitution. It is complex and strongly influenced by environmental conditions within which it occurs.
- If students are to be able to ethically encounter mass communications form, if they are to understand broadcasting or speechwriting as a social and cultural phenomenon, attention will need to be paid to their transfer in the curriculum. We must teach for transfer, and we should not expect the transfer of skills or ideas that were not developed in the first place.

---

[30]Elliot Eisner, *Educating Artistic Vision* (New York: Macmillan, 1997), 257–265. Eisner wrote this summary using the words, "art," "arts," and "artistic." The adaptation and substitution of other professional arts is an attempt to illustrate the applicability of Eisner's arguments to any other professional art.

- Evaluation, in one form or another, is necessary for making decisions in teaching and in curriculum planning. Evaluation procedures should be developed through which it would be possible to know not only what a student can do but also what he or she will do.[31] *It is through a persuasive view of the world that practice in schools begins to alter.*

The emphasis is added to the last bullet point to draw attention to the evidence that either the professions are dictating content and procedure in colleges or, in their zeal to produce graduates that get jobs, the schools are persuaded by their self-image as purveyors of skilled talent to the professional world.[32]

Many students and advocates of DBAE or DBE have developed hybrid versions of Eisner's theories. In discussing the possible implications for new ideas in curriculum and evaluation, he wrote:

> What I am suggesting here, I suppose, is something like, but not quite, a paradigm shift among those in the educational community. I say "not quite" because I am not advocating the replacement of one paradigm for another. It is not a matter of replacing a Newtonian universe with an Einsteinian one; rather, it is a willingness to recognize the essential incompleteness of any single form of representation and, hence, the desire to conceptualize and describe the world through several forms.[33]

Just as focusing on only one area within DBAE, for example, art production or art history, disallows complete access to cultural understanding and intellectual progress, a firm adherence to traditional or standardized points of view in each area is also a limitation. Precisely because culture is not static and is always evolving, academia must be open to change and reinvention.

As I attempt to provide a cause to adopt the DBE concepts in all professional and practical arts programs, I take care that my proposal remains true to the original arguments in DBAE: the arts represent the highest form of human achievements to which students should have access; the school is the primary public institution that can make such access possible for the vast ma-

---

[31]While very difficult to project or measure, this might be particularly beneficial in, say, pre-med programs.

[32]The persuasiveness that has altered school practice has been in the wrong hands for some time. Professional education programs have sought and incorporated input from those who hire their graduates. Program structure advising, curriculum writing, visiting professionals to the classroom, internship programs, and career services support have altered practice in service to the market. The industry has been making certain that teaching for transfer is being done through their persuasiveness and their recruitment and employment dollars.

[33]Elliot Eisner, *Cognition and Curriculum: A Basis for Deciding What to Teach.* (New York: Longman Inc. Company, 1982) p. 82.

jority of students in the United States; work in the arts develops unique and important mental skills, including both social and cognitive intelligence; and, the inclusion of art production, art criticism, art history, and aesthetics in curriculum encourages the development and understanding of multiple forms of literacy. Workable theories seem always vulnerable to hybridization and corruption. I provide here an example of each confronting DBAE.[34]

Charles M. Dorn attempts to redirect the discussion of DBAE positioning toward a more classic set of philosophical questions. He agrees there is no doubt that thinking is related to both the contemplation and the making of art, yet there are philosophical and aesthetic questions about the relationship between thinking about art and thinking about making art. He names thinking processes such as rationalism, empiricism, and neo-idealism as necessary in art education programs. In Dorn's rationalist view, art is in the mind of the beholder. In his empiricist view, art changes over time. His neo-idealist view is that art is essentially our experience with it. Under Dorn's philosophical constructs, students learn that art comes from experience with art, that art can be a means for social change, and that art is essentially a spirit within them.

Interestingly, and somewhat mysteriously, though Dorn seems to echo Eisner's approach to DBAE, but with a philosopher's pen, he writes in his conclusion:

> I propose that the benefits of a philosophical curricular model over a discipline-based model is that it:
>
> 1. avoids the necessity of separating art curricula into the separate domains of production, history, criticism, and aesthetics.[35]

He then returned to an Eisner-proponent stance with the remainder of his benefits:

> 2. offers a curriculum that is reflective of the values of both teachers and students;
>
> 3. provides a curriculum concept that stresses arts education as intelligent activity; and
>
> 4. stresses alternative frames of thought that encourage both teachers and students to become more intellectually empathetic and to have a greater sense of intellectual justice.[36]

---

[34] Here I turn to specific examples from graphic design schools where I will remain for the majority of the balance of the chapter. It will be of the reader's interest to plug in examples and scenarios from other professional arts, perhaps as well known to him or her as the graphic arts are to me.

[35] Charles M. Dorn, "Art as Intelligent Activity," *Arts Education Policy Review* 95, no. 2 (Nov/Dec 1993), 2–9.

[36] Ibid.

There are predictable offshoots of the DBAE and DBE model. Many are corruptions and debasements, many are reasonable adaptations to specific needs, but few outweigh the reflexive and rationalized Design Based Education proposed by Meredith Davis.[37] The proposal is clever (the acronym is even the same), but it contributes blatantly to the solipsism of the industry in general.

Davis suggests that the inherent nature of design and its activities might address national interest in integrated curricula strategies and become central in the development of interdisciplinary curricula. She believes that the design discipline can provide "all the cognitive skills necessary for life and work in the next century."[38] She urges curriculum planners who suppose themselves to be discipline based to shift their ideology to design based, paying more attention to developing competencies, skills, and qualities required for high skills, high-wage employment and for the development of analytical and problem-solving skills that produce productive members of society.

Davis relegates art and design to the service sector in support of the mainstream of society. To Davis, art provides an alternative form that serves a more dominant discipline in the curriculum, such as English, history, or science, and a new point of entry for students who excel in nonverbal communication. Still an advocate of rigor in design skills development, she outlines the reasons why a design process should be integrated into all curricula, and by implication wants us to believe that the reverse, the inclusion of four disciplines in art or design as in DBAE, is no longer necessary. She claims:

- Design problems are situated. They have a context from which students can derive information that relates to a variety of disciplines and that is critical to successful solutions.
- Design problems require both analysis and synthesis.
- Design problems are systems oriented. Solutions must be viewed as nested in a web of interactions among physical, social, cultural, technological, and economic factors.
- Design problems require the work of interdisciplinary teams of experts.

In a demonstration of single-vision-ness, Davis says, "While the Getty's[39] stance on discipline based art education carried the field through difficult

---

[37]Meredith Davis, "Design's Inherent Interdisciplinarity: The Arts in Integrated Curricula," *Arts Education Policy Review* 101, no. 1 (Sept/Oct 1999): 8–13.

[38]Ibid.

[39]The Getty Center for Education in the Arts, funding provided by the J. Paul Getty Trust, Los Angeles, CA.

political waters by carving out 'cognitive turf' and demonstrating its value in the education of children, its implementation by teachers in schools often falls short in addressing the breadth of arts practices."[40] It is important to note her focus on practice, only one of the four key disciplines in DBAE. She concludes that design is a third type of knowledge that can bridge the gap between art and science, which reads a bit like between liberal arts and the workplace.

Davis contributes significantly to the commodification of art and design. As chair of the graphic design department at a southeastern university, she typifies the metanarrative that has developed in many university art and design departments and nearly all private design and advertising schools. Her focus on design process as a basis for curriculum and pedagogy is indicative of the design field's sense of self-importance.

Perhaps in an effort to say things purposefully proprietary and impetuous, the design educators and the design professionals are wandering too far from DBE's unifying pedagogy. The schools mimic the profession in its solipsism, vainly aware of itself, its mystical reputation for perceiving problems and conceiving solutions, and its commercial indispensability.

Passion, creativity, and unique ways of living, thinking, and understanding culture define the field of design, but design often misinterprets itself as exclusive. It is a rationalization fed by a deep belief, if academically and intellectually unfounded, in its ability to lead society into its view of normalcy, what Deborah Britzman calls a "hegemonic sociality" construct.[41]

To meet the demands of the profession, design education is typified as production based, developing technological and conceptual thinking skills. Most design schools are graduate placement driven, and students are as likely to come from high schools' vocational diploma tracks as from academic or college prep tracks. For reasons of expediency, student ability (or lack of same), and limited faculty qualifications, there is a preponderance of technical and conceptual class work and dwindling evidence of liberal studies in most cases. There is also the obligatory rhetoric and hyperbole about preparing students for lucrative careers in the "real world."

I have utilized admissions catalogs and Web sites from a number of higher education organizations that include graphic design in their degree offerings.[42] Many share the same promotional messages and sentiments about the

---

[40]Davis, op. cit.

[41]Deborah P. Britzman, *Lost Subjects, Contested Objects: Toward a Psychoanalytic Inquiry of Learning* (Albany NY: SUNY, 1998), 85.

[42]Since it is not my purpose to compare or indict specific professional design education organizations, I will not cite the examples reiterated here. The examples were selected as representative of what is pervasive. I found that most, but not all, design schools are single-minded in the drive to feed skilled workers to the industry. Advice on curriculum from working professionals is solicited and incorporated into the programs. Guest professionals are put in front of classrooms to teach by real world example. Often, the technology and skills-based   (*continued*)

value of their curricula, and a representative sampling of the rhetoric includes: "teaches emerging professionals that their ideas, designs and creations do make a difference to society ... careers will likely be more global, technological, interdisciplinary, and collaborative ... students are encouraged to define their creative vision and professional practice," "stresses strong technical and presentation skills" in preparing students to be "the communications link between suppliers and consumers," "a leader in the education of artists and designers who have produced the ideas, images, and artifacts that have helped give the world both its form and function," and "educating students for professional careers."

All of these promotional messages sound quite promising and even enlightened. They use words like *society, global,* and *form and function,* which sound quite liberal arts based. But they predominantly use words like *technological, professional practice, presentation skills,* and *link between suppliers and consumers,* which sound like what they are, skills based.

Furthermore, when delving into the curriculum content of many of the schools, I found divergent attempts to provide general education content to the otherwise technological and skills-based coursework. Twenty percent of one curriculum includes liberal arts/general education requirements consisting of three art history courses and one course each in math, literature, cultural beliefs, environmental studies, and geography. One third of another curriculum (thirteen courses) are general education requirements, but six are art and design history, one is desktop publishing, one is public speaking (client based), and the students must choose between science and math. Another requires 25 percent of a graduate's coursework be in the liberal arts, including sixteen credits in art history, ten credits in humanities, ten in social science, and ten in natural science. But no math.

Consistent with the praxis I have found in most design schools, Gregory warns us, "There is constant new pressure to move education toward a skills-based curriculum ... to treat students as if they were mere mechanisms for getting the skills needed to run a post-industrial society in the marketplace."[43] What students, faculty, and colleges of all types must realize is that, in spite of the drive toward expediency, persistence, and placement, the performance of acquired job skills cannot occur, should not occur, in

content leaves less room in the curriculum for liberal education coursework. There are, however, a few public and private schools in the graphic design field that are fully accredited by organizations such as the National Association of Schools of Art and Design, and that maintain a full time academic director and faculty in general education. The evidence that there are a few, and not many, emphasizes my point that professional arts schools are not yet getting it right. Of 1,709 listed organizations in The Art School and Program Directory (Available at <http://www.artschools.com> [Accessed September 22, 2002]), just 236, fewer than 14%, are members of the NASAD accrediting body (Available at <http://www.arts-accredit.org/nasad/> [Accessed September 22, 2001]).

[43] Gregory, op. cit.

the absence of emotion, history, language, cultural understanding, and moral agency. Educational institutions should avoid any curriculum that misleads students into believing that job skills and general living have no implicit connection.

A view of typical phrases included in the mission statements reveals the pervasive commitment to preparing students for the workplace. Phrases like "transmit to students accepted knowledge" make one wonder who is doing the accepting or the deciding about what might qualify as accepted knowledge. "Prepare students for employment," "provide students with necessary technological skills," and "certify and credentialize its students"[44] may give the reader the impression that there is an education/industry consortium.

Professional education programs often rely on the advice of a group of industry representatives, typically referred to as the Program Advisory Committee (PACs) or Council or Board, that meets as often as twice yearly to bring industry trends and perspectives to the administrators, curriculum planners, and faculty. Great import is given to the advice and evaluation presented by the PACs, not only for rapid revision of curriculum and coursework, but also in promotional materials for the admissions office. The fact that programs are able to meet industry standards and project what those standards will be in three to four years is a significant marketing tool and helps in student retention.

The employers of graduates are periodically surveyed to track the suitability of these working products of the preparation program. Survey objectives generally are to determine satisfaction with technical skills and knowledge, dependability, and professionalism, to maintain the school's competitiveness in the marketplace, and to develop and confirm placement opportunities.

Professional arts programs are not blind to more traditional academic practice and liberal arts–oriented curriculum theory. Most professional arts programs have right-minded accrediting bodies available to them. In pursuing its charge by the membership to maintain the highest traditions and aims in the education of the artist and the designer, the National Association of Schools of Art and Design (NASAD) offers nationally respected accreditation to design schools. Dedicated to artistic and academic quality, NASAD states, "Every artist or designer must be, to some extent, a viewer, creator, analyst, critic, communicator, problem solver, theorist, and historian."[45] Under its General Studies criteria, NASAD requires that artists and designers develop an understanding of other areas of human achievement, including:

---

[44]Charles W. Smith, *Market Values in American Higher Education: The Pitfalls and Promises* (Lanham Maryland: Rowman & Littlefield, 2000), 104–105.
[45]National Association of Schools of Art and Design Handbook, 2001–2002.

- The ability to think, speak and write clearly and effectively.
- An informed acquaintance with math and science.
- An ability to address culture and history from a variety of perspectives.
- Basic understanding and experience in thinking about moral and ethical problems.
- The ability to respect and evaluate work in a variety of disciplines.
- The capacity to explain and defend one's views effectively and rationally.[46]

These are requirements for membership. They are *must* statements, which are to be met in practice in order for a school to gain and retain accreditation. They seem obviously beneficial toward the education of members of society. A focus on quality liberal education content, however, is expensive from both a financial and a time allotment point of view. To include a quarter of a curriculum's required credit hours, as some schools do, subtracts from the technological and skills-based content capability. The ever-expanding content needed to serve industry advice and requests puts pressure on the general education content to contract and make room. The criteria remain *must* statements, however, as I believe they should. The schools that avoid them in order to more efficiently prepare skills-based graduates must also forego NASAD's academic accreditation. More important, they deny their graduates a more complete, intelligent, and valid education.

Of the three types of knowledge, technical, interpretive, and emancipatory, most design schools are effective at delivering only the first. It may be unrealistic to expect significant, emancipatory social change from the field of applied arts, but it is rational for society to expect a designer to interpret, understand, and react to his or her environment and culture. Eisner encourages, as a developing quality toward a worldview, educational connoisseurship:

> The consequence of using educational criticism to perceive educational objects and events is the development of educational connoisseurship. As one learns how to look at educational phenomena, as one ceases using stock responses to educational situations and develops habits of perceptual exploration, the ability to experience qualities and their relationships increases. This phenomenon occurs in virtually every arena in which connoisseurship has developed.[47]

---

[46]Ibid.
[47]Elliot Eisner, *The Educational Imagination: On the Design and Evaluation of School Programs*, 2nd ed. (New York: Macmillan Publishing Co., 1985), 242.

Connoisseurship is a qualitative measure to be employed by educators, students, and professionals sensibly to blend workview and worldview. As we saw with Davis and her design-based education model, however, connoisseurship can become egocentric quite easily, dropping into self-serving myopia.

The market has since the mid-1980s been "enjoying the stature accorded to God,"[48] and the self-serving and industry-serving by higher education further bolsters the subservience. The market-driven managerial god-ness of those who advise professional education programs are responsible for the resulting quantitative standards of efficiency and productivity, the commodification of knowledge. From somewhere must come the power to insist on the agency of liberal arts to add a worldview to the workview that professional higher education serves.

Looking into the educational phenomena of market control and academic connoisseurship, considering where the power to generate a thoughtful solution can reside, will require a critical literacy that was defined by Giroux as "both a narrative for agency as well as a referent for critique."[49] It will allow education to reclaim its voice, history, and future, and to assess how power and social practice can aid in recreating a democratic educational culture rather than consenting to market influence.

How can we effect normative change? Knowing how power shapes knowledge and social practice is a critical part of the solution. Principles of corporate culture today are a power source that is intersecting and interfering with the traditional meaning of higher education.

The fourth face of power (Power$_4$), according to Foucault, says change in the ideal type is necessary and good in social and cultural terms.[50] Foucault's discussion of power acknowledges a normative cognition that utilizes the agency of both leaders and followers, and a recognition of the influence of a society's or organization's ideal types, norms, and evolutionary thought. Power$_4$ lies embedded in all social practices. It is omnipresent, it mediates all human relationships, and it enables and disables agency. Validating the leader–follower relationship and encouraging normative cognition, Power$_4$ is always accompanied by resistance.[51] Foucault sees the structure of contemporary thought shaped by conventional institutions and practices, and the ideal types affected by normative change brought about through rational discourse.

---

[48] Lears, op. cit.

[49] Henry Giroux, "Liberal Arts, Teaching, and Critical Literacy: Toward a Definition of Schooling as a Form of Cultural Politics," Contemporary Curriculum Discourses, ed. William F. Pinar (Scottsdale, AZ: Gorsuch Scarisbrick, 1988), 249.

[50] Michel Foucault, "Power and Strategies," Power/Knowledge: Selected Interviews and Other Writings 1972–1977, ed. Colin Gordon (New York: Pantheon, 1980).

[51] Digester, Peter, "The Fourth Face of Power," Journal of Politics, 54 (November 1992): 977–1007.

If Power$_4$ enables the definition of a contemporary ideal type, and if resistance steadily changes norms, then the changing norms must lead to an eventual ideal-type redefinition. Throughout all societies and organizations, norms have a tendency to evolve and to change, and, eventually, changing norms affect the perspectival ideal type.

If the contemporary ideal type is what it appears, the service of industry by higher education, then I have a problem with the definition of ideal type. I also have to wonder if higher education can mount a resistance that can indeed effect normative change. We will not be able to return to pre-1980 norms before corporations became godlike, but we might succeed in reintroducing thoughtfulness and social and cognitive intelligence to the graduating members of professional education organizations.

Can we accept the value of professional education, but insist that it be delivered in a liberal way? Liberal education and the liberal arts specifically go far beyond the acquisition of skills. Liberal education is education in and for thoughtfulness.[52] Perhaps the central question in a new curriculum theory, does the market really want thinkers?

The market has been diligent in its insistence on skilled workers who can solve the immediate problems at hand, whatever the professional discipline. Business exists to solve problems and serve its customers. The market would not exist if there were no problems to be solved. Problem solving is a not-so-liberal ability, and thinking employees could upset the apple cart.

Thinkers are questioners, and questioners make questionable employees. True, the questioners are potential business leaders, and that is potentially good for the market and its future leadership. But it is not good for the leaders who wish to hire and make a dependable profit on the skilled workers. It is through a liberal education, even (or especially) within the professional arts, that the educated become empowered to think about what they are doing, to become mindful, to share meanings, to conceptualize, and to make sense of their lived worlds.[53] Maxine Greene noted how seldom that empowerment takes place today when:

> The dominant watchwords remain "effectiveness," "proficiency," "efficiency," and an ill-defined, one-dimensional "excellence." Reforms or no, teachers are asked to teach to the end of "economic competitiveness" for the nation. They are expected to process the young (seen as "human resources") to perform acceptably on some level of an increasingly systematized world … the orientation has been to accommodation, to fitting into existing social and economic structures, to what is given, to what is inescapably *there*.[54]

---

[52]Leon Kaas, "The Aims of Liberal Education," *The Aims of Education*, Produced for the Dean of the College by the University Publications Office, University of Chicago, 1997.

[53]Maxine Greene, op. cit., 12.

[54]Ibid.

Perhaps the industry advisers to education and the industry-serving educational organizations knowingly perpetuate a skills-based, nonliberal education in the name of effectiveness, proficiency, efficiency, and excellence. Perhaps it is an underlying truth that thinking employees might affect the conscience of the industry and market.

Thoughtfulness does affect the conscience of future society. Leon Kaas wonders how both the professionally educated and the market would benefit from liberal education, and he points out that there are no courses called Liberal Education. Liberal education is a concept that can be applied to any course, professional and skills based or not. He says, "Specialization need not be incompatible with thoughtfulness, though many specialists turn out to be thoughtless".[55] Liberal education concepts in a multiplicity of courses will produce a multiplicity of worldviews that can only serve to expand the intelligence and the thoughtfulness of the student. Liberal education can be thoughtful, reflective, and conscious of what one considers good, and the process can be simultaneous with professional practice. Thoughtfulness is good for us as citizens, it is good for our lives as human beings, and it is good for our lives as social beings, which would include our relationship with the market.

Skills-based learning creates successful workers, more jobs, and practicality for schools, students, and employers. That is the claim of educational conservatives, the "establishment bulldozer".[56] Though it is now and will remain useful to professional schools, students, faculty, graduates and their recipient professions that professional skills are believed to be important, it is imperative that the purveyors of professional education maintain a liberal perspective regarding their role and cultural obligation to society. Skills do have a proper role in the "overall project of 'getting something right,' namely, life,"[57] but Gregory warns that if schools and teachers lead students to believe that they are one with their skills, and that they have value only because of their oneness with their computers, the students will one day resent not only the schools and teachers, but also society as a whole. At some point, without the benefit of being educated as a whole individual with social and cognitive intelligence, society's ever-changing values and its rapidly evolving skills expectations can only diminish and them.

There are two modes of existence within which one must direct a liberally educated life: freedom from and responsibility toward. Freedom from by itself is rather meaningless, but should be incorporated into the professional arts students' and professional skilled workers' ideology. Maxine

---

[55] Kass, op. cit., 95.
[56] Gregory, op. cit.
[57] Ibid.

Greene referred to freedom from as "negative freedom, the right not to be interfered with or coerced or compelled."[58] I accept the fact that professional education programs have allowed market values to invade, interfere, coerce, and compel, but I reject any rationale for the situation to continue as it exists today. I promote a new insistence on freedom from these detriments. We must educate for freedom, including freedom from, grounded in an awareness that we as educators, the aspiring students, and the expectant market share a world lived in common. Leading me into the claim for responsibility toward, Greene writes, "Education for freedom must clearly focus on the range of human intelligences, the multiple languages and symbol systems available for ordering experience and making sense of the lived world."[59] Responsibility toward comes from an educated worldview and an awareness that the lived world includes a workview. Responsibility toward centers our efforts on our future, our society, and ourselves. Responsibility toward combined with freedom from is difficult, but it is an existential freedom brought about by a useful liberal education. A liberal arts education allows for responsibility toward a world-inclusive view of a career, whereas skills-based learning commands blind commitment to a job. When we only have a skills-based education, we lose the perspective from which we can judge what we have lost. We no longer know what it is that we need to recover.[60]

The predominantly skills-based and profession-based curricula being forced upon students by the education/industry cohort under the guise of becoming "professionals in the real world" are a disservice, a construct we have no justification for promoting or accepting. A discipline-based education that embraces the concepts of liberal education and the liberal arts as well as the skills necessary to contribute to society while assuring a vital social and cultural life is the educational enrichment we owe our students, our institutions, and the market as well.

REFERENCES

Bracey, Gerald. 2002. *The War on America's Public Schools*. Boston: Allyn and Bacon.

Britzman, Deborah P. 1998. *Lost Subjects, Contested Objects: Toward a Psychoanalytic Inquiry of Learning*. Albany NY: SUNY Press.

Davis, Meredith. 1999. Design's Inherent Interdisciplinarity: The Arts in Integrated Curricula *Arts Education Policy Review* 101, no. 1: 8–13.

Digester, Peter. 1992. The Fourth Face of Power. *Journal of Politics* 54: 977–1007.

Dorn, Charles M. 1993. Art as Intelligent Activity *Arts Education Policy Review* 95, 2: 2–9.

Eisner, Elliot. 1982. *Cognition and Curriculum*. New York: Longman Inc. Company.

---

[58] Maxine Greene, op. cit., 16.
[59] Ibid, 125.
[60] Gregory, op. cit.

Eisner, Elliot. 1985. *The Educational Imagination: On the Design and Evaluation of School Programs, 2nd ed.* New York: Macmillan Publishing Co.

Eisner, Elliot. 1988. *The Role of Discipline-Based Art Education in America's Schools.* Los Angeles: The J. Paul Getty Trust.

Eisner, Elliot. 1997. *Educating Artistic Vision.* New York: Macmillan.

Eisner, Elliot. 1999. "Beyond Creating: The Place for Art in America's Schools," *ArtsEdNet.* E-Journal on-line. Available at <http://www.artsednet.getty.edu/ArtsEdNet/Read/Beyond/whyart.html> (Accessed 20 April 2002).

Foucault, Michel. 1972. "Power and Strategies." *Power/Knowledge: Selected Interviews and Other Writings,* ed. Colin Gordon. New York: Pantheon.

Giroux, Henry. 1988. Liberal Arts, Teaching, and Critical Literacy: Toward a Definition of Schooling as a Form of Cultural Politics. *Contemporary Curriculum Discourses,* ed. William F. Pinar. Scottsdale, AZ: Gorsuch Scarisbrick.

Giroux, Henry. 2001. Vocationalizing Higher Education: Schooling and the Politics of Corporate Culture. *Beyond the Corporate University: Culture and Pedagogy in the New Millennium,* ed. Henry Giroux and Kostas Myrsiades. Lanham, MD: Rowman & Littlefield Publishers, Inc.

Greene, Maxine. 1988. *The Dialectic of Freedom.* New York: Teachers College Press.

Gregory, Marshall. 1997. Liberal Learning vs. Professional Training, or Liberal Education Knows a Hawk from a Handsaw. Conference Paper Presented at the Annual Pedagogy Conference, Humanities and Arts Higher Education Network, Open University, Milton Keynes, England. October, 1994. Butler University.

Janus Head: Journal of Interdisciplinary Studies in Literature, Continental Philosophy, Phenomenological Psychology, and the Arts. 1998. E-Journal on-line. Available at <http://www.janushead.org> (Accessed 1 August 2002).

Jones, Marilee. 2002. There's a New Kid in Town: Observations on the Newest Generation of MIT Students *MIT Technology Review* (April): 12–14.

Kaas, Leon. 1997. *The Aims of Liberal Education.* Produced for the Dean of the College by the University Publications Office, University of Chicago.

Kliebard, Herbert. 1992. *Forging the American Curriculum: Essays in Curriculum History and Theory.* New York: Routledge.

Lears, Jackson. 2000. "The Radicalism of Tradition: Teaching the Liberal Arts in a Managerial Age," *The Hedgehog Review* 2 (Fall): 3. University of Virginia: Institute for Advanced Studies in Culture.

Levin, G. Roy. 1999. Art as Cultural Practice. *Art Journal* 58, 1 (Spring): 17–20.

Mannheim, Karl. 1971. *From Karl Mannheim,* ed. Kurt H. Wolff. New York: Oxford University Press.

National Association of Schools of Art and Design Handbook, 2001–2002.

Rorty, Richard. 1998. "Pragmatism, Relativism, and Irrationalism." In *Epistemology: The Big Questions,* ed. Linda Alcoff. Malden, MA: Blackwell Publishers Inc.

Schwartz, Barry. 1987. *The Battle for Human Nature: Science, Morality, and Modern Life.* New York: W.W. Norton & Company.

Slaughter, Sheila. 2001. Professional Values and the Allure of the Market. *ACADEME.* E-Journal on-line. Available at http://www.aaup.org/publications/Academe/01SO/so01sla.htm (Accessed 16 August 2002).

Smith, Charles W. 2000. *Market Values in American Higher Education: The Pitfalls and Promises.* Lanham Maryland: Rowman & Littlefield.

United States, National Commission on Excellence in Education. 1983. *A Nation at Risk.* Washington, DC: Government Printing Office.

Chapter 10

Controlling the Power
Over Knowledge: Selling
the Crisis for Self-Serving Gains

Lynn Wilson

Controlling knowledge about schools plays a large role in shaping public opinion about, among other things, the view that school systems are failing and are in dire need of not just reform but complete restructuring.[1] For decades, mass media has shaped public opinion on public education to influence policy and reform agendas. Since the report, *A Nation at Risk*, and more recently the No Child Left Behind Act, the general public has repeatedly heard that failing school systems are directly impacting American economic viability in the global marketplace.[2] How are the reports put together? Who puts these reports together? How are the reports funded? I wish to "push the envelope" in this chapter by highlighting the conflicts of interest among government reports and the corporation-saturated panels who produce them. Indeed, in light of the gross mishandling of funds and information revealed in recent and continuing corporate scandals, one wonders why businesses are continually turned to for advice and input on educational management issues. This chapter argues that the control of knowledge about the public school system has been and continues to be a calculated plan by neo-conservatives, who have taken hold of education reform since the Reagan and Bush eras.

---

[1] Joel Spring, *Political Agendas for Education: From the Christian Coalition to the Green Party* (Mahwah, NJ: Lawrence Erlbaum, 1997).

[2] David C. Berliner and Bruce J. Biddle, *The Manufactured Crisis: Myths, Fraud and the Attack on American Public Schools.* (New York: Perseus Books, 1995).

The conflict of interests in education centers on the fact that special-interest groups struggle for the power to define the primary purpose of education. Special-interest groups range from individuals and organizations such as teachers unions, private foundations, religious organizations, ethnic populations, and the corporate sector. Each of these groups wishes to control the flow of ideas and information about schools and in schools to further particular values and goals. Control of what students learn in schools arguably influences future decisions regarding politics, economics, consumerism, and other social and ethical issues. Controlling the knowledge that students receive in schools builds loyalty so future decisions are congruent with the needs of a particular organization.[3] In order to control the knowledge students learn in schools, special-interest groups attempt to control the knowledge the public receives about schools by using statistics and reports to support their particular ideological position in educational politics.[4] While this point is nothing new, this chapter furthers the point and argues that the exertion of power to control the knowledge about schools is most apparent in the relationships between the corporate sector and conservative foundations.

Conservative foundations (or "think tanks") like the Thomas B. Fordham Foundation, the Cato Institute, and the Brookings Institution are each committed to value systems that ostensibly privilege rugged individualism, reduced government, and free-market logic. Part of the problem I wish to point out, however, is that these (and other) conservative foundations are supported by corporate money and employ high-profile, former government officials to advance their agenda. It is the agenda, to be sure, that is most problematic, especially given that public schools are seen as an institution to destroy—albeit under the guise of "choice" and privatization plans. Herein is an important distinction: When defined, education becomes many things to many people and its purpose is a source of conflict between politicians, scholars, parents, teachers, and students alike. The most recent struggle has two primary (though not the only) players: progressives and the neo-conservatives. Progressives generally see education as a means toward social justice by providing all students equal access to schooling and redistributing funding for schools to give each student equality of opportunity. Students are engaged in problem solving in the "here and now" so that future problems are more easily solved if or when they arise.[5] Student roles are organized around becoming citizens who are able to actively participate in a more democratic society. Neo-conservative ideologies define the purpose of education as a means to shape behaviors of students to "prepare" them for the world of work and to meet the needs of the workforce. Neo-conservatives believe that

---

[3] Joel Spring, *Conflicts of Interests: The Politics of American Education* (New York: McGraw-Hill, 2002), 32.

[4] Ibid., 27.

[5] Ibid., 51.

assimilating students into a Euro-centric, basic skills–oriented, testing and accountability culture is the best way to provide equality of opportunity (via a cohesive and unified culture).[6]

From these conflicts of interests over the purposes of education stem the ongoing debates and deliberations within the education reform movement. Neo-conservatives have influenced public opinion toward defining education as preparation for the world of work through strategically controlling the flow of ideas and information about school reform to the public.[7] Well-known neo-conservative scholars like   D'Souza, William Bennett, Chester Finn, and Diane Ravitch serve as fellows in a multitude of conservative, private foundations that distribute "knowledge" about schooling and education. Corporate sponsorship of conservative foundations who are in direct support of the neo-conservative reform movement goes beyond the acquisition of knowledge for power; corporations use the foundations to influence public opinion about schools. Corporate control over the knowledge about schools has reshaped and redefined educational policy, ultimately affecting even the knowledge distributed in schools. The question arises that if corporate interests are being served by neo-conservative ideologies, and corporations strongly influence the knowledge the public receives about schools, is the general public being sold a bill of goods muddled with self-serving agendas that care more about a bottom line than a common good? Furthermore, what connection is there between corporate support of conservative foundations and corporate-owned mass media outlets?

The document that first fueled the neo-conservative movement is the infamous *A Nation at Risk*. The report was published in 1983 during the Reagan administration under the leadership of then Secretary of Education, Terrel Bell. The report created a state of crisis for American public education that (and since then) has repeatedly been a source of information for a compliant-oriented, "bad news sells" press. *A Nation at Risk* made claims backed by statistical "evidence" that U.S. schools were failing, thereby threatening our economic stability and global competitiveness. The report also spurred more than a decade-long series of reports propagating misinformation about American schools to the general public.[8]

The issue with *A Nation at Risk* and its subsequent siblings is that corporate interests are involved not only in naming the problems but also in defining

---

[6] Berliner and Biddle, 137.
[7] Ibid., 133.
[8] Berliner and Biddle discuss myths and misinformation of statistical reporting from *A Nation at Risk*. They also discuss a suppression of contradicting statistical analysis from the Sandia report by the Reagan/Bush administration so these myths could serve the neo-conservative reform agenda.

the solutions.[9] From the Reagan administration came a conservative reactionary uprising where wealthy corporate executives and family money icons such as Olin and Coors started sponsoring conservative think tank foundations to reshape public opinion regarding the purpose of education. The reshaping of public opinion was a calculated plan by private foundations to use publicly recognized intellectuals to distribute knowledge about schools in the popular press and through public speaking engagements. Fueling the already growing dissatisfaction with public education, corporate support of conservative foundations and corporate control of mass media enabled the corporate elite to maneuver themselves in key reform positions. They then supported "crisis reports" and statements regarding threats to economic stability as being directly affected by a poorly educated workforce.[10] Corporate support of conservative think tank foundations, the control of mass media by the corporate elite as a forum to distribute the report "findings," and claims of economic woes scapegoating education as a scare tactic to influence public opinion are examples of corporate interests involved in naming the problem and providing the solution.

The most common claims made by businesses regarding what they deem a failing system in the workforce include the following:

- Costs of schools are skyrocketing and investment is not bringing a return.
- Workers are unproductive and lacking skills necessary to be competitive in the global market (as a result of poor schooling and teacher incompetence).
- Unprepared workers cost business large amounts of money for remedial training.[11]

How is it that an economic superpower is pointing the finger at a poorly educated workforce as the primary cause for economic viability in a global market?[12] Even with evidence that contradicts claims against the American public school, corporate leaders and politicians continue to propagate the cause-and-effect thesis between poorly educated workforce and economic woes. Having used the education crisis to gain key reform positions, corporate elites have positioned themselves as educational experts enabling them to voice business concerns about educational problems while also defining solutions for those problems. The solutions to what are deemed failing pub-

---

[9]Susan Ohanian, "Goals 2000: What's In a Name?," *Phi Delta Kappan* (January 2000): 345–355.
[10]Berliner and Biddle, 133.
[11]Ibid., 78–102.
[12]Daniel Tanner, "Manufacturing Problems and Selling Solutions: How to Succeed in the Education Business Without Really Educating," *Phi Delta Kappan* (November, 2000): 188–202.

lic schools are in the forefront of the current educational reform movement and take shape as raising standards, standardized assessment, accountability, competition, and choice. One example of this movement is *A Nation Still at Risk: An Education Manifesto*, published by the Thomas B. Fordham Foundation.[13] The report debunks some of the manufactured crises from *A Nation at Risk* but is quick to name the current problem as "our students lack[ing] subject matter vital to our country's future." The scare tactic is similar to the 1983 parent, but the difference is that the experts naming the problem are also willing and "able" to suggest particular strategies for solving the very problems they name. Realizing who the people are who are making and solving problems may not yield skepticism, particularly if the individuals compiling the report were unbiased and had no personal capital gains at stake. Yet, present for the development of *A Nation at Risk* were approximately 40 individuals, among them business leaders, religious leaders, public policymakers, conservative foundation fellows, and administrators from the Edison Project schools, charter schools, and testing industry companies.[14] The presence of self-interested parties calls into question the integrity of the report itself.

Corporate control over the mass media has reshaped and redefined democracy in private and capitalist terms.[15] Intensified control of the mass media by the ruling elite has served the corporate agenda by advocating the dismantling and restructuring of the public schooling system to reflect business needs and interests. In contemporary U.S. society, the public depends on the mass media to provide accurate accounts of newsworthy events. Unfortunately, this expectation is not always met as reporters report on what sells, which generally is bad news. Such reporting is evidenced when education is covered in the popular press. Most stories about education inordinately focus on low achievement (with no context for evaluative findings), disproportionately emphasize conflict and failures, and strategically misuse quotes and statistics to propagate the belief that school systems are not succeeding.[16] Negativity from the popular press has influenced public confidence about public schooling, furthering advantaging elite interests.[17] Negativity from the popular press stretches back to the muckracking of Joseph Mayer Rice in 1893, but, as has been pointed out, continues to be seen

---

[13]Thomas B. Fordham Foundation, *A Nation Still at Risk: An Education Manifesto* (Washington D.C.: Opinion Papers, 1998), ERIC, ED 422455. The President of Thomas B. Fordham Foundation is Chester Finn, a neo-conservative scholar and former assistant secretary of education.

[14]At the end of *A Nation Still at Risk*, a complete list of individuals and professional of affiliations supportive of the document was included.

[15]Kenneth J. Saltman, *Collateral Damage: Corporatizing Public Schools—A Threat to Democracy* (Lanham, MD: Rowman and Littlefield Publishers, 2000), xiv.

[16]David C. Berliner and Bruce J. Biddle, "The Awful Alliance between the Media and School Critics," *Education Digest* (January, 1999): 3–10.

[17]Saltman, xviii.

and heard 20 years after the publication of *A Nation at Risk*. Does any rise in negativity coincide with the surge of neo-conservatives in the political arena and in private foundations?[18]

Corporate interests are served by the alliance between mass media, neo-conservative scholars, and public school critics. Much of the decline in public confidence is arguably due to reinforcing the idea that school systems are failing. Low confidence in the public sector enables corporate elites to become major players in shaping policy and opinion regarding what schools should look like and what they should do. Controlling the power over knowledge about schools shapes public opinion by reinforcing ideas, values, and information favorable to the underlying corporate purpose of education: a skilled and compliant workforce.[19] The alliance between corporations and mass media is evidenced in the control of mass media by a select group of corporate conglomerates. Besides the press appearing to misuse and abuse evidence by oversimplifying statistical analyses, propagating skewed conclusions to the public in the name of research evidence, and suppressing contradictory evidence regarding public school success, there seems to be an uncanny relationship between corporate control over the mass media and private capital education ventures:[20] For example:

- Viacom owns CBS. It also owns Simon and Schuster, of which Prentice Hall is a subsidiary. Prentice Hall is the nation's leading publisher and is strongly affiliated with Pearson Education, the world's leading learning company. Pearson acquired NCS, a division responsible for applications, services, and technologies for education testing and assessment, a multibillion-dollar industry. Pearson brought in $8 billion from the market in 2002.[21]
- The *Washington Post* owns a host of newspapers and magazines and has several subsidiaries in education such as Kaplan, Inc. Kaplan is a tutoring and test-preparation company responsible for publishing course material, books, software, and Web content to assist students in test preparation. Kaplan also owns other educational businesses such as Quest education and Score!Prep. The *Washington Post*'s education revenues accounted for approximately 11% of the total reve-

---

[18] Berliner and Biddle, in *Manufactured Crisis*, discuss press coverage after *A Nation at Risk* as being the beginning of the onslaught of negativity experienced through the 80s and 90s. Spring, in *Political Agendas*, discusses the neo-conservative movement taking form about the same time within its calculated plan of monopolizing information that gets to the public.

[19] Spring, *Conflicts of Interests*.

[20] Berliner and Biddle, *Manufactured Crisis*, 158–168.

[21] http://www.ncspearson.com 8/4/02, and http://www.pearson.com as noted in the CBS market watch link.

nues in 2000 and are growing with the current educational push toward assessment.[22]

- Other corporate conglomerates such as Disney (ABC) and General Electric (NBC) are more subtly invested in education ventures with operations such as Disney learning partnerships.

In addition, the Fox Network, though not directly involved in capital gains from educational ventures, has strong connections with conservatives through support for and affiliations with conservative private foundations, with values that support pro-business and free-market ideologies.[23] Pro business ideologies are based on the pursuit of profits and are concerned with reducing employment costs to increase gains. Major networks promote pro-business and elitist positions to influence the very public opinion that shapes educational policy to serve corporate interests. Consider some indicators that suggest media affiliations with pro-business positions: In 2000, 92% of all U.S. sources interviewed were White, 85% of whom were male and 75% of whom were Republican. In addition, business representatives were more than 35 times more likely to appear as a source than were labor union representatives.[24] These statistics allude to the broadcast industry serving the needs of the business elite who own them rather than providing an open forum where knowledge about public interests, like schools, is balanced and not serving a special interest. Corporate control of the mass media calls into question the use of sources and reports to serve corporate interest in reshaping educational policy. Corporate support of private, conservative think tank foundations, who are regularly the sources used by mass media regarding the alleged crisis state of American education, is one way to control the knowledge the public receives about public schools.[25]

In the 1970s, William Simon, head of the Olin Foundation called for business leaders to fund the conservative foundations that support what he termed "counterintelligensia," or the spreading of free-market ideas.[26] With the aim of shaping public agendas and the construction of a network of con-

---

[22]Margie Burns, "Washington Post to Benefit from Bush Education Bill," Online Journal, 21 January 2002. Available from http://www.onlinejournal.com/Special_Report/Burns012102/burns012102.html. Accessed 4 August 2002.

[23]Spring, *Political Agenda*.

[24]Fair Press Release, "Who's on the News: Study Shows Network News Sources Skew White, Male and Elite," *Fairness in Accuracy in Reporting*, June 2000. Available from http://www.fair.org/press-releases/power-sources-release.html. Accessed 04 August 2002.

[25]Sam Husseini, "Checkbook Analysis: Corporations Support Think-Tanks—And the Favor is Returned," *Extra!* , May/June 2000. Available from http://www.fair.org/extra/think-tanks-survey.html. Accessed 4 August 2002.

[26]One free market idea is ending the "public school monopoly" over educational services. Many services, like food preparation and busing are already privately contracted. See Deron Boyles, *American Education and Corporations: The Free Market Goes to School* (New York: Falmer, 2000), 111–171.

servative institutions, Simon and his colleagues identified one course of action: to dismantle what they perceived to be a liberal agenda in public education. To do this, they needed to get the information and ideas out to the general public, and used a strategy called the trickle-down distribution of ideas theory. This theory marks the calculated plan by conservative think tanks (and the corporate interests that sponsor them) to control and manipulate the knowledge the public receives about schools as well as to influence public policymakers within the legislative process. The trickle-down distribution of ideas theory has four broad-based strategies to disseminate and distribute knowledge:

- Create foundations and institutions that fund research and policy statements supportive of school choice, privatization of public schools, and charter schools.
- Identify scholars to do the research, write policy statements, and lecture at public forums that are favorable to school choice, privatization of public schools, and charter schools.
- Finance conferences to bring like-minded scholars together for the sharing of ideas and the creation of books.
- Pay scholars to write newspaper opinion pieces that are then distributed to hundreds of newspapers across the country.[27]

The call to businesses to fund conservative foundations resulted in large sums of money donated to support existing foundations and to start new ones. Corporate donations comprise upwards of 43% of funding sources for private foundations and 18% of conservative foundations receive 75% of all donations to foundations generally.[28] These conservative foundations appear to have overlapping missions, namely the discrediting of public institutions and lessening of corporate responsibility.[29] One result of this appears to be a loosening of corporate responsibility in terms of school funding. According to Spring, corporations do not pay their fair share of taxes to support public schools.[30] To dismantle the public institution of education using the trickle-down distribution of ideas theory, foundations solicited the help from well-known scholars such as Chester Finn, William Bennett, Diane Ravitch, and Lamar Alexander, each of whom spent time working in govern-

---

[27] Spring, *Political Agenda*, 27.
[28] See Husseini, op. cit.; and also a series of phone calls to headquarters of conservative think tanks. Many were forthright with corporate sponsorship, others would not disclose. 18% receive 75% is from "The Wealthy Conservative Think Tanks," *Covert Action Quarterly*, Winter 1998. Available from http://www.thirdworldtraveler.com/Democracy/WealthyThinkTanks.html. Accessed 4 August 2002.
[29] Spring, *Political Agendas*.
[30] Spring, *Conflict of Interests*, 20.

ment positions during the Reagan and Bush administrations and used their positions to establish a presence in the popular press. The conservative foundations affiliated with these individuals and others like them, include the Fordham Foundation, Heritage Foundation, Hudson Institute, Cato Institute, American Enterprise Institute, and Brookings Institution.[31]

The Heritage Foundation and the American Enterprise Institute are two of the largest foundations that support neo-conservative policies and reform agendas in education, including removing multicultural education and increasing standardization through testing.[32] From publishing reports designed to influence legislators to the dismantle of the Department of Education to the publication of *Illiberal Education: The Politics of Race and Sex on Campus* and *The Bell Curve*, conservative think tanks are advancing the notions of free-market logic and school choice by selling them through the press to the general public.[33] In 1999, 91% of all media citations from foundation reports came from conservative and centrist organizations whereas only 9% came from progressive organizations.[34]

What is arguably not realized by the general public is that think tanks are marketing ideas about school reform by reporting selective research findings.[35] The irony is that the conservative, pro-business scholars, as well as corporate executives, name the problem and define the solution. Foundation scholars and their reports discuss schools of excellence as those that encompass market values, and use market language to connect schools with competition and greed. Conservative reform agendas tend to use market terms such as *standards, assessment, accountability, pro-business values, data-driven, competition,* and so on, to convince the public sector that what has worked for the

---

[31] Spring, *Political Agendas.*

[32] Ibid.

[33] *Illiberal Education* was authored by Dinesh D'Souza, a John Olin Foundation and American Enterprise Institute scholar. The writing criticizes multicultural education and affirmative action because it places minority students in high risk intellectual environments where they compete against better prepared students. D'Souza also believes that multiculturalism and feminism are destroying liberal education by replacing significant books written by white males with inferior writings by minorities and women. Peter Brimelow authored Alien Nation with support from the Cato Institute which expresses concerns about the decreasing percentages of whites in the population and that US citizens have legitimate interests in the racial composition of their population. Bell Curve was authored by Charles Murray; scholar at the American Enterprise Institute attempts to show that IQs differ by race and social class and uses that as an understanding to justify the wage disparities between whites and blacks in the workforce. Spring, *Political Agendas,* 39.

[34] Fair Press Release, "The Rich get Richer," *Fairness in Accuracy and Reporting.* Available from http://www.fair.org/extra/think-tanks-survey.html. Accessed 4 August 2002.

[35] Jeffrey W. Wimer and Debra S. Vredenburg, "When Ideology Sabotages the Truth: The Politics of Privately-Funded Educational Vouchers in One Urban School District," paper presented at the American Educational Studies Association, Mexico City, Mexico, November 1, 2003. The authors were part of a Fordham Foundation grant that intended to show support for private voucher programs. The findings of the authors did not support the foundation's conclusions and was not included in any findings by the foundation.

corporate world will work for public services. But we should remember that "corporate values exist to provide a financial return to the people that own them, thus when business thinks about schools, its agenda is driven by what will maximize its profitability, not necessarily by what is in the best interest of the students."[36]

Involvement of the corporate sector in the education reform movement as a means to serve business and industry needs is not a new phenomenon. The rhetoric of business education reform agendas encapsulating market values is an offshoot of an ideology that evolved in the 19th century and reemerged in the 1950s as human capital theory (HCT). HCT argues that education should be an investment into human resources to benefit industry and fuel the national economy. Industrial support of HCT stems from the idea of maximizing profits while minimizing costs. If schools become nothing more than training grounds for the corporate sector, costs associated with training workers are dramatically reduced. It is not a difficult stretch to recognize that the interests of business in education and the interests of education toward a democratic society are not the same. Businesses are interested in profits whereas schools are interested in students.

Corporations are not the only ones interested in profit, though. Many respected educational scholars and foundation fellows are also finding ways to utilize their elite positions for private capital gain: "We examine these [self-serving interests] with reluctance. Most Americans like to think well of their fellow citizens, and some people will find it hard to believe that criticism of schools may also be motivated by hidden selfish interests; and yet, such interests often underlie campaigning of public advocacy."[37] Specifically, neo-conservative scholars and former secretaries of education have all started or involved themselves in private, for-profit companies. Their ventures include selling their ideas to parents and schools regarding how to reform education to meet the standards of "excellence" they themselves define. So we now see prestigious scholars naming the problems, defining the solutions, *and* reaping financial benefits. Regardless of their public positions in government, has an ethical line been crossed once private gain is the objective of former public servants? And furthermore, if and when personal profit becomes the motive, should the public question the information reported by these individuals? As Berliner and Biddle put it:

> We don't want to suggest that all criticisms of education or proposals for reforming public schools are motivated by crass, selfish interests. Indeed, some criticism of education comes from people with genuine concern for the problems faced by our schools and are focused on the parts of education the spe-

---

[36] Alfie Kohn, "What to Look for in a Classroom and Other Essays," in *The Five-Hundred-Pound Gorilla* (San Francisco: Jossey-Bass, 1998), 190.
[37] Berliner and Biddle, *Manufactured Crisis*, 149.

cial interests of the critics themselves; friends or business interests of the critics; or the ideological, racial, ethnic, religious, or class interests that critics represent. Such possibilities should alert us all to read criticism of the public schools with a healthy dose of skepticism.[38]

Of these neo-conservative scholars, Chester Finn, Jr., William Bennett, and Lamar Alexander are just a few of the public school critics most recognized by the general public.

Chester Finn, Jr., served as Assistant Secretary of Education under William Bennett during the Reagan years. He is currently the president of the Thomas B. Fordham Foundation and has served as a scholar with the Olin Foundation, Hudson Institute, Hoover Institute, and Manhattan Institute. Finn has published 11 books and authored more than 200 articles.[39] Finn plays a large role in naming problems and defining solutions regarding education reform through his involvement with conservative foundations and corporate-interest groups such as the Business Roundtable, New American Schools, and various committees established to involve business interests in education reform.[40] As a major architect of *America 2000*, published in 1991, Finn was instrumental in the development of suggested educational reform strategies to fix the "failing public schools."[41] Part of this reform packet called for restructuring the American public schools through choice in the form of vouchers and charters. Strangely enough, almost on the heels of the proposed *America 2000*, Chris Whittle was aided by Finn in proposing the Edison Project, a coast-to-coast network of for-profit schools.[42] As Troy notes, "Chester Finn, a former assistant secretary of education in charge of anti-public school propaganda, has the gall to write that parents should not believe what they personally experience. In other words, they are too dumb to know what a good school is. His motive? Finn is heavily invested in commercial privatization of public schools, writing the curriculum for the Edison Project, a privatization initiative."[43]

William Bennett served as the Secretary of Education under Ronald Reagan and is affiliated with many of the conservative foundations mentioned. A

---

[38]Ibid., 152.

[39]From Hoover Institutes Web site's bio on Chester Finn. Available from http://www.hoover.stanford.edu/bios/finn.html. Accessed 19 July 2002.

[40]Susan Ohanian, "Goals 2000."

[41]Finn was instrumental in also naming the problem in *A Nation at Risk* through as Berliner and Biddle state that [*A Nation at Risk*] "was far from the end of the White House criticisms of American Education. Indeed, the next decade witnessed a veritable explosion of documents and pronouncements from government leaders—two American presidents, Ronald Reagan and George Bush, secretaries of education, assistant secretaries of education, and chiefs and staff members in federal agencies—telling Americans about the many problems of their public schools ..." (p. 3).

[42]Berliner and Biddle, *The Manufactured Crisis*, 151–152.

[43]Forrest J. Troy, "The Myth of our Failed Public School System," *Church and State* (January 1999): 17–20.

conservative Catholic and Republican, Bennett connects the religious right with the American public through a private foundation called Empower America. In 1993, Bennett was hired by Empower America to promote school choice and vouchers to the public by claiming that public schools lacked morals and values. The call for vouchers to "fix" these problems enabled parents to send their kids to private Catholic schools, perpetuating special-interest ideologies in what became government-funded schools.[44]

Empower America boasts that Bennett is "continuing a high profile fight against government bureaucracy and monopolies" since leaving government office in 1990. Bennett's solution to education centers on what he calls the three C's—choice, content, and character. Bennett has authored 14 books and has written on numerous opinion-editorials, appeared on countless talk shows, and given several public appearances across the country. Empower America lists a few examples of press releases, articles, and opinion-editorials on their Web site. Most center on vouchers, technology, standards, character, and the failing school system. These and other documents flood various media outlets to become influential documents in the political and public arenas. Such a consistent stream of information about schools shapes public opinion regarding what is considered wrong with schools and how schools should change. What the public does not hear is that the "knowledge" it receives about schools is often one-sided. As Berliner and Biddle explain,

> We note only, for example, some of those who write op-ed articles and are widely quoted are not necessarily objective and have something to gain from, say, the approval of vouchers that could be used at non-public schools. It serves their interests to promote the belief that public education is a failure and that privatization is the only sensible solution. Why, when they write or talk, aren't they identified as individuals who may be compromised in regard to their objectivity?[45]

Bennett has also positioned himself to gain from the education market in the wake of the reforms developed from the reports produced by he and other conservative writers. Bennett, a one-time critic of online learning, recently founded k12.com, an online curriculum and education center for Grades K–12. Tuition fees for accessing this curriculum are approximately $1,000 per year, or $225 per course. Parents can also order standardized tests to run diagnostics on their child in specific subject areas, graded by k12.com at the cost of $50 to $100 per test.[46]

---

[44] Spring, *Political Agenda*, 50. Bennett also was revealed to have a gambling addiction, raising questions regarding his authority on morals and ethics.
[45] Berliner and Biddle, "Awful Alliance" pp. 4–5.
[46] Susan Ohanian, *What Happened to Recess and why are our Children Struggling in Kindergarten?* (New York: McGraw-Hill, 2002).

The Web site/organization k12.com received a $10 million seed grant from Knowledge Universe. Knowledge Universe Learning Group either owns or holds shares in 14 companies in the for-profit education industry.[47] Market analysts claim the education industry is a "740 billion dollar market, second only to health care as a percentage of U.S. gross domestic product" and that the for-profit sectors are cornering a mere 100 billion of that market.[48] What is the collateral cost to education? Knowledge Universe, co-founded by "former junk bond king Michael Milken and his brother Lowell" is a prime example of an entrepreneurial approach to education. The point here is "connections." Chester Finn is on the board of directors of k12.com as is Rupert Murdoch of the Fox Network.[49]

Lamar Alexander served as the Secretary of Education from 1991 to 1993 under George H. W. Bush. Alexander joined Bennett as a co-director of Empower America and was a senior fellow at the Hudson Institute.[50] Currently a U.S. Senator, in 1989 he was the governor of Tennessee and was part of a group of governors responsible for the development of Goals 2000 (then America 2000). Alexander was appointed by Bush to help implement Goals 2000 using the language of human capital and national standards to inform the general public. To appease the corporate sector and their interest in keeping education reform costs at a minimum, Bush and Alexander claimed no correlation between an increase in spending on education with an increase in student achievement. This claim enabled corporations to continue to reap huge tax benefits while calling for education to meet their needs as a human-capital commodity.[51]

In 2000, Alexander headed up an e-commerce company called Simplexis. Simplexis, an online purchasing company for K–12 schools and their suppliers, had backing from not only Alexander himself, but also other corporate sponsors such as Kaplan Inc. (*The Washington Post*) and General Electric.[52] Schools spend approximately 5 percent to 8 percent of their total operating budget on supplies and equipment totaling anywhere between $16 and $26 billion annually.[53] Not lasting long, Simplexis assets

---

[47] Gerald W. Bracey, *The War Against America's Public Schools: Privatizing Schools, Commercializing Education* (Boston: Allyn and Bacon, 2002), 143.

[48] Jeffrey A. Fromm and Todd V. Kern, "Investment Opportunities in Education: Making a Profit While Making a Difference," *The Journal of Private Equity* (Fall 2000): 38.

[49] Ohanian, *Recess*, 48.

[50] Biography on Lamar Alexander's homepage. Available from http://www.lamaralexander.com/accomplishments. Accessed 18 August 2002.

[51] Spring, *Political Agenda*, 55.

[52] San Francisco Business Times, *American City Business Journal* (4 December 2000). Available from http:// www.bizjournals.com. Accessed 4 August 2002.

[53] Anne Bridgman, "Click Here To Buy," *American School Board Journal* (April 2000). Available from http://www.asbj.com.html. Accessed 4 August 2002.

folded into Publicbuy.net and sold for an undisclosed amount, though Alexander remains as cochairman of the parent company Co-nect.[54]

Is it fair that government officials place the special-interest needs of the corporate sector over a common good of society? What does it say that former public officials partner with corporations in for-profit ventures designed to benefit the investors who already have evaded social responsibilities? It seems like a win-win situation for the elite. As Ohanian sees it:

> Advocates for vouchers, choice, charters, high stakes testing, and any other notion certainly have a right to be heard. One might even suppose they have a right to try to establish an educational marketplace that ignores any obligation to improve education for all children. But the media has an obligation to label truth in promotion, to label propaganda as such, to separate the experts from the chaff. The conclusions of Chester Finn or a William Bennett should not be given the same weight as the conclusions of a Jerry Bracey or Linda McNeil, not because of their ideologies, but because of the respectability and the peer review of their research. At the very least, the media has an obligation to indicate which research is juried, and if they ever get really courageous, the media might also point out think tank incest when it occurs.[55]

The media has the power and control over what knowledge the public receives about schools; therefore the media has the responsibility to report all sides of the issue. Should the public know of Lamar Alexander's financial ties to an industry fueled in part by his own position of power?

Teachers and administrators across the country are under enormous pressure to devote instructional time preparing for high-stakes testing under recent federal and state mandates. Why is it that under the banner of reform, school administrators and supervisors so readily follow and even embrace what they suspect are wrongheaded policies and practices? Might the response to this question be that the answer is found in the myth that problems in education can be solved by turning to big business and the business model of managerial efficiency? In an educational model of efficiency, learning becomes an outcome and teaching becomes drill and practice or teaching for the test. Demonstrated success is associated with "excellence" derived from test scores and slotting students into a bell curve. Acceptance of this process by the general public allows standardized test scores to be used as a means and an end regarding what constitutes teaching and learning. Because the public is told that standards matter (and are objective), and the validation of the point comes from the apparently unassailable arena of business and capital, business models are accepted as good for schools. Yet, do we hear about the hidden interests

---

[54] Rhea Borja, "E-Procurement Firm Simplexis Closes Door as Industry Struggles," *Education Week* (5 December 2001). Available from http:/www.edweek.org.html. Accessed 4 August 2002.
[55] Ohanian, *Recess*, 195.

of the corporate sector as much as we hear about the "benefits"? Do we ever ask ourselves whether Enron, Arthur Andersen, Qwest, or WorldCom are the models for the very "excellence" and "standards" business touts for schools? The shift toward looking to big business as the expert is a "consequence of well organized, active push by powerful economic and political forces that view standardized, regimented reading programs and nation-wide high stakes testing as tools to advance their own interests."[56]

A result of Goals 2000 and America 2000 has been the effective linking of human capital to national academic standards. This, in turn, has enabled business leaders to maneuver into key reform positions. In 1991, with the help of Lamar Alexander and Diane Ravitch (then secretary and assistant secretary of education, respectively), President H. W. Bush allocated $1 million in start-up funds for CEOs and American business leaders to use in designing new schools to meet the challenges proposed in Goals 2000. These goals as outlined in Goals 2000 were primarily concerned with national standards and national testing. The development of new schools under the Goals 2000 "Accountability Package" created a host of committees responsible for the implementation of these standards. The committees were composed of business leaders, think-tank scholars, universities, and others. The inclusion of business executives in defining the solutions in education reform is a powerful political and social force in setting the policy for a public good. The largest corporate force behind high-stakes testing and accountability measures is the highly influential Business Roundtable (BRT).

The BRT was formed in the early 1970s and is a coalition of CEOs from the nation's largest corporations. The following is a paragraph from the BRT's Web site outlining their purpose and mission:

> With the publication of A Nation at Risk in 1983, the landmark study of declining academic standards and student performance in U.S. schools, business and policy leaders began to take notice of the need to improve our education system. Realizing that too few schools were preparing students to meet world standards in core academic subjects and that too many students were graduating unprepared for work and effective citizenship, in 1989, President George Bush called for corporate CEO's to make a personal commitment to reforming education. The Business Roundtable answered that call by committing to a 50-state initiative to improve the quality of our schools. And in 1992 the Roundtable formed the Educational Excellence Partnership (EEP). The EEP fulfilled a critical need—to clearly communicate the need to reform education to the general public.[57]

---

[56]Bess Altwerger and Steven L. Strauss, "The Business Behind Testing," *Language Arts* 79, no.3 (January 2002): 257.

[57]From the Business Roundtable Web site. Available from http://www.brtable.org/document.cfm. Accessed 22 July 2002.

As Altwergen and Strauss put it, "The BRT's position on various social issues from education, to international trade, the environment, and health care, is always in the service of its stated single objective—to promote policies that will lead to sustainable, non-inflationary, long-term growth in the U.S. economy."[58]

By pushing for national standards, testing, and accountability, the BRT is part of the corporate interest in shifting and reinforcing public opinion regarding education as preparation for the workforce. The CEOs are representing corporate interests and using their own Educational Excellence Partnerships (EEP) to "communicate to" the general public how education should reform. The EEP, however, as a body formed by the BRT, is not open to public scrutiny. The EEP is also not interested in social welfare, students as dynamic human beings, or teachers as professionals. The EEP is like most corporations. As Kohn describes, "Corporations in our economic systems exist to provide a financial return to the people who own them: they are in business to make a profit.... its agenda is driven by what is in its [corporate] best interest and what will maximize its profitability."[59]

Through contrived school "report cards" and other degrading national comparisons, standardized test scores have become the major indicator the general public receives about school success and what and how much students have learned. Schools are classified on a continuum. From a "failing" school to a school of "excellence," the continuum purportedly indicates what successful schools are. Arguably, however, the rankings result in a testing tyranny that directly influences what is taught in the classroom. The BRT is one of the leading advocates for high-stakes testing and national standardization. Indeed, the following are the elements of the BRT's unfolding agenda for educational reform:

- An assembly line manufacturing process, also called a standardized curriculum (misleadingly referred to as "standards"), to manufacture a workforce with skills that big business believes will allow it to maintain a competitive edge in the global economy.
- Quality control over the manufacturing process, referred to as national testing and accountability, to measure how well the future workforce (euphemistically called students) is mastering this curriculum, to make sure that none of the parts of the manufacturing machine (called teachers, parents and schools) strays from its role in the manufacturing process, and to discard products of poor quality (students who fail) as well as machine parts (teachers and schools) that perform poorly.

[58] Altwerger and Strauss, "Business Behind Testing" p. 258.
[59] Alfie Kohn, *The Five-Hundred-Pound Gorilla,* p. 190.

- Business propaganda (called public-service announcements) to instill a mentality in which the object and target of this agenda, the U.S. public, sees itself as the subjective agent of change, expecting rewards for good performance, and accepting punishment for poor performance.[60]

Because of corporate interest in maximizing profits, business leaders are concerned with public schools serving their needs by maximizing output (preparation of the student) for minimal costs (less taxes). The push for testing and national standards as a reform measure requires little cost to the taxpayer (corporate or otherwise) while creating an image for the public that a tougher stand is being taken on school reform issues. As Tanner points out, however, "The Roundtable never gave priority in its agenda to the critical needs for state financing to equalize educational opportunity, to replace outmoded and outworn school buildings and facilities, and to reduce class size or provide adequate curricular resources."[61] These suggestions get filtered out when reported to the general public.[62] Why? Because costs associated with reducing class sizes and improving the infrastructure would require corporations to be held accountable for their social responsibilities by paying their fair share of taxes. The message behind educational standards is that the primary problems with schools are the teachers and administrators.

Standards and achievement will be the force behind driving ineffective teachers to reform instruction (teaching to a test). The identification of low academic standards as the reason for our failing educational system rather than the underfunded school, class size, or lack of resources, shifts the argument from the need to raise taxes to the need to increase the standards. An amazing cost differential exists associated with this shift in educational reform.[63] "The obscene gap between the have and have nots, between our private economy boom and our public sector bust, and this is what high-stakes testing is all about. Once the high-stakes tests have driven a standardized curriculum into the schools, politicians and their corporate cronies can claim that they have equalized education—regardless of the shameful inequities of facilities and resources."[64]

The knowledge industry itself (textbooks and testing) is a multi-billion-dollar industry. To properly fund the recent testing mandate put

---

[60]Altwerger and Strauss, 258–260.

[61]Tanner, "Manufacturing Problems," 193.

[62]Berliner and Biddle, *The Manufactured Crisis*, discuss the Sandia report as "actually looking at evidence. Not surprisingly, its findings contradict the erroneous claims that were then being made by education critics in the Bush administration, and as a result the report was suppressed until George Bush Sr. was no longer in office." (p. 26).

[63]Spring, *Conflict of Interests*, 20.

[64]Ohanian, *Recess*, 155.

forth by George W. Bush, it is estimated that $2.7 to $7 billion will be needed. Over the past 5 years, state testing expenditures have almost tripled, increasing from $141 million to $390 million, and that is expected to continue to grow. Much like the monopolies discussed earlier in the mass media, the knowledge industry has also come under control of just a few major firms, primarily McGraw-Hill, Houghton Mifflin, and Harcourt, "all identified as Bush stocks by Wall Street analysts in the wake of the 2000 elections."[65]

McGraw-Hill is the nation's leading manufacturer of K–12 classroom publications and testing materials and stands to profit immensely from the recent legislation on mandated testing. Harold McGraw III is a member of the Education Task Force of the Business Roundtable. IBM is another major American company likely to benefit from federally mandated testing. Indeed, Louis Gerstner, CEO of IBM, is a leading business executive in favor of standards and testing. According to Ohanian, "Gerstner sounds the trumpet for standards and testing, he sets up Achieve, a non-profit standards and testing consulting company; he gets his state governor cronies of all political stripes on board for mass testing. And then, IBM offers a dazzling array of for-profit services to school districts to organize and manipulate the mountains of data that the call for massive state testing has created."[66]

Corporate interests and the alliance with mass media and conservative foundations have the power to control the knowledge the public receives about schools. In this attempt to control the power over knowledge, corporations "transform public education from a public good, benefiting all students, to a private good designed to expand the profits of investors, educate students as consumers, and train young people for the low-paying jobs of the new global marketplace."[67] In order to do this, corporations have propagated the myths associated with our failing school system to create a sense of crisis among the general public. How does propagation of the myths serve the needs of the corporate sector? What might the hidden interests be that the public is not hearing? Consider a comparative critique in which the message corporations advance is in boldface. Following the corporate message is an interpretation:

- **Schools produce an inadequate workforce.** Corporations are hiding behind decades of mismanagement, production of low-quality

---

[65]Steven Metcalf, "Reading Between the Lines," *The Nation* (28 January 2002). Available from http://www.thenation.com.html. Accessed 22 July 2002.

[66]Ohanian, *Recess*, 155.

[67]Henry Giroux, "Schools for Sale," *Kappa Delta Pi Record* (2001). Available from http://www.kpd.org/publications_forum_giroux.html. Accessed 15 August 2002.

products, too much middle management, and an autocratic elitist hierarchy of overly paid executives.[68]

- **Costs of education are skyrocketing and are wasteful.** Corporations are evading social responsibility through bullying communities into tax exemptions by threatening to relocate (thus taking away jobs).[69]
- **Schools are responsible for an incompetent and unproductive workforce.** Corporations are trying to convince the general public that workforce training is the responsibility of educators, thus removing both the responsibility and cost of training from business.[70]
- **The global market needs skilled labor, especially in the areas of science, math, and technology.** Convincing the general public that this is a crisis that will create a flood of graduates in these fields in large quantities. A large supply of skilled labor will decrease demand and consequently lower wages of generally high-paying positions.[71]
- **Poor education is threatening our economic competitive edge in the global market.** Corporate executives want to shift the focus to "failing" schools and away from the failures of business while promoting business's connection to the health of the domestic economy (disregarding the widening gap between executive elites and the working class).[72]
- **Multicultural and other nonbasic studies take valuable time away from critical skills—based training.** Elite corporations (still run primarily by White men), want to keep the status quo by using knowledge as a way to convince other cultures of their subordinate positions in society.[73]
- **The Market model is the best model.** Corporations want to socialize students to be compliant workers and adopt a pro-business attitude by infusing school culture with business language.[74]

The call, then, is to advance the kind of critique that does not take for granted the messages corporations and conservative foundations send. Although corporations and conservative foundations represent the power elite and control media (and, to some degree, governmental outlets), I am not about to cede them total control. The challenge is to find both a language and a medium through which to confront the hierarchy and the privilege. By

---

[68]Jonathon Weisman, "Skills in School: Now it's Business' Turn," *Phi Delta Kappan* (January 1999): 367–369.

[69]Saltman,13; Berliner and Biddle, *The Manufactured Crisis*, 83.

[70]Berliner and Biddle, *The Manufactured Crisis*, 94–95.

[71]Ibid., 96–100.

[72]Saltman,16.

[73]Spring, *Conflict of Interests*, 42.

[74]Henry Giroux, "Education Incorporated?" *Educational Leadership* (October 1998): 12–17.

contesting the claims that conservative foundation scholars actually "care" about schools and the children who attend them, I have tried in this chapter to illustrate how certain central players are complicit in an odd form of "bait and switch." That is, the hope is that the investigation has revealed just how hypocritical it is for certain conservative scholars to argue for a free-market, rugged-individualist ideal. This is particularly true given that their livelihoods are often supported by a kind of corporate welfare state: business-supported foundations hiring conservative writers and politicians to further an agenda of rugged individualism.

REFERENCES

Altwerger, Bess and Steven L. Strauss. 2002. The Business Behind Testing. *Language Arts 79*, no.3: 256–263.

Berliner, David C. and Bruce J. Biddle. 1995. *The Manufactured Crisis: Myths, Fraud and the Attack on American Public Schools.* New York: Perseus Books.

Berliner, David C. and Bruce J. Biddle. 1998. The Lamentable Alliance between the Media and School Critics. *The School Administrator* (September): 12–18.

Borja, Rhea. 2001. E-Procurement Firm Simplexis Closes Door as Industry Struggles. *Education Week* (5 December 2001). Available at http://www.edweek.org.html. (Accessed 4 August 2002).

Boyles, Deron. 2000. *American Education and Corporations: The Free Market Goes to School.* New York: Falmer.

Bracey, Gerald W. 2002. *The War Against America's Public Schools: Privatizing Schools, Commercializing Education.* Boston: Allyn and Bacon.

Bridgeman, Anne. 2000. Click Here to Buy. *American School Board Journal* (April). Available at http://www.asbj.com.html. (Accessed 4 August 2002).

Burns, Margie. 2002. Washington Post to Benefit from Bush Education Bill. Available at http://www.onlinejournal.com/Special_Report/Burns012102/burns012102.html. (Accessed 21 July 2002).

Fromm, Jeffrey A. and Todd V. Kern. 2000. Investment Opportunities in Education: Making a Profit While Making a Difference. *The Journal of Private Equity*: 38–51.

Giroux, Henry. 1998. Education Incorporated? *Educational Leadership* (October): 12–17.

Giroux, Henry. 2001. Schools for Sale. *Kappa Delta Pi Record.* Available at http://www.kpd.org/publications_forum_giroux.html. (Accessed 15 August 2002).

Sam. 2002. Checkbook Analysis: Corporations Support Think-Tanks—and the Favor is Returned. *Extra!* (May/June). Available from http://www.fiar.org/extra/think-tanks-survey.html. (Accessed 4 August 2002).

Kohn, Alfie. 1998. *The Five-Hundred-Pound Gorilla.* San Francisco: Jossey-Bass.

Metcalf, Steven. 2002. Reading Between the Lines. *The Nation* (28 January 2002). Available at http://www.thenation.com.html. (Accessed 22 July 2002).

Ohanian, Susan. 2000. Goals 2000: What's In a Name? *Phi Delta Kappan* (January): 345–355.

Ohanian, Susan. 2002. *What Happened to Recess and Why are Our Children Struggling in Kindergarten?* New York: McGraw-Hill.

Saltman, Kenneth J. 2000. *Collateral Damage: Corporatizing Public Schools—A Threat to Democracy.* Lanham, MD: Rowman and Littlefield Publishers.

San Francisco Business Times. 2000. *American City Business Journal* (4 December 2000). Available at http://www.bizjournals.com. (Accessed 4 August 2002).

Spring, Joel. 1997. *Political Agendas for Education: From the Christian Coalition to the Green Party.* Mahwah, NJ: Lawrence Erlbaum.

Spring, Joel. 2002. *Conflicts of Interests: The Politics of American Education* New York: McGraw-Hill.

Tanner, Daniel. 2000. Manufacturing Problems and Selling Solutions: How to Succeed in the Education Business without Really Educating. *Phi Delta Kappan* (November): 188–202.

Thomas B. Fordham Foundation. 1998. *A Nation Still at Risk: An Education Manifesto.* Washington D.C.: Opinion Papers, 1998, ERIC, ED 422455.

Troy, Forrest J. 1998. The Myth of our Failed Education System. *The School Administrator* (September): 6–10.

Weisman, Jonathon. 1999. Skills in School: Now it's Business' Turn. *Phi Delta Kappan* (January): 367–369.

Wimer, Jeffrey W. and Debra S. Vredenburg, "When Ideology Sabotages the Truth: The Politics of Privately-Funded Educational Vouchers in One Urban School District," paper presented at the American Educational Studies Association, Mexico City, Mexico, November 1, 2003.

Chapter 11

The Exploiting Business:
School–Business Partnerships,
Commercialization, and Students
as Critically Transitive Citizens

Deron R. Boyles

ex•ploit (eks_ploit) *n.* [ME. & OFr. *esploit* < L. *explicitum*, neut. pp. of *explicare.* see EXPLICATE] an act remarkable for brilliance or daring; bold deed *–vt.* **1.** to make use of; turn to account; utilize productively **2.** to make unethical use of for one's own advantage or profit; specif., to make profit from the labor of (others).[1]

At the 2000 Philosophy of Education Society Conference in Toronto, Virginia Held was invited as a distinguished speaker and she delivered an address titled "The Commercialization of the Classroom." Philosophers of education in attendance seemed taken aback at some of the examples of commercial intrusion in K–12 schooling—and rightly so. Commercialization in schools is expanding at an alarming rate. According to the Center for the Analysis of Commercialism in Education, school–business partnerships have increased their presence in North America by 303 percent since 1990.[2] Examples of school leaders entering into exclusive contracts, renting advertising space on the sides of school buses, and providing businesses with a cap-

---

[1] David B. Guralnik, ed., *Webster's New World Dictionary* (New York: Simon and Schuster, 1982), 494.

[2] Alex Molnar, "Cashing in on Kids: The Second Annual Report on Trends in Schoolhouse Commercialism," Center for the Analysis of Commercialism in Education, Document # 99-21, (September, 1999): 3. The report can be accessed at the following url: <http://www.uwm.edu/Dept/CACE/kidsreport/cashinginonkids.html>

tive audience (and lucrative market) abound. In Colorado Springs, the director of school leadership for District 11 sent a memo reminding teachers and administrators that in order to profit from the exclusive contract the district had signed with Coca-Cola, students needed extra breaks from class to consume 70,000 cases of Coke products.[3] In schools throughout the United States, Pizza Hut offers "free" pizza for students who not only complete reading assignments in order to get the "free" pizza, but who are also too young to go to the restaurant to redeem their free pizza alone (resulting in an average bill of $16.50 and profit for Pizza Hut).[4] In Fresno, California, math and science lessons included the McGraw-Hill middle school textbook that used Oreo cookies, Nike shoes, and McDonald's meals as sample lessons.[5] In Georgia, Colgate-Palmolive offers dental care charts and pamphlets emphasizing "five easy steps" of gum care, replete with suggestions to buy "Colgate Junior" toothbrushes and toothpaste.[6]

Such an encroachment of commercialism and consumer materialism in schools appears to have put teachers and students in an awkward position. Because school funding has been tied so tightly to property taxes, some schools find themselves "forced" into school–business partnerships. The argument here is that it is better to get money for students in exchange for advertising and commercialism than to have students suffer in underfunded schools. Given that educational reform initiatives are based on policies of accountability that are increasingly linked to school funding (i.e., teachers must "prove" that they are "doing their jobs" where "doing their jobs" equals teaching to standardized tests based on central-office goals and objectives lists that impact budgets), teachers and school leaders have, on one view, been savvy enough to identify alternative funding sources. The problem with this kind of alternative funding source is at least twofold: (a) The giving is contingent and uncertain; and (b) it generally represents a very small percentage of overall school budgets—raising questions about the amount of time and energy put into "partnership" initiatives. This chapter uses the term *exploit* in the two major ways it is defined. The argument is that school–business partnerships exploit schools in the sense that they "make unethical use of [schools] for [their] own advantage or profit." The ultimate intention of this chapter, however, is to champion the other definition of the term in order "to make use of, turn to account, [and] utilize productively" school–busi-

---

[3]See John Bushey, "District 11's Coke Problem," *Harper's* (February, 1999); and Constance Hays, "Today's Lesson: Soda Rights; Consultant Helps Schools Sell Themselves to Vendors," *New York Times*, 21 May 1999, C1.

[4]See Hilary Stout, "Marketing: Firms Learn that Subtle Aid to Schools Can Polish Their Images, Sell Products," *The Wall Street Journal* 25 March 1991, B1.

[5]See Editorial, "Textbooks as Billboards: Commercialism Gains a Greater Hold on the Classroom," *The Fresno Bee*, 2 April 1999, F2.

[6]Deron Boyles, *American Education and Corporations: The Free Market Goes to School* (New York: Falmer, 2000), 73–74.

ness partnerships as object lessons for students' critical analysis. Specifically, this chapter asserts that standard school–business partnerships promote consumer materialism, thwart critical transitivity, and negatively alter what it means to be a citizen. The potential to transform standard partnerships, however, is latent in the standard partnerships themselves. This chapter intends to show why exploiting (in the first sense of the actual definition) the potential of the standard partnership is as important as it is difficult to achieve, nonetheless holding out hope that transformation will take place in U.S. public schools.

CONSUMERISM AND TRANSITIVITY

Consumer materialism and critical transitivity are, in relation to school–business partnerships, intertwined concepts. Consumer materialism is the focus on goods and ends only or primarily. Perhaps best characterized by students wanting to know whether they are going to "get" their "money's worth" for a course, consumer materialism circumvents process in favor of product. Consumer materialism is also the valuing of easy answers over difficult investigation. Linked to convenience, consumer materialism manifests itself in schools via business partnerships when the ends or goods (e.g., Coca-Cola, "free" pizza, trips to amusement parks, T-shirts, etc.) become the focus and where the focus is not analyzed or investigated. Said differently, consumer materialism commodifies existence by reducing searching, being, thinking, and so on, to objectified and reductionistic particulars. For schooling, it means, in part, that students see their roles as seeking "right" answers to questions instead of searching for meaning and understanding by contesting and critiquing. Similarly, teachers see their roles as seeking preordained procedures that will allow the efficient transfer of information from them (or the adopted texts/curriculum) to their students.[7] Accordingly, teachers demonstrate consumer materialism when they participate in school–business partnerships without questioning and analyzing the ideological, symbolic, and practical consequences of partnering with the private sector in overtly commercialist ways.

Critical transitivity is best understood when compared to two other levels of awareness—intransitivity and semitransitivity. The phrases come from Paulo Freire and intransitivity means "noncritical (in)action." He clarifies that intransitivity repudiates the power of individuals to change their existences when, for example, teachers claim "I can't speak out about school–business partnerships because my school might lose funding ...

---

[7]Peter McLaren uses a similar phrase, "consumer capitalist culture," to make a connection between what he calls postmodern pathologies and the constitution of the body/subject. See Peter McLaren, *Critical Pedagogy and Predatory Culture: Oppositional Politics in a Postmodern Era* (New York: Routledge, 1995). See Boyles, 33.

that's the 'real world' and I can't do anything about it."[8] Differently, semi-transitivity is characterized by individuals who see the world as changeable, but see the world in unrelated segments such that semitransitivity is two-dimensional and short term. Business groups may donate money, time, or materials, for example, but teachers do not ask whether businesses are getting tax credits, free advertising, or other "perks."[9] Whereas intransitivity and semitransitivity are visible in schools, Freire's ultimate goal—critical transitivity—is rarely evidenced. Critical transitivity is demonstrated when individuals make, according to Shor, "broad connections between individual experience and social issues.… In education, critically [transitive] teachers and students synthesize personal and social meanings with a specific theme, text, or issue."[10] Students and teachers who critique school–business partnerships (in this case) rather than seek them out and/or participate in them without question, are demonstrating, in minor form, what critical transitivity entails. The point of critical transitivity in relation to school–business partnerships is to engage students and teachers in debates and arguments over, for example, the motives for business involvement in schools, the benefits from partnerships for schools versus the benefits for businesses, and what is gained and lost in specific partnerships. Are businesses altruistic in their "support"? How much time and money is spent by school districts in "human hours" securing and maintaining partnerships? If businesses paid non-reduced taxes (i.e., many businesses get tax reductions for locating in particular areas), would the dollar amount of their "contributions" to schools be greater or smaller than what they would have paid if they had not received a tax break? These are the kinds of questions that characterize critical transitivity and are also questions that, by virtue of their being formed and asked, challenge consumer materialist assumptions regarding easy answers and convenient, simple conclusions.

Critically transitive debate and argument utilizes processes of investigation that do not accept the impervious realities that Maxine Greene calls the "givens" of an imposed "real world."[11] In this sense, students would be better off being young philosophers of education: questioning their own schooling at the very time they are engaged in it. Unfortunately, opportunities for questioning are limited as testing-, grading-, and preparation for future life-oriented curricula (i.e., pro-consumerism, job and workforce preparation, skills-oriented approaches) crowd out chances for such investigation. The concern here is that business partnerships inherently inhibit questioning

---

[8] See Paulo Freire, *Education for Critical Consciousness* (New York: Seabury, 1973); and Ira Shor, *Empowering Education* (Chicago: University of Chicago Press, 1992), 127–128.
[9] Ibid.
[10] Shor, op. cit.
[11] See Maxine Greene, *The Dialectic of Freedom* (New York: Teachers College Press, 1988), 22 *ff*.

and instead help develop uncritical consumers rather than critically transitive citizens. This happens, in part, by their institutionalized nature. Accepted by schools and reinforced in society, business assumptions that value consumer materialism and *in*transitivity become "beyond question." Accordingly, unwilling or unable to raise questions (for fear of losing funding? in- or semitransitivity?), teachers and school leaders often demonstrate for their students what it means to accede to the "given" of commercialism and consumer materialism. One result is that schools harbor noncriticality and confer diplomas to students (and employ teachers and administrators) who are unable (and/or unwilling?) to raise questions about motive, meaning, and any ultimate consequences of supporting business influences on and in schools. A cycle is established, therefore, where business expectations for schools beget schools that push products, provide free advertising, and "produce" future consumers (consumer materialists) that, in turn, favor and support business interests and corporate involvement in public schooling. Some call this a "win-win" situation, but who wins what? Who wins how much? Who wins in the long run?

Although a compelling case might be made to get rid of school–business partnerships altogether, this chapter offers a way in which schools can continue their "partnerships" yet still promote critical transitivity and critical citizenship on the part of the teachers and students alike. Three primary claims are made here:

1. Schools are currently places where commercialism is rapidly intruding.
2. Students, teachers, and leaders rarely critique commercial intrusion (resulting in uncritical consumers and uncritical citizens).
3. If schools are forced into "partnerships" with businesses,[12] one way that commercialism can be exploited to avoid uncritical consumerism and uncritical citizenship is to use the partnerships, themselves, as object lessons.

(1) COMMERCIAL INTRUSION, PROFIT MARGINS, AND (2) MISSED OPPORTUNITIES FOR CRITIQUE

In virtually every neighborhood grocery store, one will find a program where a percentage of sales will be "donated" to local schools. In Michigan, Glen's Markets has a "Save-Share 2000" plan. The store, like most others, provides a

[12]The concept "partnerships" relating to schools and businesses is explored in Kathleen Knight-Abowitz and Deron Boyles, "Private Interests or Public Goods?: Dewey, Rugg, and Their Contemporary Allies on Corporate Involvement in Educational Reform Initiatives," *Philosophy of Education* (2000): 131–139.

"value card" and customers "swipe" their card at a machine located at the register. From the total bill, 1 percent will be "donated" to a school the shopper designates. Interestingly, the store does not keep track of the individual contributions so that those who shop at the store have no idea whether their contribution was actually made.[13] Harris Teeter has a similar program. They boasted, in a letter to River Eves Elementary School (Roswell, Georgia), that they "gave away $500,000 to 1,955 schools" in 1998.[14] Each school, in other words, received $255.75. Like Glen's (and Kroger, Publix, Acme, Bruno's, Stop-n-Shop, etc.), Harris Teeter uses schools as no-cost marketing tools for their stores. In the letter to River Eves Elementary, Harris Teeter informed the school that it had only $8.78 earmarked for its school. Because the company will not cut a check for an amount less than $250 (but keeps the interest accrued on such funds?), the school was sent a list of ideas "to increase [their] dollars earned." The suggestions included posting the Harris Teeter account number on the school's marquee as well as in sight of the car pool line. Harris Teeter's account number would not, of course, be listed without the name "Harris Teeter" next to it, as an account number means nothing if it is not connected with the store name or the project that goes along with it. The suggestions also included advertising the program in the school newsletter, announcing the program at school events and PTA meetings, and copying reminder cards to be distributed to parents. For $250, Harris Teeter gets free advertising in a variety of ways (the school marquee, newsletters, handouts, and announcements) and the school spends money and time on paper, printing, and "human hours" devoted to advertising. The "River Eves Eagles Newsletter" did, indeed, include a "front page" headline proclaiming "Hooray for River Eves Business Partners."[15]

Coca-Cola has a summer "economics" institute program to expose minority students to the benefits of competitive business practices. Nissan automobile dealerships participate in "automotive services apprenticeships." CiCi's Pizza sets aside one night per month when students and parents from participating schools come to the restaurant. A percentage of the net sales (not gross) is "donated" to the school. Subway provides "free" subs to a local school and a representative from the store, in order to make an "educational" link, comes to the school as a guest speaker on "health occupations." McDonald's secures itself as part of a cafeteria "choice" program in a Colorado school and offers business credit to students who "intern" as cooks and servers. Channel One is connected to thousands of classrooms, providing students with a news program and commercials for jeans, candy, makeup, and other "targeted" products. Tucker Federal Bank and

---

[13] Glen's Market flyer, "This Year, We Plan to Share," August 30, 2000.
[14] Carol Trout to Eve Neumeister, letter dated October 27, 1999.
[15] "River Eves Elementary School Newsletter," November 5, 1999, p. 1.

Wachovia Bank participate in an "Academy of Finance" program, which claims to prepare students for "rewarding careers" in the financial-services industry. In August 2000, National Public Radio reported the case of a father in Ohio who is suing his local school (with the help of the American Civil Liberties Union) to stop the school from giving student information to local banks who contact students about setting up savings accounts. The principal of the school, demonstrating either intransitivity or semitransitivity, interpreted the suit as a nuisance and he defended the bank as being a "friend to the school."

The General Accounting Office (GAO) recently came out with a report warning of the increase in commercialization in schools. As noted in a *New York Times* article:

> The G.A.O. report cites textbook covers distributed by Clairol, Ralph Lauren, and Philip Morris with company names and logos fully displayed. In New York City, the Board of Education is considering a plan that would provide computers for all of its students, starting in the fourth grade. The computers might carry ads and possibly encourage shopping on a particular Web site.[16]

Far from being limited to supermarket programs, school–business partnerships are increasing in number and variety and arguably represent a larger, insidious agenda. The agenda is a pro-business, pro-capitalist, pro-careerist one that excludes questions about whether business is exploitative of workers and consumers (and schools), whether capitalism is the only or best economic theory, and whether elementary school students should be forced to consider their entire future based *not* on "What do you want to *be* when you grow up?" questions, but "What do you want to *do* when you grow up?" questions. To be clear, capitalism *may* be the best economic theory ("at least compared to all the rest," as the oft-cited proviso goes), but the claim here is not to have the assumption accepted (and furthered) without investigation.

To illustrate the agenda identified earlier, many city and county chambers of commerce publish booklets touting the advantages of school–business partnerships, all the while (understandably?) excluding questions or concerns or potential problems with such partnerships. One chamber of commerce lists the benefits of school–business partnerships as follows:

> Present firsthand requirements, satisfactions, and expectations of the business world.... Alert teachers to the job skills applicants need and help them find ways to develop these skills.... Help develop career awareness geared to specific local job-market needs both now and in the future.... Gain under-

---

[16]Constance L. Hays, "Commercialism in U.S. Schools is Examined in New Report," *The New York Times* (14 September 2000): C1, C25.

standing of the school systems, whose health is vital to the economic well being of the community.... Become known as a community involved company
which adds to your public relations efforts.[17]

Note the slant. The benefits are for businesses, but schools are referred
to in ways that assume them to be beneficiaries as well. Although "win-win"
situations may exist, it simply does not follow, in this particular example
anyway, that the benefits for schools are anything more than residual and
they appear always linked to the kind of fiscal policies that primarily favor
businesses. Teachers are supposed to teach their students what businesses
desire in terms of "job skills." Businesses benefit from learning more about
schools, but for the purpose of the "economic well-being of the community." To the possible question "why should my business get involved," the
chamber of commerce already provides the answer: so your business will be
perceived as being involved in the community, "which adds to your public
relations efforts."

Schools, then, are faced with programs connecting them with businesses
while also having outside forces further the idea that schools and businesses
should become even more closely aligned.[18] The problem with this is that students and teachers become subsumed in a market logic that, in part because of
its pervasiveness, appears (therefore becomes) impervious to critique.[19]

(3) COMMERCIALISM EXPLOITED: AN EXAMPLE

In university communications departments, students study television and
print advertisements for their symbolism, hidden messages, overt messages,
aesthetics, and so forth. Guided by experts in the field, meanings intended
by advertisers—as well as meanings other than those intended by advertisers—are identified, revealed, and debated. Much like textual analysis, literary criticism, and hermeneutics, the ads become fodder for investigation.
School–business partnerships offer the same opportunity. How might such
an opportunity be realized? How might public schools use school–business
partnerships as opportunities for the development of critical transitivity?
Consider one example.

---

[17]"Benefits of School Partnerships to the Business and School," Cobb Chamber of Commerce (Education Department), p. 3. For a detailed treatment of a state-wide business initiative (Michigan) to reform schools, see John W. Sipple, "Institutional Constraints on Business
Involvement in K–12 Education Policy," *American Educational Research Journal* 36, no. 3 (Fall,
1999): 447–488.

[18]See Alex Molnar, *Giving Kids the Business: The Commercialization of America's Schools* (Boulder,
CO: Westview, 1996), 166–184.

[19]See Pam Bettis, "Corporate Discourses in School: Adapting to the Prevailing Economic Climate," *Educational Foundations* (Winter, 2000): 23–49.

After studying school–business partnerships, critical transitivity, and a variety of other related topics during a recent summer term, a student returned to her classroom. Her intention was to explore the possibility that her fifth-grade students might alter the climate of their classroom by altering the school–business program she operated to fund set production for school musicals. Relating her experiences, the student noted the following:

> I had to let you know about several classroom conversations today. You'd have been proud. I introduced my fifth graders to a new concept—critical transitivity! I shared with them my dilemma regarding the "Box Tops for Education" [General Mills initiative whereby tops from cereal boxes are collected for money] fund raiser for the coming year. We talked about the large profit margin for General Mills and the free advertising I'd provided for the past two years. I then asked them why General Mills would want to "help" schools like this. After a brief silence, one little boy said, "They want to control schools." Another little girl corrected him and said, "they want to manipulate schools!" I almost fell over in amazement. From the mouths of babes! "We" decided, collectively, not to continue the Box Tops campaign. So, one small effort has been made in developing critical transitivity in the lives of 60 children.[20]

Only anecdotal evidence, and only in one classroom, the example nonetheless gives us a glimpse of the challenge. Forget for the moment that the teacher considered the change a success. One might, for example, justifiably wonder whether the teacher is accurate in her assessment that the students actually "learned" or "demonstrated" critical transitivity. They might have been led to the conclusion the teacher wanted and thus void the larger claim. Yet, there might be enough of a glimpse in what the teacher wrote to suggest that she really did demonstrate the larger point being made here. Including the students in the consideration is key, even though the setup was suggested (that the teacher had a dilemma regarding the "Box Tops for Education" program). Their responses, little cynics though they may appear, indicate a level of sophistication and understanding that, should teachers get out of the way of them, would emerge naturally.

Getting the teacher to consider a side other than the one she had been practicing for two years was not an easy process, however. This particular teacher was not initially willing to consider that the business she courted could be seen as anything other than helpful. It took a variety of examples and corresponding analyses to move the student from reactionary to contemplator. Indeed, her revelation and refutation of her preexisting beliefs— her *elenchus*, if you will—resulted in her proclaiming, as though she just realize she had been "had" or "taken," that she had been a "Captain Crunch pimp" for years.

---

[20]Shelly Hall to author, e-mail dated 17 August 2000.

Consider some guiding questions:

1. What is the primary reason for entering into a school–business partnership?
2. Whose interests are being served? Who benefits most? Who benefits in the long run?
3. How much time is given to the business part of the school–business partnership? What amount, in terms of teacher (or administrator) salary, does the time equal on an hourly basis?
4. What is learned as a result of the partnership? In addition to the claims associated with specific projects, what is the larger message or meaning being conveyed to students?
5. Are business partners willing to share financial information with teachers and students regarding their benefits from the partnership?
6. Can individual teachers or classes opt out of partnership programs?

These and other questions should form the basis of an initial analysis of school–business partnerships. The student in the example asked at least some of these and used them to guide her actions.

The overall point here is to illustrate how using school–business partnerships as object lessons goes toward, if not fully achieving, critical transitivity and critical consumerism. The teacher noted, in fact, that "one small effort has been made in developing critical transitivity." It is not a complete package to be "had" just because one program was thwarted, even though the teacher and the students came to the conclusion collectively. What other programs, inside or outside the specific school in the example, might also offer opportunities for further critique? Such a question goes to the Deweyan point that problems solved only reveal other problems to be solved in such a way that habits of the mind are formed from educative experiences. The example is not (yet) educative in the sense that we do not know whether further learning and further educative experiences obtained. Still, Dewey would have to be pleased that students were engaged, actions were taken, and a problem was identified and (temporarily?) solved.

One caution from the suggestion, of course, is that teachers have plenty of curriculum mandates to keep them chasing objectives, goals, and testable material. Adding to the curriculum is not the intention here. Instead, the point is to take what is already a part of school life—and an increasing part of school life—and raise questions about it. The not-so-covert intention here is to reveal how school–business partnerships are pushing uncritical consumerism into what businesses no longer consider schools, but markets. For the utilitarianism and reductionism of such a viewpoint to go unchallenged will mean giving over to businesses the markets they so eagerly crave. Business interests are in making money; schooling interests are not. Careerist though many public schools may be, the claim here is that we will do ourselves a favor by putting school–business partnerships and commercialism under the hypothetical microscope. The favor is one that combats oligarchical power, that is, corporate interests directing and controlling government (which leads to governmental favors for businesses). Recall Dewey in *Reconstruction in Philosophy* (1920):

> In spite of its interest in a thoroughly social aim, utilitarianism fostered a new class interest, that of the capitalistic property-owning interests, provided only property was obtained through free competition and not by governmental favor. The stress that Bentham put on security tended to consecrate the legal institution of private property provided only certain legal abuses in connection with its acquisition and transfer were abolished. *Beati possidentes*—provided possessions had been obtained in accord with the rules of the competitive game—without, that is, extraneous favors from government. Thus utilitarianism gave intellectual confirmation to all those tendencies which make "business" not a means of social service and an opportunity for personal growth in creative power but a way of accumulating the means of private enjoyments.[21]

Schools, as extensions of government, are being delivered to corporations as the favor of which Dewey spoke. Accordingly, the "social service" and "personal growth in creative power" that schools *can* offer is consistently subjugated under commercial interests. This, again, is the second definition of *exploit*—"to make unethical use of for one's own profit; specifically, to make profit from the labor of (others)." Combating the second definition is the first definition: "to make use of; to turn to account; utilize productively." In terms of school–business partnerships, teachers and students should demonstrate the first definition by investigating—in critically transitive ways—the impact and effect school–business partnerships have on their classroom, school, and lives outside of school.

At least three implications might follow from the foregoing claims: (a) Colleges of education, foundations departments, philosophers of education, and so on, should expand their analyses to include school–business partnerships and commercialism; (b) K–12 schools should avail themselves of ever-present opportunities for critique and questioning via school–business partnership programs; and (c) School–business partnerships might ebb in numbers as result of the teacher/student analyses—the ultimate point of using school–business partnerships as object lessons in the first place.

Exploitation comes in a variety of forms. Indeed, the marked increase in technology in schools is arguably another example of exploitation in the negative that can be used in "positively exploitative" ways. The next section of this chapter extends the general idea of exploitation and applies it to the ex-

---

[21]John Dewey, *Reconstruction in Philosophy* (Boston: Beacon Press, 1920), 182–183.

ample of Channel One. Important to note, Channel One offers us an opportunity to critique school–business partnerships and their exploitative nature. Channel One also represents a larger encroachment in schools of a technology industry that may have more fiscal interests than pedagogical ones.

CONSUMERISM, TECHNOLOGY, AND THE POSSIBILITY OF DEVELOPING CRITICAL CITIZENS

With an increasing emphasis on technology in the schools and the enormous amount of money being spent (both for initial outlay and seemingly ad infinitum upgrades and support), the issue of technology calls out for critical evaluation.[22] Technology that fosters commercialism in schools should be of particular concern, as it uses the technology trend to further an economic agenda rarely critiqued (like the technology itself) by those entrusted with students. By taking the specific example of Channel One, this section of the chapter intends to reveal (or reiterate) a confluence of issues that should concern those interested in pedagogy unfettered by commercialism and murky conceptions of knowledge. Another intent is to provide a broad framework for criticism of technology in the general sense—a realm that appears "uncriticizable"—paying particular attention to epistemological concerns and their connection to commercial interests. Important to note, technology is not understood here as a purely scientific "advancement," nor is it understood only or primarily as "inert" machinery or software. Instead, technology is, in addition to being machinery and software, a capital venture rife with values, presuppositions, and power. Questioning those features via the example of Channel One reveals often hidden values, presuppositions, and instances of power that impact the lives of students and teachers in arguably negative ways.

At a conference concerning technology (titled "Asking the Right Questions") Neil Postman offered six questions as ways of evaluating the merits of technology:

1. What is the problem to which technology is the solution?
2. Whose problem is it? (Who benefits from it? Who pays for it?)
3. Given a solved problem, what new problems emerge as a result of the new technology/the solving of the old problem?

---

[22]For the purpose of this paper, "technology" refers to televisions, satellite dishes, video tape players, computers, etc., and is distinct from pencils, pens, and papers which, on a broader definition, would also be "technology." Channel One is clearly not the only example that could be used. The "Zap Me" program is another and many more illustrations exist. The point here is to use Channel One, given its prevalence and its unabashed commercialism, as an exemplar of the larger problems—both epistemological and commercial. See Alex Molnar, *Giving Kids the Business* (Boulder, CO: Westview, 1996).

4. Which people/what institutions might be most seriously harmed by technological movements?
5. What changes in language are being enforced by new technology and what is being gained and lost as a result?
6. What sort of people and institutions acquire special economic and political power as a result of technology?

I amend Postman's questions for this section of the chapter in order to inquire about the epistemological implications of technology use, especially as represented by Channel One:

1. What is the epistemological problem to which Channel One is a solution?
2. Whose problem is it? (Who benefits from it/Who pays for it?)
3. Given a solved problem, what new problems emerge as a result of Channel One/the solving of the old problem?
4. Which people/what institutions might be most seriously harmed by Channel One?
5. What changes in the requirements for knowing are enforced by Channel One and what is being gained and lost as a result?
6. What sort of people and institutions acquire special economic and political power as a result of Channel One?

Question 1: What is the epistemological problem to which Channel One is the solution? De Vaney notes that "the program attempts to combat a perceived teenage ignorance and apathy about current events."[23] Channel One uses a twelve minute television news program as the means by which to rectify the lack of current events "knowledge" students are charged with not having. Indeed, Garramone and Atkin assert that "TV news exposure is generally the strongest predictor of political knowledge among youth."[24] Based in part on this claim, Greenberg and Brand hypothesized that "adolescent viewers of 'Channel One' will learn more about news events presented on the program than nonviewers."[25] They note: "To test whether viewers of 'Channel One' would gain more general knowledge than nonviewers, multiple-choice responses for 10 items were created and were interspersed among items assess-

---

[23]Ann De Vaney, ed., *Watching Channel One: The Convergence of Students, Technology, and Private Business* (Albany: SUNY Press, 1994), 2.

[24]See G. M. Garramone and C. K. Atkin, "Mass Communication and Political Socialization: Specifying the Effects," *Public Opinion Quarterly* 50 (1986): 76–86.

[25]Bradley S. Greenberg and Jeffrey E. Brand, "Television News and Advertising in Schools: The 'Channel One' Controversy," *Journal of Communication* 43, no. 1 (Winter 1993), 143.

ing [the hypothesis]. Correct responses to these 10 items were summed to form a *General News knowledge index.*"[26]

I argue that the epistemology asserted and assumed by Garramone, Atkin, Greenberg, and Brand represents—at best—only nonpropositional knowledge. Nonpropositional knowledge is, simply, "how-to." How to ride a bike, how to balance a checkbook, how to type, and so forth, are all examples of nonpropositional knowledge. Although important, nonpropositional knowledge nonetheless does not have as a requirement any version of justification. Propositional knowledge, however, does carry the requirement for justification, which simply means that those claiming to know something are obligated to provide either evidence, reasons, warranted assertions, or other forms of support and substantiation. Far too dualistic, the distinction between nonpropositional and propositional knowledge nonetheless helps us compare different kinds of knowing, rather than assuming that one version of knowing is the same as (or worse or better than) all others. In terms of Channel One, for example, Greenberg and Brand (and others) seem to confuse propositional knowledge with lucky guesses. Steup clarifies by telling us, first, that a "belief can be lucky because, in relation to certain relevant *facts*, its truth was not a likely outcome. Second, a belief can be lucky because, in relation to the subject's *evidence*, its truth was not a likely outcome.... Justification is what prevents a true belief from being a lucky guess, but not from being a lucky truth."[27]

To say, for example, that students who *view* a news program will, as a result, *know* more or even *learn* more is to reduce the complexity of knowing processes and conflate information transfer with knowing. The point here is that Postman's modified first question results in a sort of non sequitur. It asked what the *epistemological* problem is to which Channel One is the solution. Data transfer and lucky guesses (the typical result of Channel One?) underscore a reliabilism that limits students' knowledge and reinforces a consumer materialist assumption—that "getting" information equals knowing, even if the person cannot connect, interpret, or otherwise warrantably assert or make meaning of the "knowledge" they "got" from, in this instance, Channel One.

To Postman's second question: Whose problem is it? Who benefits from Channel One? Who pays for it? According to the premise (that students are lacking current events knowledge), the problem resides with schools—teachers and students more specifically. It might appear that teachers and students would also be the ones who benefit from Channel One. They do, after all, "get" "a free satellite dish and cable wiring for the building, plus video-

---

[26]*Ibid.*, 146.

[27]Matthias Steup, *Contemporary Epistemology* (Upper Saddle River, NJ: Prentice Hall, 1996), 9. A lucky guess is also noted as follows: *S*'s belief that *p* is a lucky guess *iff* (i) *p* is true; (ii) *S* believes that *p*; (iii) *S* has no evidence for believing that *p* is true.

tape recorders and televisions in exchange for the promise ... [to] view the twelve minute news program every day."[28] Consider, however, a further amendment to the second question. Instead of who benefits from Channel One, ask the question "Who benefits *most* from Channel One?" The modifier *most* raises important issues about exploitation and allows us to see Channel One in a different way.

Not only is the fundamental question about information and knowledge, it includes modes of transmitting information—and claiming it as knowledge—in the form of machinery/technology, as well as a programming format ("news show") interspersed with advertising. Assuming, for the sake of argument, that more than lucky guesses result from news show viewing, is there an imbalance in the benefits derived from Channel One? On one hand there is a moving intangible (news show viewing resulting in knowledge). On the other hand, there is the very tangible revenue generated by the company that owns Channel One. For the 30-second advertisement slots, Channel One generates over $100 million per year.[29] Schools get free equipment, however, so perhaps balance is restored. Yet, the subtle epistemological question seeps out: Because the admitted goal of Channel One is profit, what impact do advertisers have over the content of the news shows and, by extension, what students know? If Channel One can exacerbate the too-oft-cited laments of ill-informed education commentators (including parents, media, and, sadly, teachers) regarding the *"need"* for technology in schools, and if Channel One can then *supply* schools with the hardware and software (television sets and news shows), knowledge becomes the controlled purview of private-sector interests. There is nothing particularly new here, as textbooks suffer this same control, but the difference is that with books, those students who read them are at least partially active in the processes of knowledge construction (including textual visualization and meaning making). Very differently so are viewers of Channel One. They watch. Passively. Epistemologically, this means a kind of faithful reliabilism where S need not justify the claim p in order to say she knows it.[30] To this point we return momentarily.

Postman's third question gives any benefit of the doubt to Channel One: Given a solved problem (students increase their current events "knowledge"), what new problems emerge as a result of the new technology and/or the solving of the old problem? Three points to consider here: (a) further re-

---

[28] De Vaney, *op. cit.*

[29] *Ibid.*; See, also, Jonathan Kozol, "Whittle and the Privateers," *The Nation* (21 September 1992).

[30] See, for example, Keith Lehrer, *Theory of Knowledge* (Boulder, CO: Westview Press, 1990), 66–67. For the purpose of this paper, Plato's traditional syllogism (S knows that p iff: p is true, S believes that p, and S justifies that p) represents propositional knowledge. See Myles Burnyeat, *The Theaetetus of Plato*, trans. M. J. Levett (Cambridge: Hackett, 1990).

duced autonomy of teachers, (b) reified conceptualization of knowing as simple data transfer, and (c) consumer materialism.

For (a), in addition to the lack of autonomy teachers already face, Channel One designates a twelve-minute block of time wherein teachers are *required* to have the television program running (90 percent of all televisions in 90 percent of all of the rooms equipped with them). Even given Robinson's and Knupfer and Hayes' observations that teachers generally work on lesson plans or other paperwork during the news program (and students are not always attentive),[31] the fact remains that Channel One exerts a control heretofore not seen in such stark terms. It's as though the formal autonomy attributed to teachers is undermined such that informal autonomy (or resistance) takes over. Principals are known to monitor teachers in terms of the teacher's effectiveness in classroom management, but principals monitoring teachers monitoring the monitor (TV) might just be overkill. We have touched on the notion raised in (b) regarding knowing as a process of information transfer. What should be made clear, if it already has not been done so, is that knowing requires information, but on most epistemological views it requires more than information (and efficient means of transferring it). Although the traditional justified-true-belief syllogism may not ultimately hold under careful scrutiny, it nonetheless carries with it doxastic freedom and justification. Channel One and other technologies rarely if ever include either one of these notions.

Doxastic freedom means knowers are not bullied into holding beliefs they do not freely accept. Justification requires varying forms of evidence, demonstration, support, and so on. What Channel One effectively does (although it is not alone in this) is caricature news programs (also rife with contradictions and what Edward Reed called "processed second hand experiences")[32] that are developed by profit-minded entrepreneurs from the private sector. Advertisements blur viewers' versions of reality (as in what is "cool," what is beautiful, what is valuable, etc.) rendering doxastic freedom a quaint-but-arcane artifact of "*techne-episteme*."[33] Similarly, except for those rare instances when Channel One is used as the object lesson for critical discernment between facts, values, politics, perspectives, and so on, Channel One is not intended for students to demonstrate and engage in justificatory debate. It is, recall, a mechanism intended to transmit current events to passive listeners. This point brings us to (c): consumer materialism. Consumer

---

[31] See Rhonda Robinson, "Investigating Channel One: A Case Study Report," *Watching Channel One: The Convergence of Students, Technology, and Private Business*, Ann De Vaney, ed. (Albany: SUNY Press, 1994): 21–41; and Nancy Nelson Knupfer and Peter Hayes, "The Effects of the Channel One Broadcast on Students' Knowledge of Current Events," in De Vaney, *op. cit.*, 42–59.

[32] Edward S. Reed, *The Necessity of Experience* (New Haven: Yale University Press, 1996).

[33] See Molnar, *op. cit.*; and David Noble, "Selling Academe to the Technology Industry," *Thought and Action* 14 (1998): 29–40. See, also, Larry Cuban, *Oversold and Underused: Computers in the Classroom* (Cambridge: Harvard University Press, 2003).

materialism, as noted earlier in the chapter, commodifies existence by reducing searching, being, thinking, and so forth, to objectified and reductionistic particulars. For schools it means, in part, that students have roles whereby they "get" correct answers to questions instead of searching for meaning and understanding by contesting, for our purposes, Channel One "factoids."[34] The "correct answers" are material goods; "getting" is what consumers do. Commercials played for captive audiences are the vehicle for corporations to reach a specified market and the news show is an extension of that point. Students-as-consumers fits the epistemological agenda because it mirrors the larger point of having students (at earlier and earlier ages) adopt a materialist want as consumers (vs. critical consumerism). If "knowledge" can be "had" only by receptor-like listening and viewing, companies are able to dissociate justification and critique, thus making the larger consumer materialist agenda possible—and profitable.

Question 4: Which people/what institutions might be most seriously harmed by Channel One? This question may force an unwanted dualism, but it seems to pit public and private interests against one another and leaves, as usual, students and teachers as (unwitting?) pawns. The larger concern within this dualism is one detailed by De Vaney when she notes Channel One's founder Chris Whittle's larger agenda: for-profit schools. In terms of knowledge, it suggests that teachers and students are, again, displaced by an authorized and economically brokered system of information delivery (called knowledge). Debates about Channel One are largely centered in administrative circles and with the parental public. Academics are on the margin of this debate, but teachers and students are rarely heard. They may thus have the better posture, if one considers that any program that depends on students' and teachers' use of it will actually be in the ultimate power position. Channel One, however, represents a program that uses teachers and students, not the converse. It uses underfunded schools and overworked teachers to make the feeble-but-passable argument that, for "free" equipment, teachers need only have the program on 90 percent of the time. The harm may be nothing more than symbolic extortion, but one wonders if, at root, that's all the process boils down to be.

Postman's fifth question, revised, asks what changes in the requirements for knowing are being enforced by Channel One and what is being gained and lost. It's already been noted that schools gain a satellite dish, televisions, VCRs, and so on. Depending on one's perspective, teachers and students gain or lose 12 minutes per day watching, listening to, or tuning out Channel One. But this is somewhat beside the point. In terms of epistemology, that which is lost or gained includes the conditions for knowledge. My

---

[34]Deron Boyles, *American Education and Corporations: The Free Market Goes to School* (New York: Falmer, 2000), *xv.*

argument is that Channel One represents an extension of a form of reliabilism in which lucky guesses satisfy educationists' claims that students "know." Channel One literally capitalizes on this perspective and extends the problem cloaked in desirable techno-speak. Said differently, schools with Channel One rely on a form of reliabilism when they assert students "know." When reliabilists talk about justification, they talk about beliefs being justified in terms of reliable processes (generally understood in scientific terminology and exemplified in U.S. schools by standardized testing). They do not consider justification calling for evidentialist language, that is, terms like *reasonable, certain,* or *evident.*[35] To do so would be to open up the project of epistemology to justificatory claims that represent internalism, that is, "self-evident epistemic principles, beliefs, and perceptual, introspective, and memorial experiences, all of which are accessible on reflection [for foundationalism and] self-evident epistemic principles, beliefs, and coherence relations among beliefs [for coherentism]."[36] Instead, *externalism* privileges the reliabilist theory of knowledge, which maintains that the classical definition of knowledge (justified-true-belief) is wrong in requiring the justification condition. Reliabilism maintains that human knowledge requires only reliably produced true belief and that the reliability of such processes is *not* internal to the mind. Consequently, for reliabilists, according to Almeder, human knowledge does not require of a person any "awareness that the belief is reliably produced (or caused by appropriate information)."[37] A form of externalism, where inter- and intrapersonal distinctions further elaborate the problem,[38] the important point is that reliabilism does not require of a person any *awareness* or *personal reflection* in order to claim knowledge. Neither does Channel One. Students who are claimed to have increased knowledge (as noted earlier by Greenberg and Brand) as a result of Channel One viewing are claimed as "knowers" based on the reliabilism just outlined. Additionally, Channel One represents externalism because the students who take the "knowledge of current affairs tests" have applied to them criteria not contingent on their awareness or personal reflection, only criteria that represent reliably produced true beliefs that result in claims to knowledge. The fact is, researchers cannot know which of the answers are lucky guesses and thus cannot discern between knowers and lucky-guessers.

Finally, we turn to the last of Postman's questions: "What sort of people and institutions acquire special economic and political power as a result of

---

[35] See Steup, *op. cit.,* 160–176.
[36] *Ibid.,* 84.
[37] Robert Almeder, "Dretske's Dreadful Question," *Philosophia* (Spring, 1996), 24.
[38] See Robert Almeder, *Blind Realism* (Lanham, MD: Rowman & Littlefield Publishers, Inc., 1992), 64–71. Almeder notes: "On one hand, if the intrapersonalist gives reasons in order to establish the falsity of solipsism then the intrapersonalist must admit that giving reasons, or being in a position to give reasons, is sometimes a necessary condition for justification" (p. 70).

Channel One?" As has already been pointed out, Channel One reaps huge profits from advertising. Advertisers are obviously willing to pay the high costs for entry into a captive market. There is the larger issue of consumer materialism to consider here, however. It is not enough that advertisers present their images and their goods. Schools, *ipso facto* of advertisements on Channel One, have allowed their sphere to become a market. This is not to say, however, that consumer materialists are the ones who acquire special economic and political power, unless by special we mean "less" or "marginalized" because consumer materialists are *reactionary* agents of *external* stimuli and status quo expectations.

The larger point here is to highlight the technophilia impacting school programs, including Channel One, and the resulting capitalist regress that most U.S. citizens will not only be unable to escape—they will hegemonically participate in their own demise. Channel One recurs here as teachers have, by either their vocal willingness or not-so-vocal apathy, allowed (again and further) encroachment of "other-than-teacher" forces to enter *their* classrooms.

Recall Dewey's position regarding technology. He advocated a "vision of a day in which the natural sciences and the technologies which flow from them are used as servants for a humane life ..."[39] The particulars of his technology stance (objects, data, etc.) are subsumed under his larger argument about the principle of interaction.[40] For Dewey, external conditions *and* internal conditions are unified by experience. Experiences are "educative" when they result in more unification and when continued inquiry occurs (and recurs). The role of the teacher, accordingly, is as a kind of regulator. Teachers have as their "immediate and direct concern ... the situations in which interaction takes place. The individual, who enters as a factor into it, is what he is at a given time. It is the other factor, that of objective [external] conditions, which lies to some extent with the possibility of regulation by the educator."[41] The topics, coverage, commercials, and the televisions teachers (must) use, the way the "news broadcast" is presented, the way the "broadcasters" talk and what they say, for instance, all comprise the objective/external "situations" to which Dewey referred. These make up, in Dewey's words, "that environment which will interact with the existing capacities and needs of those taught to create worth-while experience[s]."[42] Yet as Seals notes,

> [Channel One], quite obviously and understandably, stand[s] Dewey's argument on its head. When incorporated into the external environment of the

---

[39] John Dewey, *Individualism Old and New* (New York: Capricorn, 1962 [1929]), 155–156.
[40] See John Dewey, *The Quest for Certainty* in Jo Ann Boydston, ed., *John Dewey: The Later Works, 1925–1939*, Vol. 13. (Carbondale, IL: Southern Illinois University Press, 1988), 3–62.
[41] *Ibid.*, 26.
[42] *Ibid.*

students' educational situation, [Channel One] present[s] a feature of that environment crucially outside the power of the educator to control, manipulate, or regulate. The inflexibility associated with [Channel One] "conversational" interaction forces the educator to practice manipulation of the other side of the educational situation. In short, the internal state of the student must be brought to the point of matching the latest member of the classroom's external environment. Since [Channel One] can't be moved from [it's] preferences concerning styles of interaction, students must be moved from theirs.[43]

At this point, we might suggest that there is no problem here after all. The purpose of schooling, so this argument goes, *is* to change the internal conditions of students. Dewey even admits to this when he suggests his companion principle to the principle of interaction—the principle of continuity. The principal of continuity holds that, like "educative experiences," changes for the better and growth as a result of interaction must obtain for "education" to be said to occur. On this point, Channel One can only be said to give teachers a new job to do: they must train students to "listen" to the program being transmitted. As a result, students are enabled to learn on their own by watching Channel One. Dewey is satisfied and Channel One no longer represents a problem. Unfortunately, as Seals points out:

This objection ... misses the point of the problem of the inversion of the principle of interaction. The problem occurs, not after students adapt to [watching Channel One], but before and during their adaptation to it. That is, the problem of the inversion of the principle of interaction cannot be used to argue about any alleged interruption or enhancement of a student's continual growth qua student. It may be true that [Channel One], inflexible and strict as [it is] in [its] interactions with humans, indoctrinate students into passivity, docility and compliance. It may also be true that [Channel One], entertaining and fascinating as [it] can be, unlock[s] untold treasures of educational interest for some students. But those problems, whatever merit they may have, have no bearing on the current issue. Instead, the problem of the inversion of the principle of interaction concerns an anthropological point and arises at the place where students are being [exposed to Channel One]. The upshot of identifying [Channel One] as an [informational and] conversational subculture, and an inflexible, strict, and narrow one at that, is that [economic] differences among users will determine differential responses to [viewing Channel One]. Therein lies the rub. As a[n informational and] conversational subculture in their own right, [Channel One is] guaranteed to interact more or less well with members of other, more or less well-adapted and adaptable subcultures.[44]

---

[43] Greg Seals, "Ritual: The Hidden Curriculum of Education in Cyberspace," *Insights* 32, no. 1 (June, 1996): 7.
[44] *Ibid.*, 7–8.

Dewey's vision is not realized under this interpretation because *humane **inter-action*** does not happen. The structure of the technology in question sub-sumes any potential *interaction* in favor of furthering the passivity required of a consumer materialist agenda—an agenda that, *de facto*, privileges those who play the game and follow along while securing the power (and profits) of those in command of the technological and commercial encroachment into schools. Even if one disagrees with the criticism of Channel One, specifi-cally, and technology, generally, the argument is nonetheless to raise serious questions about the seemingly "anointed" field of technology and the rarely-if-ever critiqued commercialism in schools.

RESTRUCTURALISM AND INCREMENTALISM—
HURRY FOR WHOM?

The stage was set for Channel One's encroachment into schools when econ-omist-minded politicos drafted *A Nation at Risk*. The 1983 document holds a unique position in the world of education policy as being far-reaching and influential. The document criticized schools at the time for being the cause of the economic ills of the United States and is still used to argue that schools are "failing." What is odd, of course, is that if the cause-and-effect rationale was to hold true, schools in the year 2000 should be applauded for reaping huge national surpluses and should get at least some of the credit for what has been called the largest economic expansion in forty years. Those who use the *Nation at Risk* report are not interested in giving credit, however, as their interests are of a different kind. Instead of a cause-and-effect rationale, what economist-minded reformers have in mind is a kind of "cause-and-a larger cause" effect. The impetus for viewing schools as economic engines (thus stu-dents and teachers are reduced to mere widgets) is itself a viewpoint that rep-resents a cause—cause as in a movement, not as in anything producing a result. Call it a hyper-capitalist cause, the stage was set in 1983 for the "new" economy of technology and the vital way schools would be used to advance that cause.

Connected with the rise in consumer materialism so clearly seen in the earlier Channel One example, the "new" economy of technology repre-sented a wave of what we call restructuralists' technophilia. As though in a hurry to grab hold of the latest fad (one that is well funded by legislatures) restructuralists wanted their cake and they not only wanted to eat it too, they wanted everyone else to gorge themselves immediately. According to Van Dusen

> [Restructuralism is founded] on the doctrine of progress and its corollary, the doctrine of regress. The doctrine of progress, heavily influenced by an ex-panding market economy and a plethora of technological innovations to fa-

cilitate it, asserts that continued economic growth and a corresponding improvement in the human condition directly depend on the nature and quality of our educational system. To restore American economic hegemony, our schools and colleges must produce skilled knowledge workers able to function in a highly competitive, technologically intensive economic environment. Failure to "fix" an educational system perceived to be on the skids, according to the corollary doctrine of regress, will result in a devastating backward slide, socially and economically.[45]

By almost, if not, literally "buying into" restructuralism, schools were (and are) faced with outside interests who considered schools "public" enough to justify their involvement, but not reciprocally so. That is, schools are used to advance the causes noted previously, but critique of those causes is rare or eschewed. The Gablers of Texas were successful in persuading the legislature not to adopt any texts that criticized capitalism,[46] and as markets go, Texas influences many other states. We should not think that the Gablers are either alone in their thinking or restricted only to textbooks. Channel One succeeds because educators, parents, and educational policymakers are willing to trade independence (of time, thought, procedures, etc.) for technology. Although excluding Channel One from schools will not automatically mean critique will emerge, using Channel One (and other technologies) as an object lesson regarding commercialism and the place/role of technology in schools and society would go further toward thwarting consumer materialism than what currently exists. Whether it is enough to stem the tide of what appears to be an overwhelming meta-narrative in favor of glitz, gadgets, and gigabytes is yet to be seen. One only trusts that highlighting the issue will open new avenues for critique and criticism—it's overdue.

Langdon Winner, at the same conference at which Postman presented his six questions, revealed (to the accompaniment of "2001 Space Odyssey") the APM (Automatic Professor Machine). It looked just like an ATM (Automatic Teller Machine) and had buttons students would be able to press for answers and inquiries (fees would be incurred for each transaction at a different-than-host machine). His point, as the tongue-in-cheek CEO of the Educational Development of User Software and Hardware Advertising/Marketing Corporation (E.D.U.S.H.A.M [pronounced edu-shaahm]), was that we are facing a period in history where the quest for technological advancement has reached a religiously fevered pitch, with few questions being raised about the value of what technological "advance-

---

[45] Gerald C. Van Dusen, *Digital Dilemma: Issues of Access, Cost, and Quality in Media-Enhanced Distance Education* (San Francisco: Jossey-Bass, 2000), 4–5. See, also, Hubert Dreyfus, *On the Internet* (New York: Taylor and Francis, 2001).

[46] See Joel Spring, *Conflicts of Interest: The Politics of American Education* (New York: Longman, 1988), 128–129.

ment" brings along with it (recall Postman's third question). Winner also made the point that the ATM replaced a human being, much the same way as he proposed the APM will replace the professor. It's a question of dislodging humans and replacing them with machines. Given the pervasiveness of movie and film strip projectors, VCRs, stereo/CDs, televisions, computers/Internet/e-mail connections, and so on, one cannot help but wonder if the trend isn't toward reducing the number of humans in authentic conversation and dialogue (Dewey's humane interaction)—and all under the supported fervor for "technological" efficiency and effectiveness. The direct implications for epistemology are as clear as they are disturbing. Reduce the difficult aspects of knowing by "streamlining" the requirements and we have, almost exactly, a replication of the reliabilism that Channel One both fosters and furthers—all the while advancing consumer materialism deeper into the classroom.

REFERENCES

Almeder, Robert. 1992. *Blind Realism*. Lanham, MD: Rowman & Littlefield Publishers, Inc.

Almeder, Robert. 1996. Dretske's Dreadful Question. *Philosophia*. Spring: 24.

Bettis, Pam. 2000. Corporate Discourses in School: Adapting to the Prevailing Economic Climate. *Educational Foundations* (Winter): 23–49.

Boyles, Deron. 2000. *American Education and Corporations: The Free Market Goes to School*. New York: Falmer.

Burnyeat, Miles. 1990. *The Theaetetus of Plato*, trans. M. J. Levett. Cambridge: Hackett.

Bushey, John. 1999. District 11's Coke Problem. *Harper's* (February).

Cuban, Larry. 2003. *Oversold and Underused: Computers in the Classroom*. Cambridge: Harvard University Press.

De Vaney, Ann. 1994. *Watching Channel One: The Convergence of Students, Technology, and Private Business*. Albany: SUNY Press.

Dewey, John. 1929. *Individualism Old and New*. New York: Capricorn.

Dewey, John. 1929/1988. *The Quest for Certainty*, in *John Dewey: The Later Works, 1925–1953*, Jo Ann Boydson, ed., vol. 13. Carbondale, IL: Southern Illinois University Press.

Dewey, John. 1920. *Reconstruction in Philosophy*. Boston: Beacon Press.

Dreyfus, Hubert. 2001. *On the Internet*. New York: Taylor and Francis.

Editorial. 1999. Textbooks as Billboards: Commercialism Gains a Greater Hold on the Classroom. *The Fresno Bee*. (2 April): F2.

Freire, Paulo. 1973. *Education for Critical Consciousness*. New York: Seabury Press.

Garramone, G. M. and C. K. Atkin. 1986. Mass Communication and Political Socialization: Specifying the Effects. *Public Opinion Quarterly*. 50: 76–86.

Greenberg, Bradley S. and Jeffrey E. Brand. 1993. Television News and Advertising in Schools: The "Channel One" Controversy. *Journal of Communication*. 43, no. 1 (Winter): 143.

Greene, Maxine. 1988. *The Dialectic of Freedom*. New York: Teachers College Press.

Guralnik, David B. ed. 1982 *Webster's New World Dictionary.* New York: Simon and Schuster.

Hays, Constance L. 2000. Commercialism in U.S. Schools is Examined in New Report. *The New York Times.* (14 September): C1, C25.

Hays, Constance. 1999. Today's Lesson: Soda Rights; Consultant Helps Schools Sell Themselves to Vendors. *New York Times* (21 May): C1.

Kozol, Jonathan. 1992. Whittle and the Privateers. *The Nation.* 21 September.

Knight-Abowitz, Kathleen and Deron Boyles. 2000. "Private Interests or Public Goods?: Dewey, Rugg, and Their Contemporary Allies on Corporate Involvement in Educational Reform Initiatives," in *Philosophy of Education.* Urbana-Champaign: University of Illinois, 131–139.

Knupfer, Nancy Nelson and Peter Hayes. 1994. "The Effects of the Channel One Broadcast on Students' Knowledge of Current Events," in *Watching Channel One: The Convergence of Students, Technology, and Private Business,* Ann De Vaney, ed. Albany: SUNY Press, 42–59.

Lehrer, Keith. 1990. *Theory of Knowledge.* Boulder, CO: Westview Press.

McLaren, Peter. 1995. *Critical Pedagogy and Predatory Culture: Oppositional Politics in a Postmodern Era.* New York: Routledge.

Molnar, Alex. 1999. Cashing in on Kids: The Second Annual Report on Trends in Schoolhouse Commercialism. Center for the Analysis of Commercialism in Education. Document # 99-21 (September). Available at http://www.uwm.edu/Dept/CACE/kidsreport/cashinginonkids.html.

Molnar, Alex. 1996. *Giving Kids the Business: The Commercialization of America's Schools.* Boulder, CO: Westview.

Noble, David. 1998. Selling Academe to the Technology Industry. *Thought and Action* 14: 29–40.

Reed, Edward S. 1996. *The Necessity of Experience.* New Haven: Yale University Press.

Robinson, Rhonda. 1994. "Investigating Channel One: A Case Study Report," in *Watching Channel One: The Convergence of Students, Technology, and Private Business,* Ann De Vaney, ed. Albany: SUNY Press, 21–41.

Seals, Greg. 1996. Ritual: The Hidden Curriculum of Education in Cyberspace. *Insights* 32, no.1 (June): 1–11.

Shor, Ira. 1992. *Empowering Education.* Chicago: University of Chicago Press.

Sipple, John W. 1999. Institutional Constraints on Business Involvement in K–12 Education Policy. *American Educational Research Journal* 36, no. 3 (Fall): 447–488.

Spring, Joel. 1988. *Conflicts of Interest: The Politics of American Education.* New York: Longman.

Steup, Matthias. 1996. *Contemporary Epistemology.* Upper Saddle River, NJ: Prentice Hall.

Stout, Hilary. 1991. Marketing Firms Learn that the Subtle Aid to Schools Can Polish Their Images, Sell Products. *The Wall Street Journal.* (25 March): B1.

Van Dusen, Gerald C. 2000. *Digital Dilemma: Issues of Access, Cost, and Quality in Media-Enhanced Distance Education.* San Francisco: Jossey-Bass.

Contributors

Carolyn Vander Schee is a doctoral student studying social foundations of education in the Department of Educational Policy Studies at Georgia State University. Her research interests focus on health and educational policy, social equity issues in education, democracy and education, and school business partnerships.

Leslee Trammell is a student at Georgia State University in the Department of Educational Policy Studies. In her research, she analyzes the relationship between education, culture, and society, employing critical and feminist theories, anthropology, philosophy, and sociology.

Randy Hewitt is an assistant professor of educational studies at the University of Central Florida. His research interests include pragmatism, critical theory, the reproduction of social class, and democratic education.

Donna Adair Breault is an assistant professor of educational leadership at Georgia State University and a former elementary and middle school teacher and school administrator. Her research focuses on inquiry in education and its implications for both teachers and administrators.

Beth M. Weiss is a doctoral student in social foundations of education at Georgia State University, a community activist, and youth services advocate.

Judy Block is a doctoral student in the social foundations of education program in the College of Education at Georgia State University and an on-campus advocate for students with special needs.

Benjamin Baez is associate professor of higher education in the Department of Educational Policy at Georgia State University. He has published books and articles on academic freedom, affirmative action, legal issues in higher education, racial diversity, and intellectual property.

Gary A. Miller served as an academic advisor and advising administrator in the Robinson College of Business at Georgia State University from 1999 until 2004. He completed a M.S. degree in social foundations of education at Georgia State University in May, 2003. He now resides in Seattle, Washington, where he continues both his work with college students and interest in the debates on the purpose of higher education.

Larry Stultz holds a Master of Arts degree in graphic design. He worked as a professional graphic designer for twenty-five years, the majority of that time operating his own studio in New Orleans and Atlanta. He is a professor and former chair of the Graphic Design and Advertising Department at The Art Institute of Atlanta. He is finishing a doctorate in social and cultural foundations at Georgia State University.

Lynn Wilson is currently completing her M.S. in social foundations of education at Georgia State University. Lynn has been an educator for over five years and is currently the founding director of Inner Harbour, an AmeriCorps program and residential treatment facility that serves youth at risk in Douglasville, Georgia.

Deron Boyles is an associate professor in the social foundations of education program at Georgia State University. His interests include philosophy of education and epistemology with a focus on school-business partnerships, commercialism, and the roles businesses play in public school settings.

Author Index

Subject Index